Malta
& Gozo

Gozo &
Comino
p113

Northwest
Malta
p75

Sliema, St Julian's
& Paceville
p65

Central
Malta
p90

Valletta
p42

Southeast
Malta
p104

D0308184

Contents

PLAN YOUR TRIP

ON THE ROAD

CARNIVAL PROCESSION,
VALLETTA P18

LES STOCKER/GETTY IMAGES ©

CHURCH OF OUR LADY OF
LOURDES, MĠARR P121

CHRISTIAN KOBER/JOHN WARBURTON-LEE PHOTOGRAPHY LTD/GETTY IMAGES ©

FALOMBINI/GETTY IMAGES ©

Contents

AZURE WINDOW, DWEJRA P126

Welcome to Malta & Gozo

Malta packs glorious variety into its small archipelago. You'll find prehistoric temples, fossil-studded cliffs, hidden coves, thrilling scuba diving and a history of remarkable intensity.

A Legendary History

Malta's geographical location in the centre of the Mediterranean made it an alluring and much-fought-over prize in times when it was impossible for sea vessels to attempt long, continuous trips, and the islands are all of majestic above- and below-ground defences. The capital, Valletta, built by the Knights of St John, is a harmonious grid, Mdina and Victoria are fortress-like hilltop towns, and watchtowers dot the coast. Even Malta's fishing boats resonate with the past, their prows painted with eyes, just like the boats of their Phoenician predecessors.

Secret Coves & Glittering Sea

Malta's landscape contrasts rocky stretches of coast that end in dizzying limestone cliffs with sheltered bays that hide gin-clear water and red-gold beaches. The islands' many marinas jostle with boats, and you can take to the water in sky-blue traditional craft, stately yachts or speedboats. Snorkellers and divers have much to explore underwater as well, in a world of caves, crags and wrecks.

A Mediterranean Cocktail

Malta is staunchly Roman Catholic but is also home to a beguiling mix of cultures that has stewed together over generations. Traditional Maltese food mixes Sicilian and Middle Eastern flavours, while making use of local ingredients such as rabbit and honey. The Maltese people are warm and welcoming: if you ask for directions, it's likely a local will walk with you to help you find the way. Plenty of 21st-century sophistication can be found, but there are also pockets where you feel you've gone back in time, especially on Gozo, where mammoth churches tower over quiet villages.

Mysterious Ancients

Malta and Gozo's astounding prehistoric sites were seemingly constructed by sophisticated temple builders, who also left miniature figurines and mammoth sculptures of 'fat ladies', which have survived millennia and are housed in Malta's fascinating museums. Out in the open, gigantic temples and towers from many different eras stand proud, continuing their endless watch over the sea. But the most extraordinary site of all lies underground: Ħal Saflieni Hypogeum, a 5000-year-old necropolis carved from the living rock.

Why I Love Malta & Gozo

by Abigail Blasi, Author

Malta is packed with interest, yet is laid-back and easy. There are boat trips, beautiful towns, periwinkle seas, friendly people and soul-feeding views, and you can go from swimming in glinting sea to a clifftop prehistoric site, to a harbourside restaurant, all in the space of a few hours. Combine sightseeing and beaches on Malta with a relaxing stay on Gozo, with its hillocks, small villages and carved-out coast, and you have the perfect holiday.

For more about Abigail Blasi, see page 192

Above: Vittoriosa, Malta (p59)

Malta & Gozo

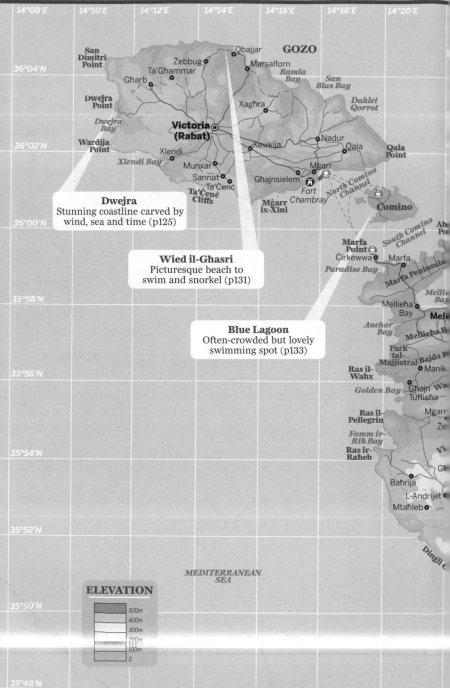

GOZO

San Dimitri Point
Żebbuġ
Ta'Ghammar
Qbajjar
Marsalforn
Ramla Bay
San Blas Bay
Gharb
Dahlet Qorrot
Dwejra Point
Xaghra
Dwejra Bay
Victoria (Rabat)
Wardija Point
Xlendi
Xewkija
Nadur
Qala
Xlendi Bay
Munxar
Qala Point
Sannat
Mġarr
Ta'Ċenċ
Ghajnsielem
Ta'Ċenċ Cliffs
Fort Chambray
North Comino Channel
Mġarr ix-Xini

Dwejra
Stunning coastline carved by wind, sea and time (p125)

Comino

South Comino Channel
Ab Po

Marfa Point
Ċirkewwa
Marfa
Paradise Bay
Marfa Peninsula

Wied il-Ghasri
Picturesque beach to swim and snorkel (p131)

Melli Bay
Mellieha Bay
Mel
Anchor Bay
Mellieha R

Blue Lagoon
Often-crowded but lovely swimming spot (p133)

Park tal-Majjistral
Bajda P
Manik

Ras il-Wahx
Golden Bay
Ghajn Wa
Tuffieha

Ras il-Pellegrin
Mġarr
Że
Fomm ir-Rih Bay
Ras ir-Raheb
Vi
Gh

Bahrija
L-Andrijet
Mtahleb

Dingli C

MEDITERRANEAN SEA

ELEVATION
500m
400m
300m
200m
100m
0

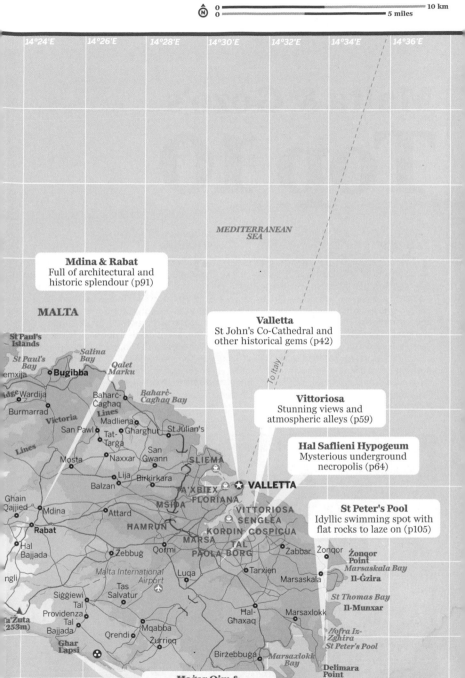

Mdina & Rabat
Full of architectural and historic splendour (p91)

Valletta
St John's Co-Cathedral and other historical gems (p42)

Vittoriosa
Stunning views and atmospheric alleys (p59)

Ħal Saflieni Hypogeum
Mysterious underground necropolis (p64)

St Peter's Pool
Idyllic swimming spot with flat rocks to laze on (p105)

Għar Lapsi
Natural swimming pool sheltered among rocks (p112)

Ħaġar Qim & Mnajdra Temples
Ancient megalithic marvels (p110)

MALTA

MEDITERRANEAN SEA

0 — 10 km
0 — 5 miles

14°24′E 14°26′E 14°28′E 14°30′E 14°32′E 14°34′E 14°36′E

St Paul's Islands
St Paul's Bay
Salina Bay
Qalet Marku
emxija
Bugibba
Baħar ic-Ċagħaq
Baħar ic-Ċagħaq Bay
To Italy
Wardija
Burmarrad
Victoria Lines
Madliena
San Pawl
Tat-Targa
Għargħur
St Julian's
Lines
Mosta
Naxxar
San Ġwann
SLIEMA
Balzan
Lija
Birkirkara
TA' XBIEX
FLORIANA
★ VALLETTA
Għajn Qajjied
Mdina
Attard
MSIDA
VITTORIOSA
SENGLEA
Rabat
HAMRUN
KORDIN COSPICUA
Ħal Bajjada
Żebbuġ
Qormi
MARSA
TAL BORG
PAOLA
Żabbar
Żonqor
Żonqor Point
ngli
Malta International Airport
Luqa
Tarxien
Marsaskala
Marsaskala Bay
Il-Gżira
Siggiewi
Tas Salvatur
St Thomas Bay
Il-Munxar
a' Żuta (253m)
Tal Providenza
Tal Bajjada
Mqabba
Qrendi
Żurrieq
Hal-Ghaxaq
Marsaxlokk
Ħofra Iż-Żgħira
St Peter's Pool
Għar Lapsi
Birżebbuġa
Marsaxlokk Bay
Delimara Point
Benghisa Point

Malta & Gozo's
Top 10

Valletta

1 Malta's capital (p42), named the European Capital of Culture for 2018, is a remarkable city. Only 1km by 600m, with every street leading to the sea, the walled city is a harmonious ensemble of 16th- and 17th-century townhouses fronted by traditional Maltese balconies. The last few years have seen Valletta bloom, with new restaurants and an emerging nightlife area in Strait St, its former red-light district. You'll feel the excitement the moment you walk through the striking City Gate, and see the cutting-edge Parliament Building and Opera House – all three monuments designed by Renzo Piano.

Dwejra

2 The thrilling coastline of Dwejra (p125), in Gozo, features astoundingly beautiful rock formations that have been sculpted by the wind and sea (they're so dramatic it's been used as a location for *Game of Thrones*). Take a boat trip through the Azure Window, an arch of rock that forms a doorway to the ocean, and visit the Inland Sea, a wonderful place to swim and snorkel when the weather is calm. Close to the coast, the great chunk of Fungus Rock rears from the piercing blue Mediterranean.

Diving

3 Malta and Gozo arguably have Europe's best diving (p22), with warm seas, astounding underwater architecture and some particularly thrilling shipwrecks (most dating from WWII). The diminutive size of the islands means that an incredible range of dives are accessible from the shore, and there's something to suit all levels, from beginners to technical divers. Multiple diving companies are on hand to ease your way underwater – recommended even for the experienced diver.

Below: Snorkelling at the Blue Hole (p126), Gozo

Vittoriosa's Backstreets

4 Vittoriosa (p59) is the most fascinating of Malta's Three Cities. This ancient town has stunning views and perfectly preserved streets. Still known locally as Birgu (its name before the Great Siege of 1565), Vittoriosa was the original home of the Knights of Malta. Their headquarters, Fort St Angelo, was opened to the public in late 2015. But this town is no museum – it's a living, breathing city with a strong sense of community. You're in luck if your visit is in October: the culmination of BirguFest sees the ancient streets lit solely by candles.

Blue Lagoon

5 The beautiful island of Comino has an eclectic history. It was written about by Ptolemy 1800 years ago, and has been a hermit's hideaway, a cholera isolation zone and a prison camp. But its most extraordinary feature is the otherworldly Blue Lagoon (p133). This serene, limpid sea pool is so blue that it looks like an over-saturated image. It attracts hoards of swimmers in the summer months, but even the crowds can't obscure its beauty still, try to head here in the afternoon, after most people have left).

Hal Saflieni Hypogeum

6 Visiting these ancient underground burial chambers (p64) is a unique, mysterious and awe-inspiring experience. Amazingly preserved, the sacred spaces hollowed from the rock are around 5000 years old – painted ochre patterns are still visible decorating the ceilings of some sections. It's a window into an enigmatic ancient world, which leaves a beguiling and perplexing resonance. You'll need to book several months ahead.

F AREI GALLAS/GETTY IMAGES ©

Ħaġar Qim & Mnajdra Temples

7 These great prehistoric structures (p110) are among Malta's finest and most atmospheric, partly due to their breathtaking location – set high on the edge of coastal cliffs that are carpeted by wild flowers in spring. There are magnificent views out to sea and over to the distant islet of Filfla, marked nature trails around the surrounding countryside, and a fascinating visitor centre that illuminates what is known about the mysterious temple builders.

Secret Coves

8 Although Malta & Gozo have some lovely sandy beaches, many of the islands' finest swimming spots are the natural inlets that punctuate the rocky coast. Highlights include the searingly beautiful St Peter's Pool (p105; great for leaping off the rocks); the sheltered, natural, rocky swimming pool at Għar Lapsi (p112); and Gozo's narrow rocky gorge that meets the sea, Wied il-Għasri (p127), reached by a staircase chiselled into the rock. All offer rewarding snorkelling as well as being relaxing places to hang out and cool down. Above: Għar Lapsi

St John's Co-Cathedral

9 The austere exterior of Valletta's cathedral (p45) is no preparation for the frenzy of baroque gold and lavish decoration in its interior. The floor alone is a carpet of many-coloured marble tombs, on which symbolic pictures are delicately rendered in stone. The chapels, each pertaining to a division of the Knights of St John, vie to outdo each other in opulence. The outstanding highlight is Caravaggio's *Beheading of John the Baptist* in the Oratory – the largest work ever produced by the artist.

Mdina & Rabat

10 Malta's tiny some-
time capital, Mdina
(p91) is a walled city
perched on a hilltop, filled
with beautiful honey-
coloured buildings. A
treasure trove of museums,
artefacts and churches
(including Malta's stunning
second cathedral) during
the day, it's appealingly
mysterious at night, when
everything's closed and the
city is dimly lit and empty.
Wander around after most
people have left and you'll
understand why it's known
as the 'Silent City'. Mdina
adjoins Rabat (p95), it-
self a lovely town with some
fascinating sights, many of
them underground.

Right: St Paul's Cathedral , Mdina

ANIBAL TREJO/SHUTTERSTOCK ©

Need to Know

For more information, see Survival Guide (p167)

Currency
Euro (€)

Languages
Malti, English

Visas
Malta is in the Schengen area. Visas are also not required for citizens of EU and EEA countries. Other nationalities should check www.foreign.gov.mt.

Money
ATMs are widespread. Credit cards are used in larger hotels and upmarket restaurants, but most smaller hotels and eateries only accept cash.

Mobile Phones
Malta uses the GSM900 mobile network (not compatible with the USA's and Canada's GSM1900).

Time
Central European Time Zone (GMT/UTC plus one hour).

When to Go

Victoria (Rabat)
GO Apr–Jun & Sep–Oct

St Julian's
GO Apr–Jun & Sep–Oct

Valletta
GO Apr–Jun & Sep–Oct

Mdina
GO Apr–Jun & Sep–Oct

Marsaxlokk
GO Apr–Jun & Sep–Oct

Warm to hot summers, mild winters

High Season
(Jun–Aug)

➡ Many resort hotels are booked solid; beaches are busy.

➡ Daytime temperatures in July and August can reach more than 35°C.

➡ Main season for village festas (feast days) and music festivals

Shoulder
(Apr–Jun, Sep–Oct)

➡ Warm and sunny; occasional rainfall or hot and humid wind.

➡ Sea is warmer in autumn than in spring.

➡ Holy Week is a wonderful time to be in Malta.

Low Season
(Nov–Feb)

➡ November and December temperatures average 12°C to 18°C.

➡ January and February are coldest; northeasterly wind (grigal) occasionally disrupts Gozo ferry service.

➡ Christmas to New Year is a mini-high season.

Useful Websites

Lonely Planet (www.lonely planet.com/malta) Destination information, hotel bookings, traveller forum and more.

Malta Tourism Authority (www.visitmalta.com) Huge official site with lots of useful information.

Gozo (www.gozo.com) All about Gozo.

Restaurants Malta (www. restaurantsmalta.com) Helpful, reliable survey-based restaurant guide.

What's on Malta (www. whatson.com.mt) Music, art, festivals, theatre and clubbing listings.

Important Numbers

International access code	✆00
Country code	✆356
Directory enquiries	✆1182
Directory enquiries (Go Mobile)	✆1187
Directory enquiries (Vodafone)	✆1189
Emergency	✆112

Exchange Rates

Australia	A$1	€0.66
Canada	C$1	€0.69
Japan	¥100	€0.73
New Zealand	NZ$1	€0.60
UK	£1	€1.42
US	US$1	€0.90

For current exchange rates, see www.xe.com.

Daily Costs

Budget: Less than €80

➡ Dorm bed: €12–20

➡ Double in budget hotel: €40–60

➡ Sandwiches, pizza or pasta: €6–12

➡ 12-journey bus pass: €15

Midrange: €80–140

➡ Double room: €60–140

➡ Car rental: average per day €25

➡ Meal in restaurant: €20–30

Top end: More than €140

➡ Double room: €140–300

➡ Meal in top restaurant: €50–100

➡ Private yacht hire: per day €400

Opening Hours

We've provided high-season opening hours; hours are sometimes shorter in the low season.

Banks 8.30am–12.30pm Mon–Fri, sometimes to 2pm Fri, 8.30am–noon Sat

Restaurants noon–3pm & 7–11pm, often closed Sun or Mon

Cafes 9am–10pm

Bars 8pm–4am

Shops 9am–1pm & 4–7pm Mon-Sat

Arriving in Malta

Malta International Airport (p174)

Bus Six express services and other buses run from the airport to all of Malta's main towns from around 5am to midnight.

At night, the N71 runs from the airport to St Julian's.

Some bus numbers and timetables were due to change at the time of research, so check www. maltapublictransport.com for current information.

Shuttle MaltaTransfer (www. maltatransfer.com) operates airport shuttle services to major hotels.

Taxi Fixed price from the airport to Valletta €15 (15 to 25 minutes).

Getting Around

Malta is small and easy to get around by bus.

Bus Reasonably priced and efficient, with frequent buses for the major towns and hourly services for smaller places.

Boat Regular, inexpensive ferries cross the Grand and Marsamxett Harbours, and serve Gozo.

Car Good for travelling at your own pace, with utmost flexibility, and for accessing the nooks and crannies the buses don't go to. Car rental is inexpensive.

For much more on **getting around**, see p174

If You Like...

Historic Towns

Malta has some beautifully preserved towns, dating from the time of the swashbuckling Knights of Malta.

Valletta Crammed with emblems of the island's history, from St John's Co-Cathedral to the National War Museum. (p42)

Mdina & Rabat Mdina's evocative walled city sits alongside an excavated Roman villa and Rabat's catacombs and necropolises. (p91)

Vittoriosa The original home of the Knights, with Fort St Angelo, the Inquisitor's Palace and the Malta at War Museum. (p59)

Victoria The walled city of Il-Kastell was where the entire Gozo population used to shelter from invaders at night. (p116)

Watersports

Malta, Gozo and Comino offer some of the world's best diving, plus parasailing, kayaking, water-skiing and SUP (stand-up paddle boarding).

Dive sites Dive wrecks, caves and reefs for beginners, experts and everyone in between. (p22)

Golden Bay Take a speedboat trip, windsurf or try SUP. (p78)

Mellieħa Bay Watersports such as windsurfing, kiteboarding, water-skiing and more. (p80)

Kayaking Take a guided kayak tour around Gozo and Comino. (p30)

Prehistoric Relics

Malta has a wealth of prehistoric temples and necropolises, constructed a millennium before the Egyptian pyramids.

Hal Saflieni Hypogeum A 5000-year-old subterranean necropolis masterfully carved out of the rock. (p64)

Ħaġar Qim & Mnajdra Clifftop temples in an extraordinary setting. (p110)

National Museum of Archaeology Malta's most dazzling and refined prehistoric relics. (p44)

Ġgantija Temples Temples on Gozo seemingly built by giants. (p128)

Tarxien Temples Built of massive stone blocks that measure up to 3m by 1m by 1m. (p64)

Beaches

Golden Bay Living up to its name, with burnished sand. (p78)

Għajn Tuffieħa Bay Even more beautiful than neighbouring Golden Bay. (p78)

Ramla Bay One of Gozo's prettiest beaches, with red-gold sand, backed by rolling hills. (p132)

San Blas Bay A gorgeous little Gozitan bay with rust-coloured sand and a steep approach. (p132)

Paradise Bay A white-sand beach looking over to Gozo. (p83)

Family Fun

Comino Take boat trips, swim and explore at this tower-topped island. (p132)

Popeye Village Sweethaven is a village-style film set turned theme park. (p82)

Valletta Choreographed fountains, the National War Museum, gardens and forts. (p42)

Buġibba & Qawra Glass-bottomed boat trips, Buġibba Water Park, and the Malta National Aquarium. (p85)

Local Cuisine

Malta and Gozo's cuisine is an enticing mix of influences, including Italian, French, British and Arabic flavours.

Valletta Everything from gourmet burgers to Maltese tapas. (p53)

Sliema & St Julian's Head for its happening buzz to eat out where locals do. (p71)

Mġarr Join in the local Sunday lunch ritual. (p79)

Dingli Eat fresh-from-the-farm and locally sourced produce. (p100)

Marsaxlokk This sometime fishing village is the place to dine on seafood for Sunday lunch. (p105)

Views

Upper Barrakka Gardens Valletta's finest viewpoint. (p52)

Dingli Cliffs Soaring views over blue horizons and the islet of Filfla. (p100)

Level 22 This bar on the 22nd floor in Portomaso is ideal for cocktails. (p72)

Dwejra Otherworldly vistas over the Azure Window and Fungus Rock. (p126)

Il-Kastell Walk around the ramparts for bird's-eye views of Gozo. (p116)

Architecture

Malta has some extraordinary built structures, from ancient to modern.

Hal Saflieni Hypogeum Incredible underground caverns, sculpted from rock over 5000 years ago. (p64)

Parliament Building Renzo Piano's state-of-the-art masterpiece, inaugurated in 2015. (p44)

Maltese balconies Seen particularly on the 16th- and 17th-century buildings of Valletta and Rabat. (p167)

St John's Co-Cathedral A stern fortress-style exterior hides a frenzy of Maltese baroque. (p46)

Top: Maltese balconies, Valletta (p42)
Bottom: Tapas with *ġbejniet* cheese (p33), Gozo

Month by Month

February

As winter draws to a close, the islands celebrate Carnival with notable verve.

⭐ Carnival

A week of celebrations preceding Lent, with traditional processions of floats, fancy dress and grotesque masks. Carnival (www.visitmalta.com/carnival) is celebrated throughout the islands but with particular flair in Valletta and Nadur.

March

Holy Week sees Malta's most spectacular and important celebrations.

⭐ Good Friday

Life-size statues depicting scenes from the Passion of the Christ are carried shoulder high in processions through towns and villages.

⭐ Easter Sunday

In contrast to the solemnity of Good Friday, this is a day of joy. Early in the morning, processions bear the statue of the Risen Christ – in the three harbour towns of Vittoriosa, Senglea and Cospicua, the statue bearers *run* with the statue.

April

Temperatures begin to warm and wild flowers carpet the countryside. It's too cold to swim for all but the hardiest, but spring is a glorious time to be in Malta.

⭐ Fireworks Festival

A noisy, colourful festival of fireworks, folk music and entertainment (www.visitmalta.com/malta-fireworks-festival), with awesome Grand Harbour views.

⭐ Medieval Mdina

A weekend of medieval events, including human chess, birds of prey, archery and cookery at the Medieval Mdina Festival (www.medievalmdina.eu).

May

Malta's weather reaches a lovely pitch in May, with warm sunshine making the occasional dip inviting. Sights remain uncrowded.

⭐ Village Festas

Every village has a festa (feast day) celebrating its patron saint. From May to September there'll be something on almost every weekend.

⭐ Lejlet Lapsi Notte Gozitana

The run-up to the feast of the Ascension of Our Lord is celebrated with a weekend of music, arts, tours and craft events on Gozo.

June

Early summer is the perfect time for piercing blue skies and less-busy beaches.

☆ Valletta Film Festival

An international competition (www.vallettafilmfestival.com), with films showing at St James' Cavalier as well as outdoors at Pjazza Teatru Rjal, Fort St Elmo, and Pjazza San Ġorġ.

⭐ L-Imnarja

Harvest festival with an agricultural show and traditional horse races; festivities are centred on and around Rabat.

☆ Għanafest

Traditional Maltese folk songs are celebrated with three days of live music in Floriana's Argotti Gardens (www.maltafolkmusicfestival.org).

July

High summer is hot and busy but it's also a joyous time of year, packed with interesting festivals.

☆ Malta Music Week & the Isle of MTV

A week of gigs (www.maltamusicweek.com) on Gozo in late June all lead up to the Isle of MTV festival (www.isleofmtv.com) in Floriana, starring international acts.

☆ Malta Jazz Festival

Outdoor shows beneath the bastions of Valletta (www.maltajazzfestival.org).

🍺 Farsons Great Beer Festival

Ten days of free live gigs at Ta'Qali in central Malta, with Maltese artists performing, food stalls, and local and international beer.

🎆 Malta Arts Festival

For three weeks from early July, the Malta Arts Festival (www.maltaartsfestival.org) incorporates music, dance, theatre, literature and art exhibitions at various Valletta venues and Argotti Gardens in Floriana.

August

Temperatures reach their height and crowds flop onto the beaches.

🎆 Feast of the Transfiguration

Lija's feast is one of Malta's most popular, marked by spectacular fireworks on the eve of 5 August.

🎆 Feast of Santa Marija

Also known as the Feast of the Assumption, 15 August marks the ascent into heaven of the Virgin Mary and is celebrated in Għaxaq, Gudja, Ħ'Attard, Mosta, Mqabba and Qrendi in Malta, and Victoria in Gozo.

September

In autumn the crowds ebb and temperatures cool; the sea has been warmed over the summer, so it's still good for swimming.

◉ Malta International Air Show

Visiting aircraft and aerial displays at the Luqa airfield in late September (www.maltairshow.com).

October

Malta's autumnal months are an ideal time to visit, with greenery returning to the parched landscape, and sunny weather.

◉ Notte Bianca

On 1 October, Valletta's museums, historical buildings and cultural institutions are open free of charge till late; plus free live gigs.

🎆 BirguFest

BirguFest (www.birgu.gov.mt) is three days of music, dance and pageantry in Vittoriosa, culminating in 'Birgu by Candlelight', when the streets are lit by candles.

🎆 Mediterranea

Mediterranea (www.mediterranea.com.mt), a 10-day festival of culture on Gozo, celebrates the history, art, crafts, opera and music of the island.

☆ Mdina Grand Prix

This classic car race is held in the stunning location of Mdina and Rabat (www.vallettagrandprix.com).

☆ Malta Military Tattoo

A weekend of marching, gymnastics and military music at Ta'Qali (www.maltamilitarytattoo.org).

November

There tends to be more rain in late autumn, but it's still a great time of year for some guaranteed sunshine, few crowds and low prices.

◉ Mdina Cathedral Contemporary Art Biennale

From November to January every two years (2017/18, 2019/20), this festival (www.mdinabiennale.org) exhibits works by international artists in Mdina.

December

Although it's cold and damp at this time of year, the Christmas period is an enchanting time to visit.

🎆 Christmas

Christmas is celebrated with fervour. Nativity scenes are set up most spectacularly in Għajnsielem (http://ghajnsielem.com/bethlehem/about.html) in Gozo, which has a 150-strong living nativity.

Itineraries

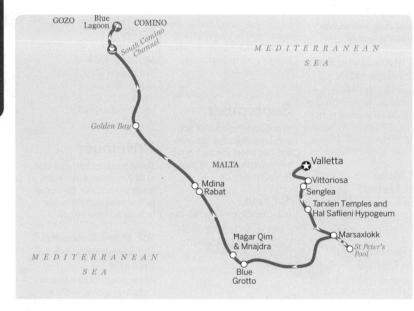

Essential Malta

Malta's diminutive dimensions (27km by 14.5km) mean that you can cover a lot of ground while taking it easy. Having your own car is an asset; otherwise, base yourself in Valletta, Naxxar, Sliema or St Julian's for the easiest bus connections.

Begin by taking in **Valletta** – explore the narrow streets, walk around the fortifications, feast your eyes on views across the Grand Harbour, and visit sights such as St John's Co-Cathedral and the Grand Master's Palace. On the second day, spend the morning at Fort St Elmo, visiting the wonderful National War Museum, before taking a scenic ferry ride across the harbour to explore the charms of **Vittoriosa** and **Senglea**. On day three visit the **Tarxien Temples** and **Hal Saflieni Hypogeum** en route south for a seafood lunch at **Marsaxlokk**, then spend the afternoon relaxing at **St Peter's Pool**, a rocky bay with crystal-clear sea and flat rocks for sunbathing. Next morning take a boat trip to the **Blue Grotto** and the magnificent clifftop temples of **Ħaġar Qim and Mnajdra**, then in the afternoon visit exquisite **Mdina** and **Rabat**. Spend day five relaxing on a beach, such as **Golden Bay** in the northwest, recharging your batteries for some physical activity on day six – a clifftop walk or maybe some scuba diving. End on a high with a day trip to Comino's spectacular **Blue Lagoon**.

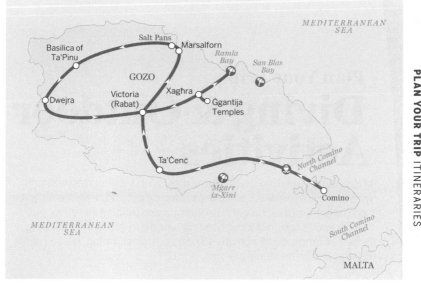

 Gozo

The island of Gozo (14km by 7km) is much smaller than Malta but you still need time to do it justice. Because of its modest size, you can base yourself almost anywhere, particularly if you have your own set of wheels (recommended). Another great way to get around is to hire a bicycle (available on Gozo) or an electric bike (to help with the hills) – the latter must be collected on Malta and brought to Gozo on the ferry. To get the most out of your stay, rent a rambling, idyllic Gozitan farmhouse.

Start your visit by spending a morning exploring **Victoria**, wandering around majestic Il-Kastell, with its astounding views, and the narrow lanes of Il-Borgo. Take a trip over to the huddled seaside resort town of **Marsalforn** for a lazy lunch with sea views and then visit the dramatically set salt pans just outside the town. On day two, head to the grand pilgrimage **Basilica of Ta'Pinu** with its poignant votive offerings, to pay your respects, then while away the rest of the day walking, swimming and snorkelling amid the fantastical moonscape scenery of **Dwejra**.

Set aside day three for walking around the soul-stirring clifftop scenery of **Ta'Ċenċ**, and for seeking out a lesser-known spot for swimming and snorkelling (nearby **Mġarr ix-Xini** is lovely, and a great place for a leisurely lunch).

It's even easier to visit the tiny island of **Comino** from Gozo than it is from Malta, so arrange your boat trip and spend an afternoon paddling around the **Blue Lagoon**.

Begin day four with a visit to the extraordinary prehistoric **Ġgantija Temples** and other attractions of **Xaghra**, then spend the afternoon reclining on **Ramla Bay** or more remote **San Blas Bay**, both of which are beautiful beaches where red sands meet blue water.

There's five days covered – but why not allocate a week and spend a few days relaxing poolside or on the beach?

Plan Your Trip

Diving & Outdoor Activities

Malta, Gozo and Comino are famed as scuba-diving destinations, with plenty of easily accessible wrecks, caves and reefs for all levels from beginner to technical. The islands are brilliant for other outdoor pursuits too, including boating, windsurfing and snorkelling, as well as land-bound activities such as rock climbing, horse riding, walking and birdwatching.

Best Time to Go

Diving – year-round

Sailing – April and November

Kayaking – April to October

Walking – October to June

Rock climbing – October to June

Best Dive Sites for Beginners

HMS *Maori*, Valletta

Għar Lapsi, Southeast Malta

Anchor Bay, Northwest Malta

Best Sites for Experienced Divers

Blenheim Bomber, Southeast Malta

Fessej Rock, Southern Gozo

Double Arch Reef, Northern Gozo

Best Sites for Snorkelling

Wied il-Għasri, Northern Gozo

San Dimitri Point, Western Gozo

Blue Hole & Chimney, Western Gozo

Diving

The calm, non-tidal nature of the sea surrounding Malta and Gozo makes for excellent visibility (25m to 30m on average). The islands are particularly renowned for their wrecks but there is a fantastic range of interesting dive sites, including caves and reefs. These sites are also remarkably easy to reach, with many accessible from the shore. If you're here for a week you could potentially dive off all three islands.

The climate is pleasant and the water warm; the main season is April to November, but you can dive all year round – in winter the water temperature rarely drops below 13°C.

There are also a large number of dive schools with qualified, professional, multilingual instructors to choose from. The following organisations' websites offer information about diving and dive qualifications, plus details of accredited diving schools:

➡ **British Sub-Aqua Club** (www.bsac.com)

➡ **Confédération Mondiale des Activités Subaquatiques** (www.cmas.org)

➡ **Professional Association of Diving Instructors** (www.padi.com)

Malta's Marine Life

Malta's marine life is richer than in many other parts of the Mediterranean, though it has suffered from the effects of boat traffic and over-fishing in recent years.

You're likely to see crabs, lobsters, octopuses, swordfish, sea bream, sea bass, grouper, red mullet, wrasse, dogfish and stingray.

Migratory shoals of sardine, sprat, bluefin tuna, bonito, mackerel and dolphin fish (lampuka) are common in late summer and autumn.

Many divers hope to see the maned seahorse; potential spots are the HMS *Maori* and Mġarr ix-Xini.

Ċirkewwa is a good place to spot barracuda, amberjack, tuna and squid, while Comino's Santa Marija Caves are good for seeing saddled bream and cow bream. San Dimitri Point off Gozo is noted for big schools of barracuda, plus dentex, grouper and rays.

The loggerhead turtle is occasionally sighted in Maltese waters. In 2012 a turtle laid eggs at Ġnejna Bay, the first time this had occurred for 100 years. Nature Trust Malta runs a turtle rescue program at the San Lucjan Aquaculture Research Centre.

The common dolphin (*denfil* in Malti) and the bottlenose dolphin are sometimes sighted on boat trips.

In April 1987 a great white shark caught by local fisherman Alfredo Cutajar off Filfla measured around 7m. Nowadays shark sightings in inshore waters are extremely unlikely.

Dive Schools

There are around 50 dive school operators in Malta, all of which are licensed by the Malta Tourism Authority. The majority are also members of the Professional Diving Schools Association (www.pdsa.org.mt), an organisation dedicated to promoting high standards of safety and professionalism.

The following dive schools all offer a similarly comprehensive menu of PADI-, BSAC- or CMAS-approved training and education courses, guided diving and the rental of scuba equipment to experienced divers. All are suitable for beginners, and most also offer technical diving.

If you're interested in wrecks, it's best to choose a centre in Malta rather than Gozo, as there's a much wider choice of wrecks.

If you're travelling with non-divers in the low season, you may also want to choose Malta, because there's more for them to do here while you're diving. If you just want to dive, Gozo is a good choice.

Nautic Team diving centre in Gozo specialises in diving for people with disabilities.

Sliema & St Julian's Area

➡ **Dive Systems** (p67)

➡ **Diveshack** (p67)

➡ **Divewise** (p71)

Northwest Malta

➡ **Buddies Dive Cove** (p87)

➡ **Dive Deep Blue** (p87)

➡ **Sea Shell Dive Centre** (p81)

➡ **Paradise Diving** (☎2157 4116; www.paradisediving.com; Paradise Bay Resort Hotel, Ċirkewwa)

➡ **Subway Dive Centre** (p87)

Gozo

➡ **Atlantis Diving Centre** (☎ 2155 4685 ; www.atlantisgozo.com; Atlantis Hotel, Triq il-Qolla)

➡ **Calypso Diving Centre** (☎ 2156 1757; www.calypsodivers.com; Triq il-Vulcan)

➡ **Nautic Team** (☎2155 8507; www.nauticteam.com; Triq il-Port)

➡ **Frankie's Gozo Diving Centre** (☎7900 9575; www.gozodiving.com; Triq Mġarr, Xewkija)

➡ **Moby Dives** (p123)

➡ **St Andrews Divers Cove** (p123)

Comino

➡ **Diveshack Comino** (☎2134 5671; www.divemalta.com; Comino Hotel)

Courses & Qualifications

Most schools offer a 'taster course' or 'beginner's dive' (around €35) which includes one or two hours of shore-based instruction, instruction in breathing underwater in a pool or shallow bay, and a 30-minute dive in the sea.

A two- or three-day resort-based scuba course (around €240) gives you shore-based instruction plus open-water dives accompanied by an instructor. Such a course would qualify you up to 12m, and with two days' more instruction you

RESPONSIBLE DIVING

The popularity of diving is placing immense pressure on many sites – more than 60,000 divers a year visit the Maltese Islands. If you dive responsibly you will help preserve the ecology and beauty of Malta's underwater world.

➡ Avoid touching living marine organisms with your body or dragging equipment across rocks. Be conscious of your fins – even without contact the surge from heavy fin strokes can damage delicate organisms.

➡ Never feed fish. You may disturb their normal eating habits, encourage aggressive behaviour or feed them something detrimental to their health

➡ Minimise your disturbance of marine animals; for example, never touch turtles.

➡ Take great care in underwater caves. Spend as little time within them as possible because your air bubbles can be caught within the roof, leaving previously submerged organisms high and dry. Taking turns to inspect the interior of a small cave will lessen the chances of damaging contact.

➡ Do not collect or buy shells or other remains of marine organisms. The same goes for marine archaeological sites (mainly shipwrecks). Respect their integrity; some sites are protected from looting by law.

➡ Plastics in particular are a serious threat to marine life. Ensure that you take home all your rubbish and any litter you may find as well.

can upgrade it to an open-water diving qualification.

A course that will give you an entry-level diving qualification (CMAS One-Star Diver, PADI Open Water Diver, BSAC Ocean Diver) takes three to five days and costs €300 to €360.

For certified divers, guided dives usually cost around €35 for one dive (including all equipment), but multidive packages are better value, costing around €170 to €210 for six dives (price dependent on the amount of gear included). Transport to dive sites may be included in these packages, but if you're staying in Malta, boat trips to Gozo or Comino will often be an additional cost.

An unaccompanied six-day dive package that includes use of cylinder, weight belt and unlimited air fills costs around €120.

Requirements

Operators usually teach junior open-water diving from 10 years of age; those under 18 must have written parental consent. Most dive schools operate PADI 'Bubblemaker' programs designed to introduce kids aged eight and nine to breathing underwater.

If you have a medical condition that may restrict your diving practices, you will be requested to have a medical to determine your fitness. The medical can be organised by the dive school, usually at a cost of €20 to €25. You should also heed medical warnings and not fly within 24 hours of your last dive.

Qualified divers wishing to lead their own groups must do so through a licensed dive centre, and must be at least an advanced open-water diver, with certification.

Safety

Speedboat and ferry traffic can be heavy, especially in peak summer months and in the Gozo Channel area. For their own protection, divers are required to fly the code-A flag and always use a surface-marker buoy. Boats are required to keep a distance of over 100m from divers' buoys, but it's wise to remain vigilant.

Ensure that your travel insurance policy covers you for diving. Some policies specifically exclude 'dangerous activities', which can include scuba-diving.

Malta's public general hospital is Mater Dei Hospital (p171), southwest of Sliema; there is a decompression chamber here. Staff at the hospital can be contacted for any diving incidents requiring medical attention on ☎2545 5269. There is another decompression chamber at Gozo's General Hospital (p171).

Snorkelling

You can sample the delights of a shallower underwater world by donning mask, snorkel and fins and exploring the rocks and bays around Malta's coastline. You can usually rent or buy the necessary equipment from hotels, lidos (recreational facilities with a swimming pool) and watersports centres in all the tourist areas. Some dive centres offer snorkelling trips, and you can also take an organised trip at Park tal-Majjistral (p78).

Top snorkelling spots are off Comino and Gozo. On Comino they include the Blue Lagoon (p133; rent equipment from the kiosk) and the crags and caves east of Santa Marija Bay. On Gozo, head for the cave-riddled coastline at Dwejra, the long, narrow inlet at Wied il-Għasri and San Dimitri Point, and along the salt pan rocks west of Xwieni Bay near Marsalforn. Good spots off Malta include the natural rocky St Peter's Pool (p105) near Marsaxlokk and Għar Lapsi.

Top Diving & Snorkelling Spots

Northwest Malta

Aħrax Point (average depth 7m, maximum depth 18m) Caverns and a tunnel opening up to a small inland grotto with good coral growth. Suitable for all levels. Shore dive; snorkellers can also view it.

Anchor Bay (average depth 6m, maximum depth 12m) Not much to see in the bay itself, but around the corner are good caves. Suitable for all levels. Shore dive.

Ċirkewwa Arch (average depth 10m, maximum depth 36m) Underwater walls and a magnificent arch, where divers can encounter a variety of fish and sometimes seahorses. Suitable for all levels.

Marfa Point (average depth 12m, maximum depth 18m) Large dive site with caves, reefs, promontories and tunnels. Can be accessed from the shore. Decent snorkelling opportunities.

P29 (average depth 30m, maximum depth 37m) Former minesweeper deliberately sunk in Paradise Bay in 2007, close to Tugboat Rozi.

St Paul's Islands (multiple sites, average depths 6m to 12m, maximum depth 25m) Popular dive sites with a wreck between the shore and inner island, a reef on the eastern side of the northernmost island, and a valley between the two islands. Suitable for all levels. The wreck can be accessed from the shore.

Tugboat Rozi (average depth 30m, maximum depth 36m) A boat deliberately sunk in 1991 as an underwater diving attraction and now colonised by thousands of fish.

Valletta & St Julian's Area

Bristol Beaufighter (average depth 33m, maximum depth 36m) A WWII aeroplane which crashed in 1941, near St Julian's; only the body, wings and undercarriage remain intact.

Carolita Barge (average depth 12m, maximum depth 22m) Possibly mistaken for a submarine, this barge was hit by a torpedo in 1942 and sank immediately. Well preserved and home to grouper and octopus. Popular training site for divers and, therefore, busy. Suitable for all levels. Shore dive.

Fortizza Reef & Coral Gardens (average depth 14m to 16m, maximum depth 18m) Close to Sliema, this reef is fantastic for beginners; profuse sea life including octopus, moray eels, damsel fish, lobsters and crabs.

Hellespont (average depth 35m, maximum depth 41m) A paddle steamer and former supply boat sunk in 1942, close to the Grand Harbour. An exposed site.

HMS Maori (average depth 13m, maximum depth 18m) Below Fort St Elmo is the wreck of the HMS Maori, sunk in 1942. Silted up, but home to fish and octopus. Suitable for all levels. Shore dive.

Tug no 2 (average depth 17m to 19m, maximum depth 21m) Scuttled at St Julian's, just off Exiles Reef, in 2013, this is the only wreck in this area, and great for beginners. Dentex and stingrays to spot. Shore dive.

Southeast Malta

Blenheim Bomber (maximum depth 42m) Exploring the well-preserved wreck of this WWII bomber, with engine and wings intact, is an exciting dive. For experienced divers only.

Delimara Point (average depth 12m, maximum depth 25m) Usually excellent visibility for divers, with vertical cliffs and many caverns. Varied and colourful flora and fauna. Suitable for all levels of experience. Shore dive.

Għar Lapsi (average depth 6m, maximum depth 15m) Popular training site for divers; a safe, shallow cave that winds through the headland.

Diving & Snorkelling Malta & Gozo

5 miles
10 km

VALLETTA & ST JULIAN'S AREA

Malta has many wrecks. The Grand Harbour in Valletta has some of the most spectacular, while St Julian's has the downed WWII plane, the Bristol Beaufighter, and Sliema has the Il-Fortizza reef.

COMINO

Comino has some incredible underwater topography and is renowned for its cave dives, featuring abundant, colourful sea life.

SOUTHEAST MALTA

This region has some great wrecks, plus safe yet dramatic diving for all levels, particularly in the area around Ghar Lapsi and Delimara.

NORTHWEST MALTA

The area around Ċirkewwa is famed for its dramatic underwater walls and arch, while Marfa Point has tunnels, caves and reefs.

GOZO

Gozo has diving for all levels with caves and reefs. Wied il-Għasri, Dwejra and Fungus Rock in particular are as breathtaking below water as they are above.

MEDITERRANEAN SEA

MEDITERRANEAN SEA

MALTA

GOZO

Xwieni Bay
Billinghurst Cave & Double Arch Reef
Reqqa Point
Wied il-Għasri
San Dimitri Point
Ghaib
Blue Hole & Chimney
Dwejra
Bay
Fungus Rock
Coral Cave
Crocodile Rock
Xlendi
Xlendi Cave & Reef
Xlendi Bay
Victoria (Rabat)
Xewkija
Ta' Ċenċ
Marsalforn
Żebbuġ
Qbajjar
Xagħra
Ramla Bay
San Blas Bay
Marsalforn
Mġarr
Xatt l'Aħmar
Ta' Ċenċ Rock
Fessej Rock
Santa Marija Cave
Santa Marija Bay
Qala
Blue Lagoon
Lantern Point
Tugboat Rozi
P29
South Comino Channel
Comino Channel
Ċirkewwa Arch
Ċirkewwa
Marfa Point
Ahrax Point
Anchor Bay
Mellieħa
Mellieħa Bay
St Paul's Islands
St Paul's Bay
Xemxija
Baħar iċ-Ċagħaq
Għajn Tuffieħa
Park tal-Majjistral
Għajn Rih Bay
Ġnejna Bay
Baħrija
Rabat
Mosta
Naxxar
San Gwann
Fortizza Reef & Coral Gardens
Tug no 2
Bristol Beaufighter
HMS Maori
Hellespont
VALLETTA
Carolita Barge
Żabbar
Tarxien
Luqa
Qormi
Żebbuġ
Siġġiewi
Bal Bajada
Tal
Ghar Lapsi
Wied iż-Żurrieq
Żurrieq
Qrendi
Birżebbuġa
Marsaxlokk
Marsaxlokk Bay
Ħal Għaxaq
Marsaskala
Delimara Point
Blenheim Bomber
Buġibba
Salina Bay

Shore dive, reasonable snorkelling and suitable for all levels.

Wied iż-Żurrieq (average depth 9m, maximum depth 30m) Close to the Blue Grotto. Underwater valley and labyrinth of caves. Shore dive, reasonable snorkelling and suitable for all levels.

Western Gozo

Blue Hole & Chimney (average depth 20m, maximum depth 45m) The Blue Hole is a natural rock formation and includes a large cave plus a fissure in the near-vertical wall. Popular, busy site. Shore dive, excellent snorkelling and suitable for all levels.

Coral Cave (average depth 25m, maximum depth 30m) Huge semicircular opening with a sandy bottom, where divers can view varied and colourful flora and fauna. Shore dive.

Crocodile Rock (average depth 35m, maximum depth 45m) Rocky reef between the shore and crocodile-shaped rock off the west coast. Natural amphitheatre and deep fissures. Shore dive, decent snorkelling and suitable for all levels.

Fungus Rock (average depth 30m, maximum depth beyond 60m) Dramatic underwater scenery with vertical walls, fissures, caverns and gullies. Good site for underwater photography and suitable for all levels.

San Dimitri Point (average depth 25m, maximum depth beyond 60m) Lots of marine life and exceptional visibility (sometimes exceeding 50m). Good snorkelling and suitable for all levels.

Xlendi Cave & Reef (average depth 6m, maximum depth 25m) Easy cave dive in shallow water and popular with beginners. Brightly coloured cave walls. Rocky headland dips steeply to the sea. An abundance of flora and fauna. Shore dive; OK snorkelling.

Northern Gozo

Billinghurst Cave (average depth 20m, maximum depth 35m) Long tunnel leading to a cave deep inside the rock, with a multitude of coloured sea sponges. There's very little natural light (torch required). Experienced divers only.

Double Arch Reef (average depth 30m, maximum depth 45m) Site characterised by a strange formation, with an arch dividing two large openings in the rock. Prolific marine life. For experienced divers.

Reqqa Point (average depth 25m, maximum depth beyond 70m) Near-vertical wall cut by fissures, caves and crevices. Large numbers of

small fish, plus groups of amberfish and grouper if conditions are favourable. Shore dive and good snorkelling.

Wied il-Għasri (average depth in cave 12m, maximum depth 30m) A deep, winding cut in the headland makes for a long, gentle dive. Possible to view seahorses in the shallows. Cave with a huge domed vault and walls covered in corals. Can be done as a shore dive; very good snorkelling; suitable for all levels.

Southern Gozo

Fessej Rock (average depth 30m, maximum depth 50m) A prominent column of rock. Vertical wall dive descending to 50m amid large shoals of fish. A popular deep-water dive.

Ta'Ċenċ (average depth 25m, maximum depth 35m) Sheltered bay – access is by 103 steps from car park of nearby hotel. Canyon with large boulders, plus cave. Good marine life, but visibility can occasionally be poor. Good spot for night dives. Shore dive; suitable for all levels.

Xatt l'Aħmar (average depth 9m, maximum depth 30m) Small bay, excellent for observing a large variety of fish including mullet, grouper, sea bream, octopus and cuttlefish. Shore dive;

BEST DIVE SITES FOR...

Caves
➡ Coral Cave, Western Gozo
➡ Wied iż-Żurrieq, Southeast Malta
➡ St Marija Caves, Comino

Wrecks
➡ HMS *Maori*, Valletta
➡ P29, Northwest Malta
➡ Tugboat Rozi, Northwest Malta

Dramatic Scenery
➡ Ċirkewwa Arch, Northwest Malta
➡ Marfa Point, Northwest Malta
➡ Delimara Point, Southeast Malta

Colourful Coral & Sea Life
➡ Xatt l'Aħmar, Southern Gozo
➡ Lantern Point, Comino
➡ Reqqa Point, Northern Gozo

Seahorses
➡ HMS *Maori*, Valletta
➡ Wied il-Għasri, Northern Gozo
➡ Mġarr ix-Xini, Southern Gozo

BEST BEACHES FOR...

Swimming

➡ Blue Lagoon (p133)
➡ St Peter's Pool (p105)
➡ Għar Lapsi (p112)

Soft Sand

➡ Golden Bay (p78)
➡ Għajn Tuffieħa Bay (p78)
➡ Ramla Bay (p132)

Watersports

➡ Mellieħa Bay (p80)
➡ Buġibba Beach (p87)
➡ Golden Bay (p78)

Peace & Quiet

➡ Fomm ir-Riħ (p102)
➡ Selmun (Imgiebah) Bay (p84)
➡ Wied il-Għasri (p127)

Scenery

➡ Paradise Bay (p83)
➡ San Blas Bay (p132)
➡ Mġarr ix-Xini (p122)

OK snorkelling; suitable for all levels. Two vessels were scuttled here in August 2006 to create an artificial dive site.

Comino

Blue Lagoon (average depth 6m, maximum depth 12m) Easy site to the north of the sheltered lagoon, very popular with divers and snorkellers. Plenty of boat traffic. Shore dive. Suitable for all levels.

Lantern Point (average depth 30m, maximum depth 45m) Popular dive site. Dramatic dive down a vertical wall. Rich fauna and an abundance of colour. OK snorkelling.

Santa Marija Cave (average depth 7m, maximum depth 10m) Large cave and cavern system; one of the most popular sites for cave dives. An abundance of fish in the area. Very good snorkelling and suitable for all levels.

Beaches & Swimming

Malta and Gozo's coastlines combine rocks and natural pools with sandy stretches.

Malta's best sandy beaches are to the northwest, including Golden Bay, Għajn Tuffieħa Bay, Mellieħa Bay and the small, white-sand Paradise Bay. Elsewhere there are great rocky swimming spots along the Sliema waterfront, and rocky coves along the southeastern coast.

Gozo's best sandy beaches – Ramla Bay and San Blas – are to the northeast, and there are rocky swimming coves and bays both north and south.

The wondrous Blue Lagoon on Comino gets extremely busy in summer, but if you head here in late afternoon you'll find it less so, and it's also better when the sun is lower in the sky as there's no shade nearby.

All beaches get busy in summer, when the weather's baking hot, though you'll often find hidden rocky coves less crowded. Wherever you swim, keep an eye on the weather. Don't swim when the sea is rough, as undercurrents can be powerful.

Sailing

Malta's magnificent harbours, sheltered coves, island scenery and great facilities make it an ideal sailing destination. It's a major yachting centre, with marinas at Msida and Ta'Xbiex, Gozo's Mġarr harbour, the Portomaso development in St Julian's, Grand Harbour Marina at Vittoriosa, and the boutique Laguna Marina at Valletta Waterfront. Many yacht owners cruise the Med in summer, and winter their vessels in Malta.

A full program of races and regattas is held between April and November (great for participants and spectators). The popular **Rolex Middle Sea Race** (www. rolexmiddlesearace.com) is a highly rated offshore classic staged annually in October. For details of events and opportunities for crewing, contact the **Royal Malta Yacht Club** (☑2133 3109; www.rmyc.org; Ta'Xbiex Seafront).

Boatlink (☑9988 2615; www.boatlinkmalta. com), **Fairwind** (☑7955 2222; www.fairwindsailing.com.mt) and the **International Maritime**

Above: Diver on a wreck off Valletta (p25)

Right: Blue Lagoon (p133), Comino

IGNATTEXX/GETTY IMAGES ©

Academy (☑2131 6160; www.imamalta.com) offer sailing courses for children and adults.

Sailing dinghies can be rented at most tourist resorts for around €15 an hour. Qualified sailors are able to hire a yacht by the day or the week from one of several charter companies. If you don't have a RYA Coastal Skipper qualification you'll need to pay extra for a skipper (around €100/180 per day/night). Try the following:

➡ **S & D Yachts** (☑2133 1515; www.sdyachts. com; per week from €2100-3000, per day €400/450 low/high season for a six-berth Bavaria 31 sailing yacht)

➡ **Blue Fin Leisure** (☑9989 0959)

Windsurfing & Kiteboarding

You can windsurf year-round in Malta, in beautiful settings and with excellent facilities. Equipment hire and instruction are available at all the main tourist resorts. Mellieħa Bay is most popular, offering flat and gusty surfing in a large sheltered bay. Experienced surfers also head to Ghallis Rock (close to St Julian's). Other locations include Armier, St Thomas Bay and the channel between Gozo and Malta (for experienced surfers). Fairwind (p28) offers windsurfing courses.

Kiteboarders are not permitted between June and September, when there are too many people on the beaches and in the sea, but the rest of the year there is plenty of choice. Mellieħa is an excellent location for kiteboarders when the wind is blowing from the east. Torri, near Armier, is a tiny bay but popular for its northeasterly winds. Golden Bay and Ġnejna Bay offer prime conditions and waves.

Kayaking & SUP

Kayaking is a great way to see the islands' coast from a different angle; to paddle through sea caves and explore hidden inlets. You can hire kayaks by the hour from resorts such as Xlendi (Gozo) and Mellieħa (Malta), but usually this means you have to stay within the bay. To explore for longer, it's best to arrange a guided kayak excursion. Two operators offer these: **Gozo Adventures** (www.gozoadventures.com)

offers a half-/full-day excursion to Comino and Gozo (€65/45); **Sea Kayak Malta** (www.seakayakmalta.com) offers day trips to Comino or St Paul's Island, with a stop at Selmun (Imġiebah) Bay, as well as longer kayaking holidays.

The re-emerging sport of SUP (stand-up paddleboarding) uses a long surfboard and a paddle and is ideally suited to Malta's flat water. Hire equipment at Mellieħa, Xlendi and Golden Bay.

Walking & Hiking

The winding backroads and clifftop paths of Malta and Gozo offer some fantastic walks. Distances are small and you can cover much of the islands on foot. A circuit of Gozo is a good objective for a multiday hike. Tourist offices have lots of walking leaflets and pamphlets that detail trails all over the islands, and you can download walking routes from www.visitmalta.com/ en/walks. If you'd like a guided long walk, **Gozo Adventures** (www.gozoadventures. com) offers half-/full-day walks (€65/45) and Malta Activities (p31) offers 2½-hour treks (€30 per person) on Malta.

A great source of information is the **Ramblers' Association of Malta** (www. ramblersmalta.org), which organises informal guided country walks for like-minded folk from October to early June (the best time for walking). This organisation is dedicated to safeguarding public access to the Maltese countryside; read about its campaigns on its comprehensive website.

Birdwatching

A stop-off point for migrating birds and with many local species, Malta has some fascinating birdlife. *Where to Watch Birds & Other Wildlife in the Maltese Islands,* written by Alex Casha and published by BirdLife Malta, is a comprehensive guide.

Birdlife Malta (☑2134 7646; www.birdlifemalta.org) is the best contact for birders visiting Malta. The organisation manages the Ghadira Nature Reserve (p81) at Mellieħa Bay and the Is-Simar Nature Reserve (p84) at Xemxija, and monitors activity that threatens wild birds. Its website details recent sightings and documents the campaign against illegal hunting.

Rock Climbing

The Maltese Islands are a thrilling destination for climbers, though you're advised to avoid high summer when temperatures can hit 40°C. There are more than 1500 established rock-climbing routes (all on limestone), with some of the most popular sites for climbers below the Dingli Cliffs in the west, at Għar Lapsi and near the Victoria Lines below Naxxar. Gozo alone has more than 300 sport climbs, with many concentrated in the Munxar-Xlendi Valley (for all abilities) and Mġarr ix-Xini, and others at spectacular coastal locations such as the Wied il-Mielah Sea Arch. There's an incredible variety of climbs for such a small area, all within a short drive of each other. You can learn to climb here and there's plenty for experienced climbers too, with multiple climbs at grades 7 and 8. The **Malta Rock Climbing Club** (www.climbmalta.com) and **Gozo Climbing** (www.gozo-climbing.com) can provide information for visiting climbers, and you can organise climbing, bouldering and abseiling trips through Gozo Adventures (p30).

Malta Activities (☑9942 5439; www.maltaoutdoors.com; per person €30-100) facilitates 2½-hour climbing or abseiling trips for all levels. Trips include opportunities to traverse sea cliffs, and all equipment is provided.

MARATHONS

Several major running events are held each year in Malta, including triathlons and half-marathons, culminating in the Malta Marathon (www.maltamarathon.com) and half-marathon, held in late February/early March.

Horse Riding

Horses have long played an important part in Maltese life, and you can often see owners out exercising their favourite steeds. Horse riding is a fun way to explore the islands' rugged countryside, with routes along the northwest coast and in Gozo, and it's possible to arrange sunset tours. Recommended stables, offering rides for adults and children, include Golden Bay Horse Riding (p78), and Bidnija Horse Riding School (p101) outside Mosta. On Gozo, contact Lino's Stables (p130) to arrange rides for all levels.

PLAN YOUR TRIP DIVING & OUTDOOR ACTIVITIES

Plan Your Trip
Eat & Drink Like a Local

Like the Malti language, Maltese cuisine is an exotic mix of flavours. Different occupiers introduced their foodstuffs and dishes, with Italian, French, British and Arabic cooking proving particularly strong influences. Locals usually feast on home-cooked Maltese food on special occasions, and eat anything from gourmet burgers to fusion when dining out.

The Year in Food

Spring (Mar–May)
Lent specialities include *warezimal* (almond cakes without fat or eggs), and for Easter there's the almond-studded *qagħqa tal-appostli* (apostle's bagel).

Summer (Jun–Aug)
The first fig crop is 'tin ta San Gwann' (of St John) and starts on St John's day (24 June). Drinkers head for July's Marsovin Wine Festival and Farsons Great Beer Festival.

Autumn (Sep–Nov)
St Martin's Day (11 November) calls for recipes involving walnuts, almonds, hazelnuts and dried figs. *Lampuki* (dolphin fish) is at its most plentiful.

Winter (Dec–Feb)
Christmas dishes include *gaghh tal-ghasel* (pastry honey rings) and *imbuljuta* (sweet chestnut soup). It's the time for famously luscious and fragrant blood oranges. Carnival sweets include *prinjolata* (pastry, candied fruit, cream, pine nuts, chocolate and meringue).

Food Experiences
Meals of a Lifetime

Trattoria da Pippo (p55) An old-boys'-club feel and simple yet fine Italian cooking.

Black Pig (p55) Complex, creative food in an intimate, 16th-century setting.

Tmun Mġarr (p121) Gozo's best restaurant, nestled among fishing boats.

Cheap Treats

Crystal Palace (p98) Malta's best *pastizzi*, fresh from the oven.

Fontanella (p94) Try a *ftira* (sandwich in traditional Maltese bread) while enjoying the soaring views from atop the city walls.

Mekrens (p132) and **Maxokk** (p132) Famous across Gozo for their freshly baked *ftira* and pizza.

Dare to Try

Fenek (rabbit) The islands' national dish, usually served fried.

Bebbux (snail salad) Local snails are boiled then dipped in olive oil, herbs, garlic and chilli, and served with salad.

Local Specialities
Bread, Cheese & Pastizzi

Malta's national gap-filler is the *pastizzi,* a small parcel of flaky pastry, Arabic in origin, which is filled with either ricotta cheese and parsley or mushy peas and onions. It's served warm, and is around €0.30 apiece. A couple of *pastizzi* make for a tasty and substantial breakfast or afternoon filler. They're available in most bars or from *pastizzerijas* (hole-in-the-wall takeaway *pastizzi* shops – follow your nose).

For bread-and-cheese picnics, bakeries sell the famously delicious traditional bread *ħobż,* made in a similar manner to sourdough bread, using a scrap of yesterday's dough to leaven today's loaves. You'll see it on menus as *ħobż biż-żejt,* slices of bread rubbed with ripe tomatoes and olive oil until they are pink and delicious, then topped with a mix of tuna, onion, capers, olives, garlic, black pepper and salt.

Ftira is traditional Maltese bread baked in a flat disc. It makes for delicious sandwiches when stuffed with a substantial, punchy mixture of olives, capers and anchovies, together with the tangy local tomato paste made from sun-dried tomatoes ground with rosemary, sugar and other secret ingredients.

Gozo is famous for its cheeses, especially *ġbejniet,* a small, hard, white cheese traditionally made from unpasteurised sheep's or goat's milk. It's often steeped in olive oil and flavoured with salt and crushed black peppercorns. The best is said to come from Żebbuġ.

Another delicious snack is stuffed olives (*Żebbuġ mimili*) filled with tuna, breadcrumbs, capers, garlic and herbs.

Soups & Pasta Dishes

Soups are popular in traditional local cooking, with several recipes cooking meat in the broth, so the soup is served as a starter, followed by the meat as a main course. This was a practical measure, and many homes still don't have traditional ovens.

Aljotta, a delicious fish broth made with tomato, rice and lots of garlic, is most commonly served in restaurants. In spring, you may encounter *kusksu,* a soup made from broad beans and small pasta shapes, often served with soft fresh *ġbejniet* (Gozo cheese), ricotta and an egg floating in the middle.

Soppa tal-armla means 'widow's soup' (probably named because of its inexpensive ingredients). It's traditionally made only with components that are either green or white: a tasty mix of cauliflower, spinach, endive and peas, with protein provided by a poached egg, *ġbejniet* and a lump of ricotta.

Minestra is a thick soup of tomatoes, beans, pasta and vegetables, similar to some variations of Italian minestrone, but thicker and more golden in colour, as it includes pumpkin.

Two other Italian-influenced dishes are *ravjul/ravjuletti* (pasta pouches filled with ricotta, Parmesan and parsley; a Maltese variety of ravioli) and *timpana,* a rich pie filled with macaroni, cheese, egg, minced beef, tomato, garlic and onion (a Sicilian dish similar to the Greek *pastitsio*). *Timpana* is usually cooked for special occasions but appears on menus in Maltese restaurants.

Meat Dishes

Maltese main courses are hearty. Meat pies and roast beef, lamb, pork, quail and duck feature heavily.

Most typical of all is *fenek* (rabbit). Introduced by the Normans, the bunny became a symbol of feudal repression when the Knights, to save enough game for the hunt, banned the peasantry from eating it. Adding insult to injury, rabbits persistently attacked the farmers' crops. The Maltese have certainly got their own back: it's now the island's favourite national dish, whether fried in olive oil, roasted, stewed, served with spaghetti or baked in a pie. *Fenek bittewm u l-inbid* is rabbit cooked in garlic and wine, *fenek moqli* is fried rabbit and *stuffat tal-fenek* is stewed rabbit.

A *fenkata* is a rabbit feast – usually spaghetti with rabbit sauce, followed by fried rabbit. This is for special occasions, particularly L-Imnarja on 29 June, the Feast of St Peter and Paul, when locals celebrate through the night at Buskett Gardens with *fenkata* and lots of wine. (It used to be written into the marriage contract that a husband had to take his wife to L-Imnarja.) On non-special occasions you can find it at places such as Ta'Marija (p101) in Mosta.

Braġioli (beef olives) are prepared by wrapping thin slices of beef around a stuffing of breadcrumbs, chopped bacon, hard-boiled egg and parsley, then braising them in a red wine and tomato sauce. *Tigieja* is roast chicken stuffed with beef, pork, ham, eggs, parsley and basil. *Stuffat tal-Laham* (beef stew) is cooked with mushrooms, onions, carrots and potatoes.

Maltese sausages *(zalzetta tal-malti)* are notably good, showing English and Portuguese influence and made in either fresh (which have more garlic) or cured versions.

Seafood

Unsurprisingly in these Mediterranean islands, fresh seafood is a staple. The most favoured of fishes is the *lampuka* (dolphin fish), and *torta tal-lampuki* (also known as *lampuki* pie) is the classic dish. It's typically baked with tomatoes, onions, black olives, spinach, sultanas and walnuts – although there are lots of other recipes too. *Ċerna* (grouper), *pagru* (sea bream), *dentiċi* (dentex), *spnotta* (sea bass) and John Dory are other versatile and popular fish that you'll find on lots of menus. Cod is not found in the Mediterranean, so Maltese recipes sometimes make use of *bakkaljaw* (salt cod). Octopus and cuttlefish are also excellent menu additions.

COOKING CLASSES

To learn more about Maltese cooking, read the *Food & Cookery of Malta,* by Anne and Helen Caruana Galizia, which includes recipes.

You can learn cooking with Patti at Thirtyseven (p144) on Gozo, and Julie at Julesys's B&B (p138) in Copiscua – but both specialise in a range of cuisines rather than local cooking. UK-based bespoke tour company **Tabona & Walford** (www. tabonaandwalford.co.uk) offers a week-long tour of Malta that combines cooking with sightseeing.

Sweets

Kannoli are Sicilian but are widely found in Malta. These tubes of crispy, fried pastry are best eaten when they've been freshly filled with ricotta (to avoid the tubes going soggy); sometimes they're also sweetened with chocolate chips or candied fruit. *Mqaret* are almond-shaped pastries stuffed with chopped, spiced dates and deep-fried – they're particularly good accompanied by vanilla ice cream.

Deliciously chewy Maltese nougat, flavoured with almonds or hazelnuts and traditionally sold on festa (feast) days, is known as *qubbajt. Gaghh tal-għasel,* honey or treacle rings made from a light pastry, are served in small pieces as an after-dinner accompaniment to coffee.

Drinks

Alcoholic Drinks

Maltese bars serve every kind of drink you could ask for, from pints of British beer to shots of Galliano liqueur. Malta has a long tradition of beer making, brought over by the British. The top locally made (from imported hops) beers, Cisk Lager and Hopleaf Ale, are cheaper than imported brews. **Lord Chambray** (www.lordchambray.com.mt; Gozo) is an artisanal brewery that opened on Gozo in 2014 – it produces the unpasteurised pale and golden ales San Blas and Golden Bay, Blue Lagoon (Belgian White), and Fungus Rock, a stout.

The main players on the local wine scene are Camilleri Wines, Emmanuel Delicata, **Marsovin** (www.marsovin.com), **Meridiana** (http://meridiana.com.mt) and Maria Rosa Winery (p103). These companies make wine from local grapes and also produce more expensive 'special reserve' wines – merlot, cabernet sauvignon, chardonnay and sauvignon blanc – using imported grapes from Italy. There are some excellent results and the quality is improving all the time. The vineyards offer worthwhile tours and tastings; check their websites for details.

Maltese liqueurs pack a punch and make good souvenirs. Look out for Zeppi's potent liqueurs concocted from local honey, aniseed or prickly pear. Gozo-produced *limunċell* (a variant on the Italian lemon liqueur *limoncello*) is delicious; there are orange and mandarin varieties too.

Water & Nonalcoholic Drinks

Good Italian coffee and a strong British-style cup of tea are widely available in cafes and bars.

Malta's tap water is safe to drink, if a little unpalatable because of its high chloride and sodium levels.

Cold soft drinks are available everywhere. Kinnie (its advertising signs are all over the place in Malta) is the brand name of a local soft drink flavoured with bitter oranges and aromatic herbs, drunk on its own or as a mixer.

How to Eat & Drink

When to Eat

Breakfast is usually a coffee or tea with a biscuit, croissant or cereal, but some Maltese will skip an early breakfast and grab a sweet tea and a *pastizzi*. Older people like a breakfast of good Maltese ħobż (bread).

Lunch was once the largest meal of the day, eaten between around 1pm and 3pm, but few people get home for lunch these days, and so will eat a sandwich, wrap or *pastizzi* (though people are becoming increasingly health conscious). Nowadays dinner tends to be the main meal, with people dining out from around 8pm.

The time for a big lunch is on Sunday. In summer, locals will spend all day at the beach, grazing on picnics and wrapping it up with a beach barbecue in the evening.

Where To Eat & Drink

Restaurants

Restaurants range from laid-back to quite formal. It's common for fine-dining restaurants to open only in the evening, and many don't accept young children, so the atmosphere is restrained and peaceful. For an excellent guide to Malta's restaurants, buy the **Definitive(ly) Good Guide to Restaurants in Malta & Gozo** (www.restaurants-malta.com; €8) online or at local bookshops.

Portions in Maltese restaurants are usually huge. If you order a starter portion of, for example, pasta, it's likely to be more than enough, or you can share a main course between two. A starter followed by a main course is likely to be overwhelming.

PLAN YOUR TRIP EAT & DRINK LIKE A LOCAL

VEGETARIANS & VEGANS

Until relatively recently, meat was a rare luxury on many Maltese tables, so there are plenty of traditional Maltese vegetable dishes, using ingredients such as artichokes, broad beans, cauliflower and cabbage, depending on the season. However, these often use meat stock or tuna, so check before you order. Some restaurants offer meat-free dishes as main courses, and most have vegetarian pizza and pasta options (these usually include egg and/or dairy ingredients). At the Electro Lobster Project (p69) there's a separate vegetarian menu.

While vegetarians are reasonably well catered for, vegans are less so, though there are a few places offering vegan options, including the Grassy Hopper (www.thegrassyhopper.com) in Valletta and Mint (p67).

Try to leave room for desserts, which are usually very good.

Kiosks

Kiosks are a common sight in Malta: small roadside or waterside restaurants in huts with outdoor tables and chairs. You'll find them on the Qawra, Sliema and Ta'Xbiex promenades, and in Upper Barrakka Gardens in Valletta. They're usually good, cheap places to eat, serving up greasy-spoon-style menus including such meals as pork chops or fish and chips. They're a great choice for families.

Cafes

Cafes in Malta are relaxed and are usually open all day. Some, like Café Jubilee (p119) in Victoria, morph from daytime cafe to night-time cafe-bar, staying open until midnight or later and serving cocktails, wine and snacks.

Pastizzerijas

Look out for small hole-in-the-wall *pastizzerijas* selling authentic *pastizzi* and other pastries. Most larger towns have at least a couple.

Plan Your Trip

Travel with Children

Sun and sea, boat trips and snorkelling, countryside and caves, forts and castles: there's lots for the young 'uns to see and do in Malta and Gozo. Add pedestrianised town centres, friendly locals, lots of laid-back, open-air restaurants, and short distances between places, and you have an ideal destination for a family holiday.

Best Regions for Kids

Valletta
Pedestrianised lanes, piazzas, forts, fountains, boat trips and museums.

Sliema, St Julian's & Paceville
Rocky beaches, one small sandy bay, and child-friendly cafes and restaurants.

Northwest Malta
Malta's best beaches, with lots of watersports facilities, boat-trip opportunities and Malta National Aquarium.

Southeast Malta
Marsaxlokk's fun Sunday market, natural swimming pools, caves and hilltop temples.

Gozo & Comino
Malta's neighbours are fun to get to (by boat) and once there you can slow your pace, swim, explore, snorkel, boat and dive.

Malta for Kids

As in most Mediterranean countries, families will receive a warm welcome, and the sunny weather and easygoing lifestyle make it easy to entertain children without too much effort. There's a good health-care system here and most people speak English; a smaller proportion also speak Italian and sometimes French. The **Malta Baby & Kids Directory** (www.maltababyand-kids.com; €8) lists lots of useful information, including days out, activities and general advice. You can buy the directory online or register to obtain its listings.

Open Spaces

Malta's sandy beaches tend to be the best for younger children, as they have gentle approaches and shallow areas for swimming. The more popular ones have watersports and boating facilities, which makes them especially good for older children too. The rocky bays that dot the coast are better for older children and adults only, as these natural sea pools do not always have shallow areas for less-confident swimmers.

Although Malta's main roads are busy, the main square of each town is almost always closed to traffic, and village and town promenades are often pedestrianised, which means there's space to run about even in a town centre. Valletta's pedestrianised centre has choreographed fountains, on Pjazza San Ġorġ.

By the coast, long, wide promenades often have playgrounds (there's one at Sliema and a great one at Qawra as part of the Malta National Aquarium complex) and kiosks for snacks. Marsaskala, in the southeast, has the large, free Sant'Antnin Park, which includes a climbing wall. Mdina has a large playground just outside the city walls, and the city's Ditch Garden is a good place to run around in. There's a small playground next to the ferry stop in Copiscua (Three Cities) and a recommended playground in Paola (close to the Hypogeum and Tarxien Temples).

As for parks, some of the best include San Anton Gardens in Attard and the Argotti Botanical Gardens in Floriana, and Valletta has the Upper Barrakka Gardens, Lower Barrakka Gardens and Hastings Garden. The wooded Buskett Gardens near Dingli on Malta are somewhat wilder and a great place to explore.

On less-busy Gozo there are lots of walking trails and beaches, but Dwejra, with its rocky moonscape coast, inland sea and boat trips, is one of the most spectacular areas for kids.

Dining Out

Children are welcome at most restaurants, though many of the smarter places don't permit very young children. In child-friendly restaurants, high chairs are usually available, there's normally a children's menu, and sometimes changing facilities. Children's menus tend to offer a similar roll call of chicken nuggets, pizza and so on; if you want to provide more variety, ask for a half-portion of an adult dish instead. As in Italy, people won't blink an eye at children staying up late, particularly in summer when many children will have had a siesta in the heat of the afternoon.

Children's Highlights

Theme Parks & Aquariums

➡ **Buġibba Water Park** (p85) A free water play park, with colour-coded areas for different ages (up to age 12).

➡ **Malta National Aquarium** (p85) Qawra's state-of-the-art glimpse into the world of the sea.

➡ **Splash & Fun Park** (p89) Waterslides and playground, at Baħar iċ Ċagħaq.

➡ **Sweethaven** (p82) Film set from the 1980 film *Popeye* turned into a fun theme park; take boat trips and make a movie.

Forts, Castles & Cannons

➡ **Fort St Elmo** (p51) A parade ground, missiles and the Malta National War Museum.

➡ **In Guardia** (p51) Costumed reenactments in Fort St Elmo.

➡ **Fort St Angelo** (p59) Restored by Heritage Malta, with magnificent views.

➡ **Fort Rinella** (p64) Costumed fort, enthusiastic volunteers and cannon- and rifle-firing.

➡ **Upper Barrakka Gardens & Saluting Battery** (p52) Get up close when they fire the cannon.

➡ **Inquisitor's Palace** (p61) Prison cells and cesspits.

➡ **Red (St Agatha's) Tower** (p82) Mini-fortress with a chance to try on armour.

➡ **Old Prison** (p118) Prison cells in Gozo's castlelike capital.

Caves & Tunnels

➡ **St Agatha's Crypt & Catacombs** (p95) and **St Paul's Catacombs** (p95) Older children will enjoy these mysterious caverns.

➡ **Ninu's Cave** (p129) and **Xerri's Grotto** (p129) Gozo caves under ordinary houses, full of stalagmites and stalactites.

➡ **Mellieħa Air-Raid Shelters** (p80) Tunnels where Maltese residents sheltered during WWII air raids, with waxworks to bring the experience alive.

➡ **Għar Dalam Cave** (p108) Malta's largest cave, full of fossilised animal remains.

Child-Friendly Museums

➡ **National War Museum** (p52) In Fort St Elmo, a fascinating museum with lots of imaginative audiovisual exhibits.

➡ **Armoury** (p47) Older children will get a kick out of the audioguides and weaponry.

➡ **Pomskizillious Museum of Toys** (p130) and **Toy Museum** (p51) Both museums house historic toys in glass cases.

➡ **Maritime Museum** (p62) Lots of model boats and the chance to role-play in the mock sailors' bar.

➡ **Malta Aviation Museum** (p98) Impressive array of engines and aircraft.

➡ **National Museum of Natural History** (p94) A classic natural history museum, with stuffed birds and skeletons.

Beaches & Coves

➡ **Golden Bay** (p78) Gentle sandy beach with lots of facilities.

➡ **Għajn Tuffieħa Bay** (p78) A bit hard to reach (186 steps) but gentle and sandy.

➡ **Mellieħa Bay** (p80) Sandy, with safe paddling and swimming, and lots of facilities.

➡ **St Peter's Pool** (p105) Limpid sea pool; confident swimmers only.

➡ **Għar Lapsi** (p112) Natural sea swimming pool.

➡ **Ramla Bay** (p132) A lovely red-sand beach with cafe.

➡ **San Blas Bay** (p132) Another great beach, less crowded than Ramla; steep approach but you can hop on a jeep.

➡ **Mġarr ix-Xini** (p122) A gorgeous little cove with good swimming.

➡ **Wied il-Għasri** (p127) Great cove with azure sea and adventurous steep approach.

➡ **Blue Lagoon** (p133) The ultimate sea-swimming pool.

Outdoor Activities

➡ **Boat trips** Round the islands in a glass-bottomed boat; speedboats to see coves or to Comino and Gozo (see individual locations).

➡ **Diving** Great beginners' diving (p22) and centres dotted all over the islands (over 10s).

➡ **Horse riding** Golden Bay, Mosta and Gozo have some good riding centres (p31).

➡ **Jeep safaris** A fun way to explore the islands (p67).

➡ **Watersports** All the major resorts offer canoeing, dinghies for hire, pedaloes etc

➡ **Rock climbing** Beginners' climbing or abseiling offered by local organisations (p31).

➡ **Kayaking** Take an organised sea kayaking trip (p30) to explore the coast.

Exhibitions

➡ **Audiovisual exhibitions** Cinematic presentations such as the Malta Experience (p52; Valletta) and the **Mdina Experience** (⏺2145 4322; www.themdinaexperience.com; Misraħ Mesquita; adult/child €6/3; ⏱10am-5pm) will entertain kids aged around seven to 12.

➡ **Waxworks** Vivid evocations of the past are found at the Knights Hospitallers (p52) .

➡ **Rampila** (p55) More waxworks can be seen at this restaurant with its own waxwork Maltese folkloric museum.

Planning

When to Go

If you're travelling in July and August, when the weather is at its hottest, easy access to the sea or a pool is recommended. Plan an afternoon siesta to avoid the heat of the early afternoon; there's usually a lull in activity from around 1pm to 4pm.

In spring, early summer and autumn (June and September) the sea is warm, the weather milder, prices lower and places less crowded. Children will enjoy the colourful parades at Carnival (February) and Easter (March/April), and the living nativity on Gozo at Christmas, but swimming will be chilly in these months.

Accommodation

As Malta and Gozo are such family-centred destinations, there are lots of suitable, reasonably priced options, including self-catering accommodation. The farmhouses for rent on Gozo are ideal; they offer plenty of space and often a pool. Most boutique hotels in Valletta only take older children.

What to Pack

You'll find everything you need available in Malta, so don't panic about forgetting something: formula, nappies (diapers), wipes, clothes, toys and English-language children's books are all easy to find. Mosquitoes are an issue – pack some child-friendly repellent or there's a chance kids will get badly bitten on their first night.

Regions at a Glance

Valletta, Malta's beautiful little capital, is rich in history and culture, and has some of Malta's best restaurants and bars. Nearby lie Sliema, St Julian's and Paceville, seafront settlements that together form Malta's gastronomic and nightlife capital. To the northwest are Malta's best beaches and the island's major resorts. Central Malta is the most traditional-feeling area of the main island, home to the historically fascinating towns of Mdina and Rabat. The southeast has more gorgeous coast, a vibrant fish market and some of Malta's finest prehistoric temples. To slow down, head to Gozo and Comino for epic scenery, walks, outdoor activities and relaxation.

Valletta

History
Food
Prehistory

Knights & Fortresses

Valletta was built after the triumph of the Knights of St John at the Siege of Malta in 1565, and the city's narrow grid of baroque streets and fortifications remain intact.

Creative Dining

You can dine spectacularly in Malta's capital, which holds some of the islands' best restaurants, serving a range of cuisines from Maltese tapas to earthy Roman cooking.

Mysterious Temples

Close to Valletta are two of Malta's most amazing prehistoric sites: the Hal Saflieni Hypogeum and Tarxien Temples, a 5000-year-old necropolis and a temple complex.

p42

Sliema, St Julian's & Paceville

Food
Nightlife
Boat Trips

Maltese, Italian & Fusion

Buzzing, chic Sliema and St Julian's are packed full of restaurants – encompassing Maltese, Italian and creative fusion cuisine – and sleek bars.

Bars & Clubs

If you're under 25 and looking for a party, Paceville could be heaven, with a fiesta-style atmosphere on summer nights, as swarms of international students, tourists and young locals descend.

Yachting & Cruising

Sliema's promenade looks across to Valletta's grand fortifications. From here you can explore the harbours by boat – or go further afield, encircling the entire island or taking a trip to Gozo and Comino.

p65

Northwest Malta

Beaches
Views
Food

Golden Sands

Malta's finest sandy fringes lie on the northwestern coast. The beaches here may not be huge but they are beautiful, backed by hills and with soft sand underfoot.

Remote Clifftops

You may think it's hard to get away from it all on Malta, but a short drive or walk along the headland to Ras il-Qammieħ will leave you feeling like you've reached the end of the world.

Contemporary Maltese

The elegant resort town of Mellieħa has escaped the rampant development seen on other parts of the coast, and you can dine on Maltese haute cuisine at some excellent local restaurants.

p75

Central Malta

History
Architecture
Scenery

Romans, Knights & Catacombs

In central Malta you'll feel as though you have travelled back in time. Here is the silent city of Mdina, the Roman villa excavated at Rabat, and Rabat's intriguing catacombs.

Medieval Meets Baroque

Whether it's the jumble of medieval and baroque architecture in Mdina and Rabat, or the great dome at Mosta, central Malta yields some illustrious architectural splendours.

Dizzying Cliffs

The Dingli Cliffs feature some of the islands' most sumptuous scenery. The 60m cliffs drop into royal-blue sea, and their heights offer endless views over the Mediterranean.

p99

Southeast Malta

Food
Prehistory
Coastline

Seaside Food

Southeast Malta is the place to go for fresh-off-the-boat seafood. The seafront at Marsaxlokk is lined by restaurants overlooking bobbing boats, while Marsaskala, off the tourist path, is a favourite of foodie locals.

Clifftop Temples

Ħaġar Qim and Mnajdra temples have the most thrilling location of any of Malta's prehistoric sites. The great ruins are perched on cliffs overlooking the islet of Filfla.

Natural Pools

There are some lovely spots along the southeastern coast to have a dip: take a trip to the Blue Grotto, swim in the natural pool of Għar Lapsi and seek out St Peter's Pool.

p104

Gozo & Comino

Swimming
Scenery
Activities

Red Sand & Rocky Bays

As well as its distinctive red-sand beaches on the northeast coast, Gozo has some glorious rocky bays to swim in, including Mġarr ix-Xini and Wied il-Għasri. Comino's Blue Lagoon can't be missed.

Hills & Cliffs

Nineteenth-century nonsense artist and poet Edward Lear invented new words to describe the beautifully strange landscape of Gozo, calling it 'pomskizillious and gromphiberous'.

Diving, Horse Riding & Boating

Gozo is a particularly beguiling destination for underwater exploration, and also yields fantastic horse riding, boat trips and other watersports opportunities.

p113

On the Road

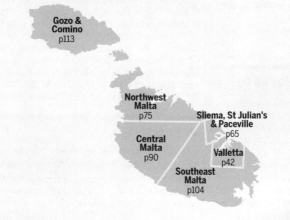

Valletta

POP 6445

Best Places to Eat

➡ Black Pig (p55)

➡ Scoglitti (p53)

➡ Rubino (p53)

➡ Harbour Club (p53)

➡ Trattoria da Pippo (p55)

Best Places to Stay

➡ Casa Ellul (p137)

➡ Palazzo Prince d'Orange (p136)

➡ Trabuxu Boutique Living (p137)

➡ Palazzo San Pawl (p136)

Why Go?

Valletta is Malta's lilliputian capital, built by the Knights of St John on a peninsula that's only 1km by 600m. Its founder decreed that it should be 'a city built by gentlemen for gentlemen', and it retains its 16th-century elegance. It may be small, but it's packed full of sights; when Unesco named Valletta a World Heritage Site, it described it as 'one of the most concentrated historic areas in the world'.

The Renzo Piano–designed City Gate, Parliament Building and Opera House have changed the cityscape and galvanised it into life. These sights, along with Valletta's status as European Capital of Culture for 2018, have seen the city reborn, with new museums, restored golden-stone fortresses, and new hotels, bars and restaurants in converted 16th-century mansions. Valletta's outskirts are even worth a visit: take the beautiful ferry trip to the Three Cities or visit the astounding prehistoric Hal Saflieni Hypogeum.

When to Go

➡ April, May, June, September and October are the balmiest months, with lower prices, sunshine and fewer crowds.

➡ The Malta Firework Festival is at the end of April, and in June there is the Film Festival and Għanafest, which celebrates traditional music.

➡ Summer is hot and lively, with the Malta Arts and Jazz festivals in July.

➡ Look out also for the Notte Bianca in October, when Valletta stays up particularly late.

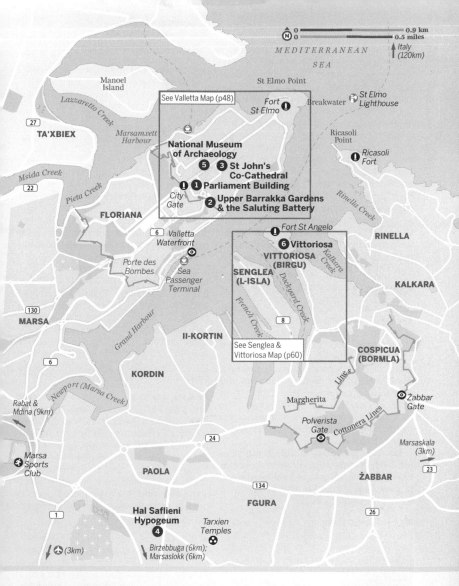

Valletta Highlights

1 Enjoy the many different angles of Renzo Piano's new **Parliament Building** (p44).

2 Check out the view that puts the 'grand' in Grand Harbour, from the **Upper Barrakka Gardens & the Saluting Battery** (p52).

3 Discover the glories of **St John's Co-Cathedral** (p46).

4 Visit the extraordinary underworld of the **Hal Saflieni Hypogeum** (p64).

5 Admire the delicate modelling of the 'fat ladies' at the **National Museum of Archaeology** (p44).

6 Get lost in the charming backstreets of **Vittoriosa** (p59), followed by a cruise of the Grand Harbour.

History

Before the Great Siege of 1565, the Sceberras Peninsula was uninhabited and unfortified, except for Fort St Elmo at its furthest point. Fearing another attack by the Turks, Grand Master Jean Parisot de la Valette (of the Knights of St John) began the task of building a new city on what was then just a barren limestone ridge. Valletta was the first planned city in Europe, with buildings tall enough to shade the streets from the hot sun, and straight streets to allow cooling sea breezes to circulate. A great ditch – 18m deep, 20m wide and nearly 1km long – was cut across the peninsula to protect the landward approach, and massive curtain walls were raised around the perimeter of the city. Spurred on by the fear of a Turkish assault, the Knights completed the fortifications in a mere five years.

◎ Sights

★ City Gate   MONUMENT
The Renzo Piano–designed City Gate forms part of the architect's dramatic and harmonious new development. It echoes the dimensions of the original 1633 entrance, rather than the 1960s gate that it replaced, allowing passers-by to have the sensation of crossing a real bridge, and giving them views of the ditch and fortifications. The architecture is pared down and stark, and the gate is framed by a pair of metal blades, each 25m high.

Inside the gate, a pair of wide, gently sloping flights of steps, inspired by the stairs that framed the original gate, link the bastions of St James' Cavalier and St John's Cavalier to the lower-level Republic St.

★ Parliament Building   BUILDING
Renzo Piano's breathtaking new Parliament Building was completed in 2014. Its design includes two massive volumes of stone that

---

❶ MUSEUM PASS
If you're going to visit more than a few historical sites and museums in Valletta, it's well worth investing in a multisite pass from **Heritage Malta** (www. heritagemalta.org), which offers a total discount of €200. This covers you for admission to all 22 Heritage Malta sites (except the Hypogeum), as well as the **Malta National Aquarium** (p85).

LOCAL KNOWLEDGE
CORNER MONUMENTS
You'll notice that on almost every corner of Valletta there is some kind of statue or monument. When the Knights of St John planned Valletta, they issued regulations, called *capitoli*, that all corners had to be embellished by statues or niches.

look suspended in air, but are supported by stilts. The blocks have been machine-cut to lighten their appearance, while reducing solar radiation and letting in daylight. Covering the rooftop are 600 sq metres of photovoltaic panels, which generate most of the energy required to heat the building in the winter and cool it in summer.

The northern block contains the parliament chamber, while the south block accommodates MPs' offices. As little has changed architecturally in Valletta since it was established in the 16th and 17th centuries, it's unsurprising that Renzo Piano's dramatic new additions, including the Parliament Building, City Gate and Opera House, have proved controversial, and everyone has an opinion on the buildings.

Royal Opera House   BUILDING
(Triq ir-Repubblika) Built in the 1860s, the once imperious Opera House was destroyed during a German air raid in 1942. Its gutted shell was left as a reminder of the war, and now acts a framework for the Renzo Piano–designed open-air performance space, where bottle-green seating is raised above the ruins. It's a wonderful place to catch a concert, which are most frequent during the Arts Festival.

Malta 5D   AUDIOVISUAL
(☑ 2735 5001; malta5d.com; Triq l-Ifran; adult/child €9/6; ☉ 9.30am-4.30pm Mon-Sat, 10am-2pm Sun) The newest of Valletta's audiovisual evocations of the past, this 20-minute show enlivens Malta's history with 3D effects, smells, gusts of air and moving seats.

★ National Museum of
Archaeology   MUSEUM
(☑ 2122 1623; Triq ir-Repubblika; adult/child €5/3.50; ☉ 9am-7pm) The National Museum of Archaeology is housed in the impressive Auberge de Provence.

Exhibits include delicate stone tools dating from 5200 BC and Phoenician amulets,

ST JOHN'S CO-CATHEDRAL

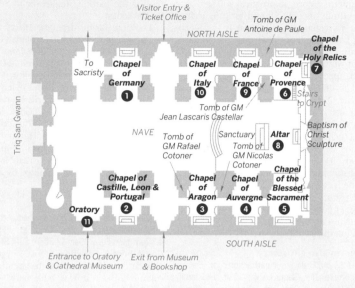

Visitor Entry &
Ticket Office

Tomb of GM
Antoine de Paule

NORTH AISLE

Chapel
of the
Holy Relics
7

To
Sacristy

Chapel
of
Germany
1

Chapel
of
Italy
10

Chapel
of
France
9

Chapel
of
Provence
6

Stairs
to Crypt

Triq San Gwann

Tomb of GM
Jean Lascaris Castellar

NAVE

Tomb of
GM Rafael
Cotoner

Sanctuary

Tomb of
GM Nicolas
Cotoner

Altar
8

Baptism of
Christ
Sculpture

Chapel of
Castille, Leon &
Portugal
2

Chapel
of
Aragon
3

Chapel
of
Auvergne
4

Chapel
of the
Blessed
Sacrament
5

Oratory
11

Entrance to Oratory
& Cathedral Museum

Exit from Museum
& Bookshop

SOUTH AISLE

Church Tour
St John's Co-Cathedral

START CHAPEL OF GERMANY
END ORATORY
LENGTH TWO HOURS

The cathedral has eight chapels allocated to the various *langues* (nationality-based divisions). Enter and turn to your right. You'll see the **1 Chapel of Germany**; look out for the German Langue's emblem of a double-headed eagle. Cross the nave to the **2 Chapel of Castille, Leon & Portugal**, with its Mattia Preti altarpiece and monuments to Grand Masters Antonio Manoel de Vilhena and Manuel Pinto de Fonseca. Next is the **3 Chapel of Aragon**, with another Preti altarpiece and the extravagant tombs of the brothers (and consecutive Grand Masters) Rafael and Nicolas Cotoner. Next is **4 Chapel of Auvergne**, with the tomb of Grand Master Fra Annet de Clermont de Chattes Gessan. Beyond is the **5 Chapel of the Blessed Sacrament**, which once contained an icon of the Virgin brought from Rhodes, removed from here when Napoleon expelled the order. It contains a 15th-century crucifix from Rhodes and keys of captured

Turkish fortresses. Opposite is the dark **6 Chapel of Provence**, with the tombs of Grand Masters Antoine de Paule and Jean Lascaris Castellar. The crypt (usually closed) contains the first 12 Grand Masters, including Jean Parisot de la Valette. The **7 Chapel of the Holy Relics** guards a wooden figure of St John, said to be from the galley in which the Knights departed from Rhodes in 1523. The **8 Altar** is dominated by the *Baptism of Christ* by Giuseppe Mazzuoli; Preti's paintings of St John decorate the vaulted ceiling. The austere **9 Chapel of France**, with a Preti altarpiece of St Paul, houses lavish funerary monuments, including to Grand Masters Adrien de Wignacourt and Fra Emmanuel de Rohan. Preti's painting, *The Mystic Marriage of St Catherine*, hangs in the exquisite baroque **10 Chapel of Italy**, overlooking a bust of Grand Master Gregorio Carafa. The **11 Oratory** was built in 1603 as a building for novices, and later redecorated by Preti. It contains Caravaggio's menacing *Beheading of St John the Baptist* (c 1608), the artist's largest painting, and his *St Jerome*, full of quiet power and pathos.

and there's an amazing temple model from Ta'Ħaġrat – a prehistoric architectural maquette. More impressive still are the beautifully modelled prehistoric figurines that were found locally. Best is the Sleeping Lady, found at the Hypogeum, which is around 5000 years old. It shows a recumbent woman with her head propped on one arm, apparently deep in slumber.

The 'fat ladies' sculptures, found at Ħaġar Qim, have massive rounded thighs and arms, but tiny, doll-like hands and feet. They wear pleated skirts and sit with their legs tucked neatly to one side. The so-called Venus de Malta, also from Ħaġar Qim, is about 10cm tall and displays remarkably realistic modelling. There are also beautiful stone friezes from the Tarxien Temples.

Upstairs the new displays showcase the coarser pottery from the Bronze Age, animal figurines and jewellery, as well as information on the island's mysterious cart ruts.

Valletta Living History AUDIOVISUAL
(☑2722 0071; www.maltaattraction.com; Embassy Complex, Triq Santa Luċija; adult/child/family €9.75/4/25; ☺10am-4pm, shows every 45min) A glossy, entertaining 35-minute sweep through Malta's eventful history (available in eight languages).

National Museum of Fine Arts MUSEUM
(☑2122 5769; Triq Nofs in-Nhar; adult/child €5/3.50; ☺9am-5pm) Take the icing-sugar-white sweeping staircase to explore this fascinating yet undervisited 15th- to 20th-century art collection. Highlights include room 8, with Guido Reni's *Risen Christ,* and the sinister *Judith & Holophernes* by Valentin de Boulogne, as well as rooms 12 and 13, which display an excellent

collection of works by Italian Mattia Preti, who was a Knight of St John and responsible for the baroque makeover of St John's Co-Cathedral.

Look out for his dramatic *Martyrdom of St Catherine* and St John the Baptist dressed in the habit of the Knights of St John. Downstairs, room 14 contains portraits of several Grand Masters by the 18th-century French artist Antoine de Favray. Room 18 has scenes of Malta by 19th-century British artists, including lovely paintings of Gozo by poet Edward Lear, and a small Turner watercolour depicting a Grand Harbour scene (1830) – the museum's pride and joy. Interestingly, Turner never visited Malta; the work is based on scenes painted by another artist.

★**St John's Co-Cathedral** CHURCH
(☑2122 0536; www.stjohnscocathedral.com; Triq ir-Repubblika; adult/child €6/free; ☺9.30am-4.30pm Mon-Fri, 9.30am-12.30pm Sat) St John's Co-Cathedral, Malta's most impressive church, was designed by the architect Gerolamo Cassar. It was built between 1573 and 1578, taking over from the Church of St Lawrence in Vittoriosa as the place where the Knights would gather for communal worship. The interior was revamped in the 17th century in exuberant Maltese baroque style, and it's an astounding surprise after the plain facade. One of its greatest treasures is a huge painting of John the Baptist by Caravaggio.

The nave is long and low and every wall, pillar and rib is encrusted with rich ornamentation, giving the effect of a dusty gold brocade. The floor is an iridescent patchwork quilt of marble tomb slabs, and the

VALLETTA IN...

Two Days

Start the day with alfresco coffee and *pastizzi* (filled pastry) at **Caffe Cordina**, before wandering Valletta's history-loaded streets. Be sure to visit major attractions evoking the island's illustrious history, **St John's Co-Cathedral**, the **Grand Master's Palace** and the **National Museum of Archaeology**. Then wander through and wonder at Renzo Piano's new **Parliament Building** and **City Gate** before taking in the astounding Grand Harbour views from **Upper Barrakka Gardens**.

On the second day, visit the **National War Museum** at Fort St Elmo, then take a tour of the **Hal Saflieni Hypogeum** (having pre-booked a few weeks' ahead, if it's open), enjoy a boat trip around the harbour, and spend the afternoon exploring the beguiling Three Cities area. Take in an evening show in Valletta at **Manoel Theatre** or **St James' Cavalier Centre for Creativity**, or dine somewhere splendid and then enjoy the air in revitalised **Strait St**.

LOCAL KNOWLEDGE

VALLETTA'S REBIRTH

Over the last few years, Valletta has been undergoing a renaissance. From its construction until WWII, the city was home to the nobility and businesspeople. However, WWII resulted in a lot of damage, and after the war, the city's empty houses were used for social housing, with around 3000 units spread across the empty mansions. The demographic changed – the rich all moved to their seaside homes in Sliema, and by the 1980s and '90s many of Valletta's beautiful houses were empty and falling apart.

Chris Briffa is Valletta's foremost architect, with works that include the installation Prospettiva (Ġlormu Cassar Av). An angular 2D interpretation of the city's five different gates, it celebrates Valletta as European City of Culture for 2018. Briffa says, 'Malta's suburban development, which had spread all over the island, had resulted in a bit of a chaotic hodgepodge, whereas in the old towns, such as Valletta and the Three Cities, the envelope and the urban quality remained the same.'

People began to buy up Valletta's houses with views first, but now even the inner-city ones are selling. Prices have gone up and estate agents are sprouting. The Renzo Piano buildings have also given the city a different feel. Briffa says, 'the last time we had something of that scale and detail and that technically advanced were the 18th-century bastions... It's a statement that Valletta is not just a museum city, but it's vibrant and a city of the 21st century.'

vault dances with paintings by Mattia Preti that illustrate events from the life of St John the Baptist.

Beyond here, the Oratory contains two paintings by Caravaggio, and the Cathedral Museum houses the beautiful 16th-century Graduals of L-Isle Adam, illuminated choral books and a magnificent collection of 17th-century Flemish tapestries based on drawings by Rubens.

St John's was raised to a status equal to that of St Paul's Cathedral in Mdina – the official seat of the Archbishop of Malta – by a papal decree of 1816, hence the term 'co-cathedral'.

Visitors should dress appropriately for a house of worship. Stiletto heels are not permitted, to protect the marble floor.

★ **Grand Master's Palace**   HISTORIC BUILDING
(Pjazza San Ġorġ; adult/child incl Palace State Rooms & Armoury & free audioguides €10/5; ⊗ Armoury 9am-5pm daily, State Apartments 10am-4pm Fri-Wed) The stern exterior of the 16th-century Grand Master's Palace conceals a sumptuous interior. This was once the residence of the Grand Masters of the Knights of St John. From Malta's independence until 2015 the building was the seat of Malta's parliament, before it moved into the new Parliament Building (p44). The Armoury is housed in what was once the Grand Master's stables. Originally, the armour and weapons belonging to the Knights were stored at the Palace Armoury (the Great Hall), and when

a Knight died these became the property of the Order.

The collection of over 5000 suits of 16th-to 18th-century armour is all that remains of an original 25,000 – Napoleon's light-fingered activities, overenthusiastic housekeeping by the British and general neglect put paid to the rest.

Some of the most interesting pieces are the breastplate worn by la Valette, the beautifully damascened (steel inlaid with gold) suit made for Alof de Wignacourt, the captured Turkish Sipahi (cavalry) armour, and reinforced armour with bullet marks (the development of guns marked the beginning of the end for armour). There are also displays of some beautiful weapons, including crossbows, muskets, swords and pistols.

In the State Apartments, five rooms are open to the public. The Grand Masters' Palace remains the official residence of the Maltese president, so rooms are occasionally closed. The long Armoury Corridor, decorated with trompe l'œil painting, scenes of naval battles and the portraits and escutcheons of various Grand Masters, leads to the Council Chamber on the left. It is hung with 17th-century Gobelins tapestries gifted to the Order in 1710 by Grand Master Ramon de Perellos. They feature exotic scenes of Africa, India, the Caribbean and Brazil, including an elephant beneath a cashew-nut tree; an ostrich, cassowary and flamingo; a rhino and a zebra being attacked by a

Valletta

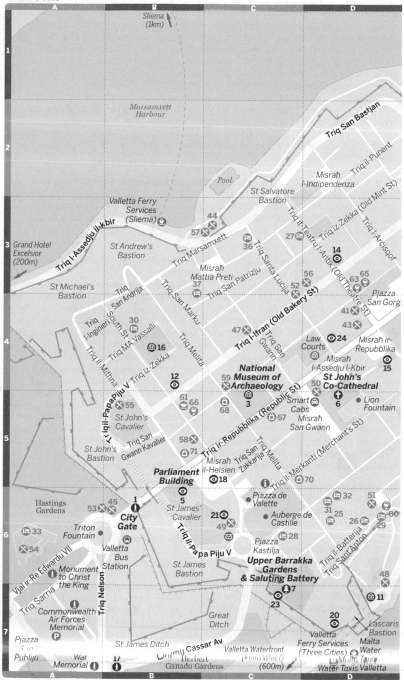

Sliema
(1km)

Marsamxett
Harbour

Pool

St Salvatore
Bastion

Valletta Ferry
Services
(Sliema) 🚢

44

57 ✗

Misrah
I-Indipendenza

Triq San Bastjan

Triq il-Punent

Triq iz-Zekka (Old Mint St)

Triq I-Arcisqof

Grand Hotel
Excelsior
(200m)

Triq I-Assedju il-kbir

St Andrew's
Bastion

St Michael's
Bastion

36

Triq Marsamxett

Misrah
Mattia Preti
37

Triq San Marku

Triq San Andrija

Triq San Patrizju

Triq Santa Lucia

27

Triq it-Teatru I-Antik (Old Theatre St)

14

56

52

63 65

Pjazza
San Gorg

Triq
I-Inginier

Triq
South St

Triq MA Vassalli

30

Triq Melita

47

Triq I-Ifran (Old Bakery St)

Triq San
Gwann

41
43

16

Triq iz-Zekka

12

National
Museum of
Archaeology
3

59 ✗

Law
Courts

24

Misrah ir-
Repubblika

Misrah
I-Assedju I-Kbir

St John's
Co-Cathedral

15

Triq il-Papa Piju V

Triq il-Mithna

St John's
Cavalier

55

61 66

68

Misrah
San Gwann

50

Smart
Cabs

6

Lion
Fountain

St John's
Bastion

Triq San
Gwann Kavalier

58 ✗

71

Triq ir-Repubblika (Republic St)

67

Triq San
Zakkarija

Triq Melita

Triq il-Merkanti (Merchant's St)

Parliament
Building

18

Misrah
il-Helsien

70

Hastings
Gardens

53 ✗

45

1

City
Gate

5

St James
Cavalier

Piazza de
Valette

Auberge de
Castille

21

49

32

31 25

26

51

60

29

33

54

Triton
Fountain

Valletta
Bus
Station

St James
Bastion

Triq il-Papa Piju V

Pjazza
Kastilja

28

Upper Barrakka
Gardens
& Saluting Battery

Triq il-Batterija

Triq Sant'Anton

48

Vjal ir-Re Edwardu VII

Triq Nelson

Monument
to Christ
the King

Triq Sarria

Commonwealth
Air Forces
Memorial

Great
Ditch

7

23

20

11

Lascaris
Bastion

Malta
Water

Pjazza
San
Publiju

War
Memorial

St James Ditch

Triq Girolamo Cassar Av

Herbert
Ganado Gardens

Valletta Waterfront
(Town Wharf)
(600m)

Valletta
Ferry Services
(Three Cities)

Water Taxis Valletta

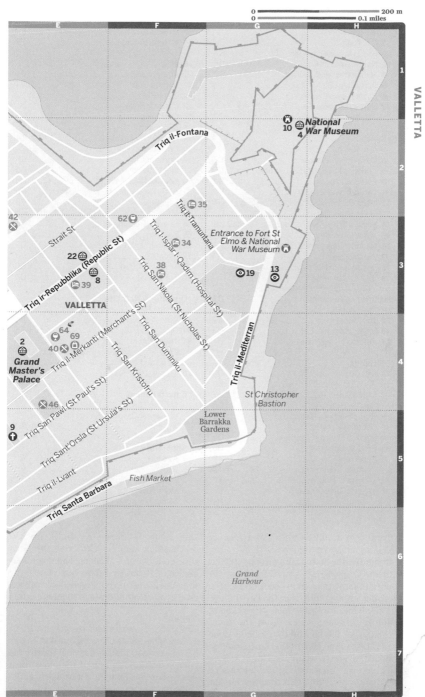

0 ━━━━━━━━━━━ 200 m
0 ━━━━━━━━━━━ 0.1 miles

Triq il-Fontana

10 National
4   War Museum

Triq it-Tramuntana

35

62

Strait St

Triq I-Isptar I-Qadim (Hospital St)

34

Entrance to Fort St
Elmo & National
War Museum

22

8

38

19

13

39

VALLETTA

Triq San Nikola (St Nicholas St)

Triq il-Mediterran

2
Grand
Master's
Palace

64
69

40

Triq il-Merkanti (Merchant's St)

Triq San Duminiku

Triq San Kristofru

St Christopher
Bastion

46

9

Triq San Pawl (St Paul's St)

Triq Sant'Orsla (St Ursula's St)

Lower
Barrakka
Gardens

Triq il-Lvant

Triq Santa Barbara

Fish Market

Grand
Harbour

Valletta

leopard; and a tableau with palm trees, a tapir, a jaguar and an iguana.

Beyond lie the State Dining Room and the Supreme Council Hall, where the Supreme Council of Order met. It is decorated with a frieze depicting events from the Great Siege of 1565, while the minstrels' gallery bears paintings showing scenes from the Book of Genesis. At the far end of the hall a door gives access to the Hall of the Ambassadors, or Red State Room, where the Grand Master would receive important visitors, and where the Maltese president still receives foreign envoys. It contains portraits of the French kings Louis XIV, Louis XV and Louis XVI, the Russian Empress Catherine the Great and several Grand Masters. The neighbouring Pages' Room, or Yellow State Room (despite the abundance of greenish tones), was used by the Grand Master's 16 attendants.

Manoel Theatre THEATRE
(☎ 2559 5523; www.teatrumanoel.com.mt; 115 Triq it-Teatru l-Antik; tours €4; ⊙ 9.30am-4pm Mon-Fri, 9.30am-noon Sat) Malta's national theatre was built in 1731 and is one of the oldest theatres in Europe. Take an entertaining audio-guide tour (in multiple languages) to see the

CARAVAGGIO IN MALTA

The Italian painter Michelangelo Merisi (1571–1610) is better known by the name of his home town, Caravaggio, in northern Italy. His realist depictions of religious subjects and dramatic use of light shocked and revolutionised the 16th-century art world.

He made his name in Rome with a series of controversial works, but was also notorious for his volatility and violence. Numerous brawls culminated in Caravaggio murdering a man during an argument over a tennis game. He fled Rome and went into hiding in Naples for several months. Then, towards the end of 1607, he moved to Malta.

Here, Caravaggio was welcomed as a famous artist and produced several works for the Knights of St John, including the famous *Beheading of St John the Baptist* for the Oratory of **St John's Co-Cathedral** (p46). In July 1608 he was admitted into the Order as a Knight of Justice, but only two months later he was arrested for an unspecified crime, and imprisoned in Fort St Angelo.

He escaped to Sicily, but was expelled from the Order and spent the next two years on the run. He created some of his finest paintings – ever darker and more twisted – during this period. He died in Italy; the cause of his death remains unknown.

restored baroque, gilt-twinkling auditorium with its huge chandelier.

National Library   LIBRARY
(⊙8.15am-1.15pm Mon-Sat mid-Jun–Sep, to 5pm Mon-Fri Oct–mid-Jun) This grand classical edifice was the last building erected by the Knights. It's worth popping in to admire the booklined stacks, and there are occasional temporary exhibitions.

Church of St Paul's Shipwreck   CHURCH
(Triq San Pawl, enter from Triq Santa Luċija; donations welcome; ⊙9.30am-noon & 3.30-6pm Mon-Sat, 10.45-11.45am & 4-6pm Sun) **FREE** In AD 60 St Paul was shipwrecked on Malta and brought Christianity to the population. This church has a 19th-century facade, but the interior dates from the 16th century and houses many treasures, including a dazzling gilded statue of St Paul, carved in Rome in the 1650s and carried shoulder-high through the streets of Valletta on the saint's feast day (10 February).

There's also a golden reliquary containing some bones from the saint's wrist, and part of the column on which he is said to have been beheaded in Rome.

Casa Rocca Piccola   HISTORIC BUILDING
(☑2122 1499; www.casaroccapiccola.com; 74 Triq ir-Repubblika; adult/under 14s €9/free; ⊙hourly tours 10am-4pm Mon-Sat) The 16th-century palazzo Casa Rocca Piccola is the family home of the 9th Marquis de Piro, who still lives here and has opened part of the palazzo to the public. Visits allow a unique insight into the privileged lifestyle of the aristocracy,

and include the family's WWII air-raid shelters, which lie 30m underground.

Toy Museum   MUSEUM
(☑2125 1652; 222 Triq ir-Repubblika; adult/child €3/free; ⊙10am-3pm Mon-Fri, to 1pm Sat & Sun) This doll-sized museum houses an impressive private collection of model toys, such as tin cars from 1950s Japan, tin toys from 1912 Germany, as well as Matchbox cars, farmyard animals, train sets and dolls.

Fort St Elmo   FORTRESS
(⊙9am-6pm Mon-Sat, noon-6pm Sun) **FREE**
Guarding the entrance to both Marsamxett and Grand Harbours is Fort St Elmo, named after the patron saint of mariners. Although now much altered, this fort was built by the Knights in 1552 in a mere four months to guard the harbours on either side of the Sceberras Peninsula, and was the fort that bore the brunt of Turkish arms during the Great Siege of 1565. After restoration and renovation, the fort opened to the public in 2015, containing the stunning National War Museum (p52).

The courtyard outside the entrance to the fort is studded with the lids of underground granaries. You can visit the parade ground, and the 1559 chapel where Knights fought to the death during the siege trying to protect the altar, as well as the later 1729 church.

In Guardia (☑2123 7747; adult/child €7/3; ⊙11-11.45am most Sun mornings) is a colourful and photogenic military pageant in 16th-century costume, which includes a cannon-firing demonstration. Check upcoming dates at the tourist office.

MATTIA PRETI – THE KNIGHT OF CALABRIA

The artist Mattia Preti was born in 1613 in a small town in Calabria, in southern Italy, and honed his craft in Rome and Naples. In 1659, Preti, having been made a Knight, travelled to Malta in search of patronage, and lived here for the rest of his life. He undertook the decoration of St John's Co-Cathedral, which had been very plain beforehand; after painting an altarpiece for the Chapel of the Langue of Aragon, Grand Master Raphael Cotoner commissioned him to decorate the vaulted ceiling of the church with scenes from the life of St John the Baptist. Completed over six years, the work transformed the church. You can see many more of his works in the **National Museum of Fine Arts** (p46). He died in 1699, and is buried in the cathedral.

★**National War Museum**   MUSEUM
(☑2123 3088; Triq il-Fontana; adult/child €10/5.50; ☺9am-6pm Mon-Sat, noon-6pm Sun) This fabulous museum reopened in 2015 in the renovated Fort St Elmo. It covers Malta's wartime history, from the Great Siege and the country's ordeal during WWII, right up to Malta's role in the Cold War and today's Europe. There are absorbing audiovisual displays, which bring history to life and illustrate aspects of war such as the struggle to get supplies through to the islands under German bombardment.

Artefacts include the Gloster Gladiator biplane called Faith (minus wings), the sole survivor of the three planes that so valiantly defended the island when Italy declared war in 1940. Pride of place goes to the George Cross medal that was awarded to the entire population of Malta in 1942. The entrance is close to the Malta Experience.

Sacra Infermeria & Knights Hospitallers Exhibition   EXHIBITION
(☑2124 3840; www.knightshospitallers.com.mt; Triq it-Tramuntana; adult/child €4.50/3; ☺9.30am-5.30pm Jul-Oct, to 4.30pm Nov-Jun) In the impressive former Sacra Infermeria, a 16th-century hospital of the Order of St John, this exhibition brings the sometimes alarming achievements of medieval medicine to life through waxworks, and allows a glance inside this fascinating building.

Malta Experience   AUDIOVISUAL
(☑2124 3776; www.themaltaexperience.com; Triq il-Mediterran; adult/child €10/5, hospital tour €4/free; ☺hourly 11am-4pm Mon-Fri, 11am-2pm Sat & Sun) A whip through 7000 years of history, this 45-minute show also highlights Malta's scenic attractions. It's screened in the Mediterranean Conference Centre, which occupies the Sacra Infermeria, the 16th-century hospital of the Order of St John. For a small extra charge you can take a worthwhile tour

of the hospital, visiting the Grand Hall that once housed around 300 patients.

★**Upper Barrakka Gardens & Saluting Battery**   PARK
These colonnaded gardens perched high above Grand Harbour were created in the late 16th century as a relaxing haven for the Knights from the nearby Auberge d'Italie. They provide a shady retreat from the bustle of the city, and the balcony has one of the best views in Malta.

The terrace below is occupied by the **Saluting Battery** (☑2180 0992; www.wirtartna.org; adult/child €3/1, includes audioguide; ☺10am-5pm, guided tours 11am, 12.15pm & 3pm), where a cannon once fired salutes to visiting naval vessels. The battery has been restored, and a cannon is fired every day at noon and 4pm with great ceremony. It's well worth making time to see this – children will enjoy it. Try to time your visit for a tour – the enthusiastic, costumed guides explain how the cannon is loaded and fired.

Upper Barrakka Lift   LIFT
There was a lift between the Grand Harbour and the Upper Barrakka Gardens from 1905 to 1973. In 2012, this was finally replaced by the marvellous panoramic lift that connects Upper Barrakka Gardens with the Lascaris Ditch, a short walk from Valletta Waterfront and ferries and water taxis to the Three Cities. It's 58m high and can carry 21 passengers. You have to pay on the way up (€1), but not on the way down; if you have a ferry ticket, it's free.

Lascaris War Rooms   MUSEUM
(☑2123 4717; www.lascariswarrooms.com; Lascaris Ditch; adult/child/family €10/5/25; ☺10am-5pm) A mechanically ventilated underground tunnel complex that lies 40m beneath the Upper Barrakka Gardens, it housed Britain's top secret command in Malta during WWII

and remained in use until 1977. Lovingly restored in 2009, the rooms are laid out as they would have been, staffed by waxwork figures, and provide a fascinating behind-the-scenes glimpse. Reach here by going to the Saluting Battery in the Upper Barrakka Gardens – the staff there will direct you.

St James' Cavalier ARTS CENTRE
(☑ 2122 3216; www.sjcav.org; Castille Pl) This 16th-century fortification has been transformed into a dazzling arts centre encompassing galleries, theatre and a cinema. Recent exhibitions have encompassed contemporary Libyan art.

Valletta Waterfront (Pinto Wharf) AREA
(www.vallettawaterfront.com) The Valletta Waterfront was once a run-down dockside area, but is now renovated and lined with waterside restaurants. Most of the services here, including shops, restaurants and bars, cater to the passengers of the cruise ships that dock here. There's a small tourist information booth, plus operators offering bus and boat trips around Valletta.

🍴 Eating

Fresh Produce Market MARKET €
(Triq il-Merkanti; ⊘ 7am-1pm Mon-Sat) Fruit, vegetables and deli items are upstairs, and fish, meat and poultry are on the ground level.

Legliglin MALTESE €
(Triq l-Ifran; tasting menu €23.95; ⊘ 6pm-midnight Sat-Thu, 1pm-late Fri) With tiled floors and brick arches, this is an intimate cellar wine bar, serving Maltese tapas alongside a fine list of tipples. The name means 'glug' in Malti.

Caffe Cordina CAFE €
(☑ 2123 4385; 244 Triq ir-Repubblika; mains €8.25-13.50; ⊘ 8am-7pm Mon-Sat, 8am-3pm Sun) Cordina was established in 1837 and is now a local institution. You have the choice of waiter service at the sun-shaded tables in the square or inside, or joining the locals at the zinc counter inside for a quick caffeine hit.

Inspirations CAFE €
(St James' Cavalier; snacks €2.50-10.50; ⊘ 9.30am-8pm Mon-Wed, 9.30am-10pm Fri-Sun) The cafe of the St James' Cavalier arts centre, it has a long menu of sandwiches, pizzas, *ftiras* (Maltese bread) and salads, but the main reason to come here is the outdoor terrace that overlooks Valletta's opera house.

QUICK EATS

Cheap, tasty fare can be found at the kiosks beside the Valletta bus terminus. **Millennium** (pastizzi €0.30; ⊘ 7am-7pm), just to your right after you exit City Gate, sells hot *pastizzi* (pastry parcels filled with either ricotta cheese or mushy peas); next door, the **Dates Kiosk** (mqaret €0.20; ⊘ 9am-7pm Mon-Fri, 9am-1pm Sat) sells traditional *mqaret* (deep-fried pastries stuffed with spiced dates).

Follow your nose to the many hole-in-the-wall places dotted around town, where you can pick up fresh hot *pastizzi* for around €0.30 from about 7.30am Monday to Saturday.

⭐ **Rubino** MEDITERRANEAN €€
(☑ 2122 4656; 53 Triq l-Ifran; mains €13.50-24; ⊘ noon-2.30pm Tue-Fri, 7.30-10.30pm Tue-Sat) White-tableclothed Rubino is a classy place that earns rave reviews for its dishes such as spaghetti with sea urchins or sea bass *involtini* (rolls) stuffed with pine nuts and mint. The velvety risotto is particularly renowned. Leave room for dessert – the house speciality is *cassata siciliana* (sponge cake soaked in liqueur, layered with ricotta cheese). Over 5s only.

⭐ **Harbour Club** MEDITERRANEAN €€
(☑ 2122 2332; Barrierra; mains €16-24; ⊘ noon-3pm Tue-Sun, 7-11pm Tue-Sat) Converted from 17th-century boathouses, the Harbour Club has been designed by Malta's foremost architect, Chris Briffa, and has a superb terrace and wonderful harbour views, as well as a bar and a subterranean jazz club created from a cistern.

Scoglitti ITALIAN €€
(☑ 2123 5548; 8 Triq il-Lanca Marsamxett; mains €15-22; ⊘ 12.30-3pm & 6.30-11pm Fri-Mon, to 10pm Tue-Thu) Set by the periwinkle blue waters, next to the ferry for Sliema, this fabulous restaurant focuses on fish and seafood, and is a great place to linger over a long lunch or dinner while watching the boat traffic chugging across the sea.

Guze Bistro BISTRO €€
(☑ 2123 9686; Triq l-Ifran; mains €15-20; ⊘ noon-2.30pm Tue-Sat, 6-10.30pm Mon-Sat) In the flagstone interior of a 16th-century house, hung with antique chandeliers and decked with

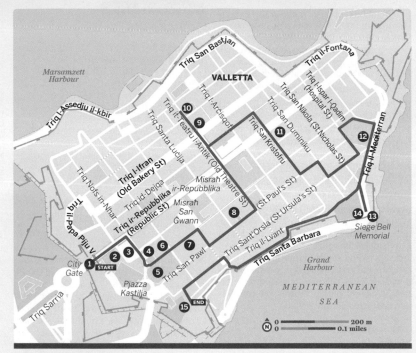

🏃 Walking Tour
Valletta

START CITY GATE
END UPPER BARRAKKA GARDENS & SALUTING BATTERY
LENGTH 2.25KM; ONE HOUR

This walk explores some of Valletta's back-streets, and affords some great views.

Begin at ❶ **City Gate**. Just beyond it are the Renzo Piano–designed ❷ **Parliament Building** and ❸ **Royal Opera House**. Walk past the Opera House and turn right into Triq Nofs in-Nhar. You'll pass through the new ❹ **Pjazza de Valette**, dedicated to Grand Master Jean Parisot de la Valette. Next turn left at Triq il-Merkanti. You'll see the ❺ **Palazzo Parisio** on your right, where Napoleon stayed during his six days on Malta, and the ❻ **Auberge d'Italie** on your left. Walk another few blocks and you'll see ❼ **Palazzo Castellania**, which house Valletta's law courts. The figures above the 1st-floor balcony represent Justice and Truth. Turn right into Triq San Ġwann, then left into Triq San Pawl, passing the 16th-century ❽ **Church of St**

Paul's Shipwreck. Turn left along Triq it-Teatru l-Antik, to see the ❾ **Manoel Theatre** on the right, and the domed ❿ **Carmelite Basilica** beyond. Double back and then turn left down Triq id-Dejqa. Note the faded old bar signs dating from its years as the city's red-light district, then turn right along Triq San Krist-ofru, passing the 16th-century ⓫ **Palazzo Messina and Palazzo Marina**. Follow Triq San Kristofru, then turn left on Triq San Pawl, right on Triq San Duminiku then left again down Triq Sant'Orsla. Walk around the Knights' 16th-century hospital ⓬ **Sacra Infermeria**. Heading southwards, you'll see the ⓭ **Siege Bell Memorial**, commemorating those who lost their lives in the convoys of 1940 to 1943. Follow Triq il-Mediterran past the ⓮ **Lower Barrakka Gardens**, which contain a Doric temple commemorating Sir Alexander Ball, the naval captain who took Malta from the French in 1800. Continue along Triq Santa Barbara, with fabulous harbour views. Cross the bridge above Victoria Gate and turn left to climb steep Triq il-Batterija to the ⓯ **Upper Barrakka Gardens & Saluting Battery**.

VALLETTA FOR CHILDREN

Valletta is a great city to wander through with kids. Much of the centre is pedestrianised, there are plenty of child-friendly restaurants (though note some only accept older children), and some places have baby-change facilities. The **Upper Barrakka Gardens** (p52; with the entertaining Saluting Battery) and Lower Barrakka Gardens are a good place for a run around, as is Pjazza San Ġorġ (St George's Sq), with its choreographed fountains. Excellent museums include the state-of-the-art **National War Museum** (p52) and the **Toy Museum** (p51), and there's an impressive collection in the Armoury in the **Grand Master's Palace** (p47). Audiovisuals include **Malta 5D** (p44) and **Malta Experience** (p52), and there are also historical re-enactments at **Fort St Elmo** (p51), cannon firing at **Fort Rinella** (p64; just outside Valletta), and exhibitions like the **Knights Hospitallers** (p52). Taking a boat across the harbour makes for a fun trip.

wooden tables, Guze offers a short menu of spectacular dishes, such as rabbit wrapped in *guanciale* (pig cheek) and stuffed with leek and cabbage.

Ambrosia   MEDITERRANEAN €€
(⌨2122 5923; 137 Triq I-Arċisqof; mains €15-23; ⊙12.30-2.30pm Mon-Fri, 7-9.30pm Mon-Sat) This is one of Valletta's loveliest restaurants, with paintings covering the walls and a relaxed, intimate feel. Locals love this place and the welcome is warm (the chef might just pop by to see how you enjoyed your meal). They use mainly local produce, farmed and cooked according to the Slow Food philosophy, and create Maltese dishes that play with traditions. Older children only.

Cockneys   MEDITERRANEAN €€
(⌨2123 6065; Marsamxett Wharf; mains €9-25; ⊙noon-3pm & 7-11pm daily Mar-Sep, noon-3pm daily & 7-11pm Sat & Sun Oct-Feb) Cockneys, in a great location just next to the water taxi and ferry stop, is a Valletta institution. There's a wooden cabin with a cosy interior, and a sunny terrace. Food is tasty and traditional, such as spaghetti with rabbit.

La Sicilia   ITALIAN €€
(⌨2124 0659; 1a Triq San Ġwann; mains €8-20; ⊙noon-3pm Tue-Sat) You're sure to find something to fill a gap at this unpretentious Sicilian-owned eatery with seating out on a tranquil square. There are lots of hearty Italian pasta dishes, grilled meats and fish; the swordfish is particularly good. It's a good place to eat with kids as they can play on the surrounding steps when they've finished.

Kantina Cafe & Wine   CAFE €€
(⌨2723 0096; Triq San Ġwann; mains €12.50-17.50; ⊙8am-10.30pm Mon-Sat, 8am-3pm Sun)

This friendly cafe has a great location – its outdoor tables are scattered under the trees in the pedestrianised area outside St John's Co-Cathedral. The menu stretches from bagels, *ftira,* sandwiches and salads to cocktails and local wines.

Badass Cafe   BURGERS €€
(Triq it-Teatru I-Antik; burgers €10-16; ⊙11am-midnight) Part of the local Badass Burger chain, this place offers its signature gourmet burgers, including the Obama, with bacon, onion relish and Marie Rose sauce. It's in a particularly good location, with chairs and tables out on the main square.

★**Black Pig**   FRENCH, INTERNATIONAL €€€
(⌨7922 1606; Old Bakery St; mains €24-28; ⊙12.30-2pm Tue-Fri, 7.30-10pm Tue-Sat) Considered by many to be Valletta's finest restaurant, Black Pig offers foodie heaven in a historic yet funky room and sophisticated cuisine that's mostly French with a twist, with dishes such as ceviche of tuna belly with melon and sea urchin. Over 8s only.

★**Trattoria da Pippo**   MEDITERRANEAN €€€
(⌨2124 8029; Triq Melita; mains around €20; ⊙11.30am-3pm Mon-Sat) This hidden-away, informal Valletta hub, all green woodwork and gingham tablecloths, is a local favourite, with something of an old boys' club feel, and is the place for those in the know. The food is a delightful mix of Maltese, Sicilian and Italian. Book ahead.

Rampila   MALTESE €€€
(⌨2122 6625; St John's Cavalier, Il-Belt Valletta; mains €12.50-28; ⊙noon-10.30pm) Rampila offers delicious food on a wonderfully set outside terrace that overlooks the City Gate – book ahead. There's also the interior tunnel

VALLETTA DRINKING & NIGHTLIFE

STRAIT STREET

Strait St was once the notorious haunt of sailors on shore leave. In *Strait Street: Malta's 'Red Light District' Revealed* (2013), an interesting book on the street, the authors John Schofield and Emily Morrissey describe hole-in-the-wall bars, where the toilet was a bucket behind a curtain. But there was also bohemian theatricality amid the squalor, and the street is coming alive once again to celebrate this. The street's artistic director, Giuseppe Schembri Bonaci, who comes from the area, says, 'It developed into a cultural hub from its initiation. It used to house artists that were working at the Grand Master's (Manoel) Theatre. It developed into 'the Gut', in a sense like a microscopic version of Montmartre (in Paris). You had a mix of bohemian characters, painters, jazz musicians, live bands competing with each other, so it was a hectic, beautiful street.'

As local people moved out of Valletta post-WWII and the British Navy left in 1979, Strait St became a shadow of its former self, with faded vintage bar signs the only clue to its past. But this is now changing fast, as people have begun to realise the appeal of Valletta's fine architecture and the city has been renovated to take the mantle of European Capital of Culture for 2018. See local listings for upcoming events, or just wander past and see what's going on. It's no nostalgic trip, but a rebirth, with regular concerts, gigs and art exhibitions.

restaurant, with a cavelike feel, and a curious Maltese folk history museum of around 40 waxworks.

Trabuxu Bistro BISTRO €€€
(2122 0357; Triq Nofs in-Nhar; mains €16-26; noon-3pm & 7-11pm Mon-Sat) An offshoot of the nearby Trabuxu wine bar, this place feels Parisian, and the setting entices you to linger, with dark red walls hung with paintings. The Mediterranean menu is up to scratch too, and there's a fine range of wines. Over 12s only.

Drinking & Nightlife

Valletta is awaking from a long sleep to become a place to hang out at night, with a growing cluster of bars, centred on narrow Strait St. Closing times vary depending on how busy the venue is.

★ **Bridge Bar** BAR
(8pm-4am Fri May-Oct) The Bridge Bar is a weekly event, with brightly coloured cushions all over a junction of steps in the eastern part of Valletta, with views, live jazz from 8.30pm to midnight, and the feel of an impromptu party. An Aperol Spritz costs €5.50.

Café Prego CAFE
(Triq Nofs in-Nhar; 7am-7.30pm Mon-Fri, 8am-1pm Sat) Step back in time at this atmospheric cafe, where the decor hasn't changed since 1004. It's been open since 1947, and the owners have stuck with the look that's worked for them; a rare true vintage experience.

The Loop BAR
(Strait St; noon-late) The Loop mingles with its neighbouring bar, another tiny hole-in-the-wall place, and has a vintage feel inside, with the original tiled floor. There are chairs and tables outside along the narrow street.

Tico Taco BAR
(Strait St; noon-late) Tico Taco is one of the pioneering bars along this tiny street, with outside tables and relaxed drinking and snacking in Malta's newest yet oldest nightlife hub.

Trabuxu WINE BAR
(2122 3036; 1 Triq id-Dejqa; 7pm-late Tue-Sat) Trabuxu ('corkscrew') is housed in a cool 350-year-old cellar – an atmospheric place to munch on perfect platters and quaff wine.

Django BAR
(www.djangojazzbar.com; 221 Triq ir-Repubblika; 7pm-1am Tue-Sat, to midnight Sun) Red-walled, intimate hole-in-the-wall bar with regular live jazz, swing and samba gigs crammed into its basement.

The Pub PUB
(7980 7042; 136 Triq l-Arċisqof; 11am-late) Fans of the late British actor Oliver Reed might want to raise a glass to their hero in this succinctly named watering hole. This is the homely little hostelry where the wild man of British film enjoyed his final drinking session before last orders were called forever in 1999.

⭐ Entertainment

Manoel Theatre   THEATRE
(☑2124 6389; www.teatrumanoel.com.mt; 115
Triq it-Teatru l-Antik; ⊗booking office 10am-1pm
& 5-7pm Mon-Fri, 10am-1pm Sat) This beautiful
place is Malta's national theatre, and the
islands' principal venue for drama, concerts,
opera and ballet, with a season running
from October to May (tickets €10 to €40).
It also organises performances at other Valletta venues, for events such as the Baroque
Festival, at wonderful places like Fort St
Elmo or the Biblioteca.

**St James' Cavalier Centre
for Creativity**   THEATRE, CINEMA
(☑2122 3200; www.sjcav.org; Triq Nofs in-Nhar)
Has a cinema that regularly shows National
Theatre, Royal Shakespeare Company and
Met Opera Live broadcasts. Also has regular
classic and creative theatre.

🛍 Shopping

Triq Santa Luċija, located behind Misrah
ir-Repubblika, is home to a number of jewellery stores offering silver filigree – the most
popular souvenir here is a silver eight-pointed Maltese Cross on a chain.

⭐ Blush & Panic   VINTAGE
(http://panic-at-strait-street.tumblr.com; 46a Triq
Melita; ⊗10am-2pm & 3-5pm Mon & Thu, 10am-
2pm & 4-7pm Tue & Fri, 10am-2pm Wed, to 4pm Sun)
This is a gorgeous clothes shop selling exquisite vintage and vintage-inspired womens-
wear, as well as wonderfully unusual pieces
of costume jewellery. These are beautiful
quality items – there's no musty secondhand
feel here.

C Camilleri & Sons   FOOD & DRINK
(Triq il-Merkanti; ⊗9am-7pm Mon-Sat, 9am-1pm
Sun) Historic dessert and sweets shop, open
since 1843, selling 'pick and mix' and beautifully decorated, delectable cakes as well as
homemade biscuits tied in ribbon.

Mdina Glass   CRAFTS
(☑2141 5786; 14 Triq il-Merkanti; ⊗10am-6pm
Mon-Fri, 10am-4pm Sat) Mdina Glass features
hand-blown glass produced by craft workshops near Mdina, from traditional styles
and colours to decidedly modern – vases,
bowls, paperweights, collectables and more.

Agenda   BOOKS
(☑2123 3621; 26 Triq ir-Repubblika; ⊗8.30am-
7pm Mon-Sat, 9am-1pm Sun) A cramped shop

with an excellent selection of travel guides
and fiction, history and reference books.

Street Market   MARKET
(Triq l-Ordinanza; ⊗9am-1pm Mon-Sat) This
market sells mainly clothes, shoes, watches,
jewellery, pirated CDs and computer games.

ℹ Information

EMERGENCY

Police Station (☑2294 3101; 111 Triq l-Arċisqof) Valletta's main police station.

MONEY

There are plenty of ATMs, plus places to change
money and cash travellers cheques on and near
Triq ir-Repubblika in Valletta.

Bank of Valletta (cnr Triq ir-Repubblika & Triq
San Ġwann; ⊗8.30am-2pm Mon-Thu, 8.30am-
3.30pm Fri, 8.30am-12.30pm Sat) ATMs are
available.

HSBC Bank (32 Triq il-Merkanti; ⊗8.30am-
1.30pm Mon-Thu, to 4.30pm Fri, to 12.30pm
Sat) ATMs.

POST

Main Post Office (Pjazza Kastilja; ⊗8.15am-
3.45pm Mon-Fri, 8.15am-12.30pm Sat) Found
under the St James' Cavalier, opposite the
Auberge de Castille.

TOURIST INFORMATION

Tourist Information Branch (☑2369 6073;
Malta International Airport; ⊗10am-9pm) Helpful tourist office in the arrivals hall, where you
can access the internet and print documents
(useful for boarding passes).

Tourist Information Office (☑2291 5214;
www.visitmalta.com; Auberge d'Italie, Triq
il-Merkanti; ⊗9am-5pm Mon-Sat, 9am-1pm
Sun & public holidays) Helpful tourist office
with plenty of maps, walking trail pamphlets
and brochures.

ℹ Getting There & Away

BOAT
Ferry

Valletta Ferry Services operate from Valletta
Waterfront to the Three Cities and from Marsamxett Harbour to Sliema.

Valletta Ferry Services (Three Cities)
(☑2346 3862; www.vallettaferryservices.
com; single/return adult €1.50/2.80, child
€0.50/0.90; ⊗half-hourly 7am-7pm Oct-May,
to midnight Jun-Sep) Operates ferries from
near Valletta Waterfront to Cospicua (Bormla)
and on to Senglea (L'Isla) in the Three Cities.
To reach the Three Cities ferry, take the Upper
Barrakka Lift (p52) and cross the road. If
you take the ferry, the lift is free on the way up.

Valletta Ferry Services (Sliema) (☑2346 3862; www.vallettaferryservices.com; single/ return adult €1.50/2.80, child €0.50/0.90; ☺7.15am-7.15pm Oct-May, to 12.45am Jun-Sep) Operates ferries between Valletta's Marsamxett Harbour and Sliema, which take around five minutes.

Water Taxi

Water taxis are operated by **Malta Water Taxis** (☑9993 9443; www.maltawatertaxis.com.mt; Valletta–Three Cities €3, harbour cruise €10) and **A&S Water Taxis** (☑9812 9802; www. maltesewatertaxis.com; Valletta–Three Cities/ Sliema/St Julian's €3/10/12, harbour cruise €30), though they are not always ready and waiting to take passengers (you can call ahead). They also offer half-hour harbour cruises in a *dgħajsa* (traditional rowing boat; pronounced 'die-sa'). They dock close to the ferry stops.

BUS

The Valletta bus station has buses for all over the island. A two-hour ticket in winter/summer/ at night costs €1.50/2/3. You can also buy a block of 12 tickets for €15 or a one-week Explorer pass for €21. At the time of research some timetables and numbers were due to change; check www.publictransport.com.mt for updates.

DESTINATION	ROUTE NOS
Airport	X4, X5, X7
Buġibba	12, 31
Ċirkewwa	41, 42
Marsaxlokk	81, 85
Mdina & Rabat	51, 52, 53
Mellieħa	41, 42
Mosta	31, 41, 42, 44
Paceville	12, 13
St Julian's	12, 13
Sliema	12, 13, 15
Vittoriosa	2, X7
Żurrieq	71

You can also take a hop-on, hop-off tour with either CitySightseeing Malta (p177) or Malta Sightseeing (p178), whose tours make a circuit of Valletta before heading off around the island.

ⓘ Getting Around

TO/FROM THE AIRPORT

Express buses X4, X5 and X7 connect with Valletta (25 minutes, every 15 minutes). As for everywhere in Malta, buses cost €1.30/1.50 for a two-hour/day ticket.

You can arrange for a direct transfer from the airport to most hotels in Malta using **MaltaTransfer** (☑2133 2016; www.maltatransfer. com; per person from €5), which has a desk in the airport baggage reclaim hall.

You'll find a taxi information desk in the airport arrivals hall and you can organise and pay for your taxi there. The set fare from the airport to Valletta or Floriana is €15.

TO/FROM THE SEA PASSENGER TERMINAL

The Upper Barrakka Lift (p52) connects Valletta to the Sea Passenger Terminal at the Valletta Waterfront. There are also regular buses, as well as stops for the hop-on, hop-off services.

As at the airport, there's a taxi information kiosk on Valletta Waterfront where you organise and pay the set rate for your taxi journey upfront. The cheapest fare (to an address in Valletta or Floriana) is €10.

BUS

Bus 133 is a circular bus route that zips half-hourly around Valletta's city walls, calling at Castille, Marsamxett and Floriana. As well as being a good way to get around, this route offers some great views.

CAR & MOTORCYCLE

If you're driving, parking is limited within the city walls, but not impossible – look for a space that's not demarcated by green lines; otherwise there's a big underground car park just outside the City Gate in Floriana, near the Phoenicia Hotel. Valletta is eminently walkable so you don't need a car to get around.

TAXI

There is a taxi rank just outside City Gate, and, within the city walls, electric cabs that can be picked up outside St John's Co-Cathedral. **Smart Cabs** (☑7741 4177; 3 people within city perimeter/to cruise-ship terminal €5/8) Smart Cabs is a fleet of ecofriendly electric-powered taxis that ply the streets of Valletta and can access pedestrianised areas. Trips can be extended outside the walls on request; book a cab by phone (at least 15 minutes' notice needed), or hail one in the street.

AROUND VALLETTA

Floriana

POP 2205

The threat of a Turkish attack in 1634 prompted Grand Master Antoine de Paule to begin the construction of a second line of landward defences, the Notre Dame Ditch, about 1km southwest of Valletta's Great Ditch. These were designed by the Italian engineer Pietro Paolo Floriani, who gave his name to the town (Floriana) that grew up within these walls in the 18th century. The northern part is taken up with government buildings and offices, while the south side is mostly residential.

✕ Eating

Phoenix Restaurant   MEDITERRANEAN €€€
(Phoenicia Hotel; mains €10-30; ⊘ 12.30-3.30pm & 7-10pm) Ideal for a wedding reception, this grand, high-ceilinged restaurant will make you feel like you're at some kind of occasion. There's a terrace overlooking the gardens. The hotel is closed until March 2016 for a €15 million refurbishment.

❶ Information

The Malta Police headquarters (p172) is at Pjazza San Kalcidonju.

❶ Getting There & Away

Floriana is just a five-minute walk from Valletta. All buses to and from Valletta also pass through Floriana.

There are two ferry terminals in Floriana. The Gozo cargo ferry (used primarily by trucks, but with some foot passengers) departs from Sa Maison wharf at Pieta Creek in Marsamxett Harbour, while passenger ferries to/from Sicily dock at the Sea Passenger Terminal by the Valletta Waterfront, where cruise liners moor.

Vittoriosa, Senglea & Cospicua (the Three Cities)

Despite their picturesque narrow streets and stunning views, the village-like 'Three Cities', Vittoriosa, Senglea and Cospicua, are surprisingly off the tourist radar and lovely places to absorb some local atmosphere. Vittoriosa and Senglea occupy two narrow peninsulas, and are now connected by a pedestrian bridge. Cospicua merges into Vittoriosa and lies just south of it. Regular ferries from Valletta make it a pleasure to visit.

After the Great Siege, Birgu was renamed Vittoriosa (Victorious), L'Isla became Senglea (after Grand Master Claude de la Sengle), and Bormla turned into Cospicua (as in conspicious courage). Local people and signs often still use the old names.

History

When the Knights of St John first arrived in Malta in 1530, they made their home in the fishing village of Birgu, on a finger of land on the south side of Grand Harbour. This spot, overlooking the inlet (now known as Dockyard Creek), was called the Port of the Arab Galleys. Here they built their auberges and repaired and extended the ancient defences. By the 1550s, Birgu (Fort St Angelo) and the neighbouring point of L-Isla (Fort St Michael) had been fortified, and Fort St Elmo had been built on the tip of the Sceberras Peninsula.

From this base, the Knights withstood the Turkish onslaught during the Great Siege of 1565, but in the years that followed they moved across the harbour to their new city of Valletta. Throughout 1941 and 1942, during WWII, the Three Cities and their surrounding docks were bombed almost daily, and suffered terrible damage and bloodshed.

❶ Getting There & Away

BOAT
Valletta Ferry Services (p57) operate from Vittoriosa to Valletta Waterfront, stopping at Senglea en route.

Near to the Cospicua/Vittoriosa stop, water taxis are operated by Malta Water Taxis (p58) and A&S Water Taxis (p58).

BUS
Buses 2 and X7 run between Valletta and Vittoriosa (Birgu) and Senglea (25 minutes). The X7 goes on to the airport, via Paola.

Vittoriosa

POP 2630
Vittoriosa is only 800m long and 400m at its widest, so it's hard to get lost – it's a sheer pleasure to wander aimlessly through its flower-bedecked alleys. There are several interesting sights, and stunning views across to Valletta. There's good information on Vittoriosa at www.birgu.gov.mt. Fort St Angelo, on the tip of Vittoriosa's peninsula, has been restored and is now open to the public. The promenade stretching down from Vittoriosa's Cottonera Waterfront has been revamped and makes for a gorgeous amble.

◉ Sights & Activities

Fort St Angelo   FORTRESS
(www.heritagemalta.com) The Knights took over this medieval fort in 1530 and strengthened it – Fort St Angelo served as the residence of the Grand Master of the Order until 1571 and was the headquarters of la Valette during the Great Siege. At the time of

Senglea & Vittoriosa

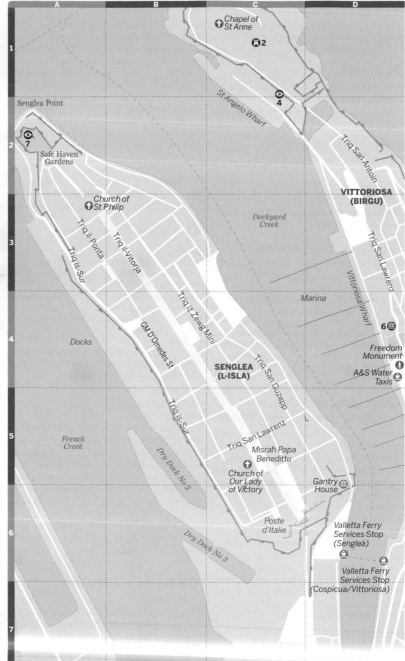

Chapel of
St Anne

2

St Angelo Wharf

4

Senglea Point

7

Safe Haven
Gardens

Church of
St Philip

Triq il-Ponta

Triq il-Vitorja

Triq is-Sur

Dockyard
Creek

VITTORIOSA
(BIRGU)

Triq San Anton

Triq San Lawrenz

Vittoriosa Wharf

Marina

Triq iz-Żewġ Mini

GM D'Omedes St

Docks

SENGLEA
(L-ISLA)

Triq San Ġużepp

6

Freedom
Monument

A&S Water
Taxis

Triq is-Sur

Triq San Lawrenz

French
Creek

Dry Dock No 2

Misrah Papa
Benedittu

Church of
Our Lady
of Victory

Gantry
House

Dry Dock No 3

Poste
d'Italie

Valletta Ferry
Services Stop
(Senglea)

Valletta Ferry
Services Stop
(Cospicua/Vittoriosa)

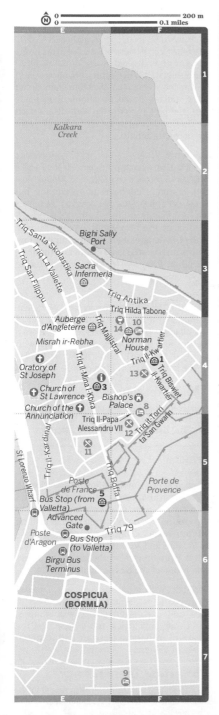

Senglea & Vittoriosa

◎ Sights

🛏 Sleeping

✕ Eating

🍷 Drinking & Nightlife

research Heritage Malta was due to open sections of the fort to the public, with hands-on interpretative exhibits and access to amazing harbour views. The British occupied the fort from the 19th century, and from 1912 until 1979 it served as the headquarters of the Mediterranean Fleet, first as HMS *Egmont* and from 1933 as HMS *St Angelo*. The upper part of the fort, including the Grand Master's Palace and the 15th-century Chapel of St Anne, is now occupied by the modern Order of St John. The tip of the Vittoriosa peninsula has been fortified since at least the 9th century; before that it was the site of Roman and Phoenician temples.

Inquisitor's Palace HISTORIC BUILDING
(📞 2182 7006; Triq il-Mina l-Kbira; adult/child €6/3; ⏰ 9am-5pm) The Inquisitor's Palace was built in the 1530s and served as law courts until the 1570s, when it became the tribunal (and prison) of the Inquisition, whose task it was to find and suppress heresy. Today the palace houses a small ethnographic museum, but the most fascinating part of the building is the former prison cells, with elaborate carvings by prisoners on the walls. Particularly sinister is the torture chamber, with its rope contraptions for extracting confessions.

The building was strengthened in 1698, as before then a prisoner managed to dig his way out eight times in one year. Outside the prison warden's room there is a delicate sundial, carved by an 18th-century warden.

Malta at War Museum
MUSEUM

(☑2189 6617; www.maltaatwarmuseum.com; Couvre Port; adult/under 16s including audioguide €10/5; ☉10am-5pm) This museum, housed in a wartime police station, and the labyrinthian tunnels that lie beneath it, pays testament to Malta's pivotal part in WWII, and brings vividly to life the suffering of the islanders. As well as displays in glass cases, there is a stirring film, with lots of original footage, narrated by Sir Laurence Olivier. Plus there's the opportunity to descend into the former air-raid shelters, which bring to life the underground existence necessary during the islands' fierce bombardment.

Maritime Museum
MUSEUM

(☑2166 0052; adult/child €5/2.50; ☉9am-5pm) The old naval bakery, built in the 1840s and operating until the 1950s, now houses a wealth of material on Malta's maritime past. The collection includes huge Roman anchors, traditional Maltese fishing boats, and models of the Knights' galleys. The small details of naval life are among the most fascinating: hashish pipes used for whiling away hours at sea, plus local prostitutes' licences indicating the lifestyle back on land.

Armoury
HISTORIC BUILDING

Built in the 16th century, this was used by the knights to store ammunition, and had a door on each of its four sides for ease of access. It was later used as a hospital during the Great Siege and the British converted it into a permanent hospital later; it's now used as offices.

🍴 Eating & Drinking

There are several restaurants lining the scenic, sun-splashed Cottonera Waterfront development facing the marina in Vittoriosa, which are great for a light meal and a snack. For something more distinctive, head into the town.

Del Borgo
MALTESE €

(☑2180 3710; Triq San Duminku; ☉6.30pm-1am) Settle into comfortable sofas in what used to be the cellar of the Prince of Wales' Own band club, with high stone-work arches. This is an atmospheric wine bar with bottle-lined walls and a fine selection of local and international wines; simple traditional dishes, such as *bil gunglien* (Maltese bread stuffed with pork belly, ricotta and oregano), are also available.

★ Osteria VE
ITALIAN €€

(☑7734 7136; osteriave.com; Triq Il-Papa Alessandru VII; mains €8-16; ☉5pm-midnight Mon, Wed-Fri, 10am-4pm & 6pm-midnight Sat & Sun) This lovely restaurant is tucked away down a Birgu backstreet in a 17th-century townhouse, and is run by a convivial Venetian pair, doing what Italians do best – simple food made with the best ingredients, with dishes such as beef with rosemary or tagliatelle with sausage and tomato.

Tal-Petut
MALTESE €€

(☑7942 1169; www.talpetut.com; 20 Triq Pacifiku Scicluna; 5-course menu €28; ☉6.30-10pm Tue-Sat) Intimate, characterful restaurant Tal-Petut occupies a former grocery but feels like a home away from home. It is presided over by the host-with-the-most, Donald, who's passionate about the restaurant's emphasis on seasonal local dishes and produce, including *lampuki* (fish) in white wine or slow-cooked pork.

Il-Forn
WINE BAR

(☑2182 0379; 27 Triq it-Tramuntana; ☉7.30pm-late Tue-Sun) Il-Forn, an alluring wine bar in Il Collachio (almost opposite the Norman House), also functions as an art gallery, with plenty of fabulously colourful art on display by the bar's Austrian-born owner.

ℹ️ Information

Tourist Information Branch (☑2180 0145; Inquisitor's Palace; ☉9am-5pm Mon-Sat, 9am-1pm Sun) Useful tourist office in Vittoriosa.

Senglea

POP 5395

Senglea is even more difficult to get lost in than Vittoriosa, as the streets form a grid pattern. The town was pretty much razed to the ground during WWII, so little of historic interest remains, but there are great views of Valletta and Vittoriosa, and the little vedette (watchtower) at the tip of the peninsula is one of the classic sights of Malta.

Vedette (Watchtower)
LANDMARK

The vedette is decorated with carvings of eyes and ears, symbolising watchfulness, and commands a view to the west over the length of the Grand Harbour and southern flanks of Valletta.

🚌 Getting There & Away

It's a 15-minute walk from the main gate at Vittoriosa around to the main gate at Senglea.

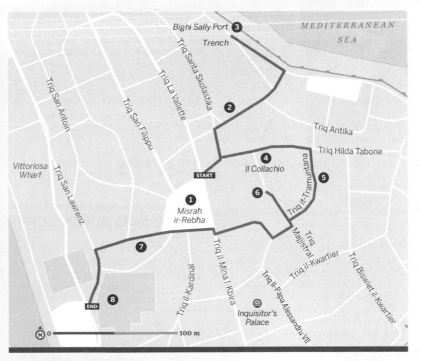

Bighi Sally Port ③
Trench
MEDITERRANEAN SEA
Triq Santa Skolastika
Triq La Vallette
②
Triq San Antoin
Triq San Filippu
Triq Antika
Triq Hilda Tabone
④
Il Collachio
Triq it-Tramuntana
⑤
Vittoriosa Wharf
Triq San Lawrenz
START
⑥
①
Misrah ir-Rebha
Triq Majjistral
⑦
Triq il-Kardinal
Triq il-Mina l-Kbira
Triq il-Kwartier
Triq il-Papa Alessandru VII
Triq Biswiet il-Kwartier
END
⑧
Inquisitor's Palace
Ⓝ 0 — 100 m

🏃 Walking Tour
Vittoriosa

START MISRAH IR-REBHA
END WATERFRONT
LENGTH 1KM; ONE HOUR

Start at ① **Misrah ir-Rebha** (Victory Sq) with its two monuments: the Victory Monument, erected in 1705 in memory of the Great Siege; and a statue of St Lawrence, patron saint of Vittoriosa, from 1880. You'll notice a magnificent building (from 1888) on the eastern side of the square; it's home to the Band Club of St Lawrence. From the square head east on Triq Hilda Tabone, then take the first left (Triq Santa Skolastika) towards the massive blank walls of the ② **Sacra Infermeria**, the first hospital to be built by the Knights on their arrival in Malta. It's now a convent. Turn right down an alley (signposted Triq il-Miratur) and walk along the wall's perimeter. The stepped ramp descending into a trench in front of the Infermeria leads to the ③ **Bighi Sally Port**, where the wounded were brought by boat to the infirmary under the cover of darkness during the Great Siege. Next, head back onto

Triq Hilda Tabone. To your right lies a small maze of charming alleys, collectively known as ④ **Il Collachio**, with some of the city's oldest surviving buildings. Wander up Triq it-Tramuntana to the so-called ⑤ **Norman House** at No 11 (on the left) and look up at the 1st floor. The twin-arched window, with its slender central pillar and zigzag decoration, dates from the 13th century and is in a style described as Siculo-Norman. Also in this area are the first auberges built by the Knights in the 16th century – the ⑥ **Auberge d'Angleterre** on Triq il-Majjistral, the auberge of the English Knights, now serves as the local library. From here, turn back to Misrah ir-Rebha, from where you can walk down to the waterfront. Turn left into the nearby chapel where the little ⑦ **Oratory of St Joseph** contains relics of Grand Master la Valette, and continue down past the ⑧ **Church of St Lawrence**. Built on the site of an 11th-century Norman church, St Lawrence's served as the conventual church of the Knights of St John from 1530 until the move to St John's Co-Cathedral in Valletta.

Hal Saflieni Hypogeum & Tarxien Temples

The suburb of Paola, 2km southwest of Cospicua, conceals two of Malta's most important prehistoric sites.

★ **Hal Saflieni**
Hypogeum   ARCHAEOLOGICAL SITE
(☑ 2180 5019; www.heritagemalta.org; Triq iċ-Ċimiterju; adult/child €30/12; ☉ 50min tours hourly) The Hypogeum (from the Greek, meaning 'underground') is a subterranean necropolis, discovered during building work in 1902. To visit is to step into a mysterious and silent world. Its halls, chambers and passages, immaculately hewn out of the rock, cover some 500 sq metres; it is thought to date from around 3600 to 3000 BC, and an estimated 7000 bodies may have been interred here.

At the time of research the site was due to close from September 2015 until April 2016 for maintenance; check locally or online to verify it has reopened.

The ancient workers mimicked built masonry in carving out these underground chambers, and exploited the rock's natural weaknesses and strengths to carve out the spaces by hand and create a safe underground structure. Carbon dioxide exhaled by visiting tourists did serious damage to the delicate limestone walls of the burial chambers, and it was closed to the public for 10 years up to mid-2000. It has been restored with Unesco funding, and its microclimate is now strictly controlled. For this reason, when it is open, the maximum number of visitors to the site is limited (10 per tour).

Pre-booking is essential (try to book around two months before your visit). As well as online, tickets are available in person from the Hypogeum and the National Museum of Archaeology; a few are available on the day, but it's better not to chance it.

Tarxien Temples   TEMPLE
(☑ 2169 5578; Triq it-Templi Neolitiċi; adult/child €6/3; ☉ 9am-5pm) The Tarxien Temples (Tarxien is pronounced tar-*sheen*) are hidden up a backstreet several blocks east of the Hypogeum. These megalithic structures were excavated in 1914 and are thought to date from between 3600 and 2500 BC. There are four linked structures, built with massive stone blocks up to 3m by 1m by 1m in size, decorated with spiral patterns, pitting and animal reliefs.

The large statue of a broad-hipped female figure was found in the right-hand niche of the first temple, and a copy remains in situ. In 2015 works took place to add a new visitor centre and erect a new cover to protect the temples.

ⓘ Getting There & Away

Myriad buses pass through Paola, including buses 1, 2 and 3 from Valletta (15 to 20 minutes). They stop at various points around the main square, Pjazza Paola.

From the main square, the Hypogeum is a five-minute walk; the Tarxien Temples are 10 minutes away.

Fort Rinella & Smart City

Fort Rinella   FORTRESS
(☑ 2180 9713; fortrinella.com; Triq Santu Rokku; adult/child/family €12/5/29; ☉ 10am-5pm Mon-Sat, guided tours on the hour) Built by the British in the late 19th century, Fort Rinella has been lovingly restored and converted into an interesting military museum with hands-on displays of fighting skills and signalling (up to 1.30pm). At 2pm there is an impressive military re-enactment outside the fort, plus the thrilling chance for visitors to fire a cannon or rifle (for a donation). The fort, 1.5km northeast of Vittoriosa, was one of two coastal batteries designed to counter the threat of Italy's new ironclad battleships.

The batteries (the second one was on Tigné Point in Sliema) were equipped with the latest Armstrong 100-tonne guns – the biggest muzzle-loading guns ever made. Their 100-tonne shells had a range of 6.4km and could penetrate 38cm of armour plating. The guns were never fired in anger, and were retired in 1906.

Xghajra Smart City   AREA
This Dubai-style development has been created along the coast east of Ricasoli Point to serve the burgeoning local interactive gaming (iGaming) industry, and combines restaurants, spanking-new apartment blocks and office space. The restaurant-lined centrepiece is Laguna Walk, which has a musical fountain that's spectacular at night.

ⓘ Getting There & Away

To get to Fort Rinella or Xghajra Smart City, take bus 3 from Valletta (35 minutes, half-hourly Monday to Saturday, hourly Sunday). Birgu or Paola. It stops outside the fort and at Smart City.

Sliema, St Julian's & Paceville

Best Places to Eat

➡ Electro Lobster Project (p69)

➡ Mint (p67)

➡ Sciacca (p71)

➡ Zest (p71)

Best Places to Stay

➡ Hotel Juliani (p140)

➡ Hostel Jones (p139)

➡ Hostel 94 (p138)

➡ Hotel Valentina (p140)

➡ Corner Hostel (p139)

Why Go?

Malta's cool crowd flocks to these areas to eat, drink, shop and party, and if you're looking for a base that mingles cosmopolitan sparkle with quiet backstreets, this is the perfect choice. Connected by a gracious seafront promenade, with shimmering Mediterranean views, this collection of districts merge into one another, and are packed with shops, restaurants and bars.

St Julian's was once a pretty fishing village, but now five-star hotels and apartment complexes dominate its scenic bays. It adjoins the small nightlife enclave of Paceville, which springs to life at night after a couple of shots. This, coincidentally, is where many of Malta's English-language schools are located.

More exclusive-feeling Sliema has long been associated with the Maltese upper classes, and makes an enticingly more peaceful base, just far enough from the action. Gracious townhouses sit along backstreets, while burgeoning swish apartment blocks line the seafront, which is blessed by sun-trapped rocky beaches and swimming spots.

When to Go

➡ Come in May, June, September and October if you're looking for lower prices, guaranteed sunshine and few crowds.

➡ If you're after a party atmosphere and lots of action, however, head here during the peak summer months of July and August.

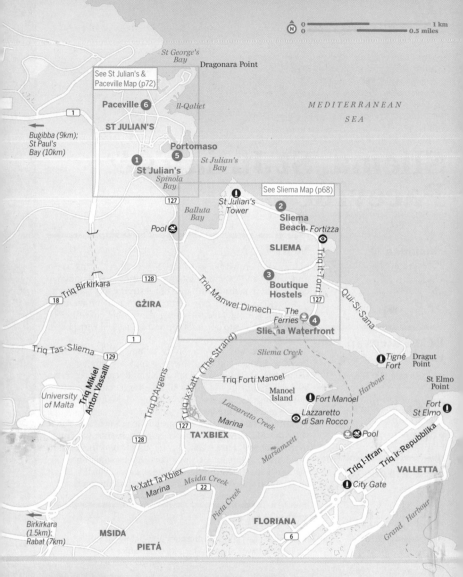

Sliema, St Julian's & Paceville Highlights

1 Wine and dine alfresco in **St Julian's** (p70), Malta's gastronomic epicentre.

2 Swim off the flat rocky stretch of **Sliema Beach** (p67).

3 Stay in one of Sliema's fabulous **boutique hostels** (p138).

4 Take to the waters on a **boat trip** (p67) from Sliema waterfront.

5 Enjoy a marina-side drink in **Portomaso** (p70).

6 Experience Malta's liveliest nightlife hub in **Paceville** (p72).

SLIEMA & AROUND

Once a summer bolt-hole for Valletta's movers and shakers, Sliema is one of the island's most sought-after neighbourhoods, a melange of golden-stone townhouses and swish apartment blocks. Covering its own peninsula, it merges into the district of St Julian's to the northwest, and Gżira and Ta'Xbiex to the south, and is separated from Valletta by narrow Marsamxett Harbour. The main seafront drag is Triq it-Torri (which turns into Qui-si-Sana further south) and is marked by two towers: St Julian's Tower is one of the network of coastal watchtowers built by Grand Master de Redin in the 17th century, and Il-Fortiżża was built by the British in Gothic style. Most of the seafront is public, so you can swim off the rocks. The district has some excellent restaurants, but for nightlife head to St Julian's and Paceville.

☉ Sights

Sliema Beach
BEACH

(Triq it-Torri) The Sliema waterfront is edged by flattish rocks, with stepped access at various points. It's a good place to swim from, though the water tends to be deep. There are also facilities for hire (sunbeds, watersports) at the private lidos scattered along the coast; admission costs around €10 per day.

In places along Triq it-Torri and at Qui-si-Sana, square pools have been cut into the soft limestone. These were made for the convenience of leisure-loving upper-class Maltese ladies, and are good for smaller children.

Tigné Point (The Point)
AREA

(www.thepointmalta.com; ☉9.30am-7.30pm) Tigné Point, a promontory east of Sliema, was one of the sites where the Turkish commander Dragut Reis ranged his cannons to pound Fort St Elmo during the Great Siege in 1565. The tip of the peninsula is still known as Dragut Point, and now has some of the area's swankiest residential apartments, and Malta's largest shopping mall, the Point. Tigné Fort, built in 1793 by the Knights of St John, is being restored as a cultural, heritage and commercial venue.

Manoel Island
HISTORIC SITE

Manoel Island, which can be accessed via a short bridge from Gżira, is largely taken up by boat-building yards and the partly restored Fort Manoel. The island was used as a quarantine zone by the Knights of St John;

the shell of their 17th-century plague hospital, the **Lazzaretto di San Rocco**, can still be seen on the south side. There's a summer funfair on the island.

Fort Manoel was built in the early 18th century under Grand Master Manoel de Vilhena, and suffered extensive bomb damage during WWII, when nearby Lazzaretto Creek was used as a submarine base. There are redevelopment plans afoot, but these are controversial, and although restoration has taken place the plans seem to be stalled indefinitely.

Ta'Xbiex
AREA

Ta'Xbiex is an upmarket seaside neighbourhood, featuring gracious villas, mansions and embassies, that loops around Malta's largest yacht marinas, with lovely views across the bobbing craft. There are some good places to eat along the waterfront.

☆ Activities

Dive Systems
DIVING

(☑2131 9123; www.divesystemsmalta.com; Exiles, Triq it-Torri) Excellent dive school with fantastic facilities and helpful staff.

Diveshack
DIVING

(☑2133 8558; www.divemalta.com; Ix-Xatt Ta'Qui-si-Sana) A PADI 5-star diving centre.

Captain Morgan Cruises
BOAT TOUR

(☑2346 3333; www.captainmorgan.com.mt) As well as its extensive program of boat trips, from harbour cruises (adult/child under 12 €16/13) to full-day catamaran rides, Captain Morgan Cruises runs popular 4WD jeep safaris exploring the more remote parts of Malta and Gozo (all day combined catamaran and jeep safari adult/child under 12 €95/79).

Hera Cruises
BOAT TOUR

(☑2133 0583; www.heracruises.com) Various boat tours leaving from Sliema waterfront, including all-day cruises (adult/child €58/30), and trips to Comino and the Blue Lagoon (€30/20) or Comino and Gozo (€50/30, includes lunch) in a regular boat, or to the Blue Lagoon in a Turkish *gulet* (old-style sailing boat; €58/30, includes lunch).

✕ Eating

★ Mint
CAFE €

(☑2133 7177; www.mintmalta.com; Triq Stella Maris; snacks €3-7; ☉8am-4pm Tue-Sun; ☎⏸) To see where Sliema's yummiest mummies

Sliema

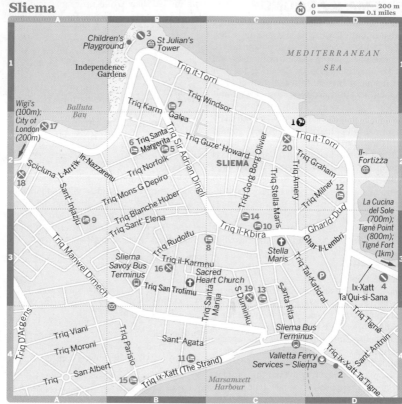

hang out, head to this chic New Zealand–owned cafe that provides laid-back Kiwi style and home cooking. Its food is smashing, with some really sumptuous snacks – quesadilla, vegan stew, savoury muffins, and delicious homemade cakes and cookies. There's outdoor seating under minty-green sunshades. It's kid-friendly.

L-Ahwa Bakery
BAKERY €

(bread loaves from €0.50; ☺11pm-6.30pm) This bakery opened over 125 years ago and has been run by Carmelo Micallef since 1968. It uses traditional rather than electric ovens, and has delicious jam tarts. At Christmas, lots of locals bring in their meat to be roasted here, as many homes don't have ovens.

Bus Stop Kiosk
FAST FOOD €

(Triq ix-Xatt; snacks €1.50-7.50; ☺7.30am-midnight) This harbourside kiosk is south of Sliema, in Ta'Xbiex, and is a great choice for a cheap meal with the locals. It's right

by the waterfront, so it's scenic too. It's ideal for families, with a greasy-spoon-style menu ranging from sandwiches to full meals of pork chops or fish and chips.

Simler's
BAKERY €

(Triq San Ġwann Battista; pastizzi €0.30; ☺7.30am-6pm Tue-Sat, to noon Sun) This bakery was established in 1945, and unlike most *pastizzerijas,* it freshly bakes everything on site, rather than baking pre-prepared *pastizzi* (filled pastries). You can see the machinery in the back of the diminutive shop. It also sells chicken pies and the like.

Piccolo Padre
ITALIAN €

(☎2134 4875; Triq il-Kbira; mains €7.20-22; ☺6.15-11pm daily & noon-3pm Sun) This casual, family-friendly pizzeria has fabulous sea views; try to snare a coveted table on the enclosed balcony. Pizzas are crunchy and tasty – the house speciality is decorated with tomato, mozzarella, Maltese sausage and

Sliema

Gozo cheese. Also available are good pasta options, salads and burgers.

Wigi's ITALIAN €€
(Triq Ġorġ Borg Olivier; mains €15-23; ⊙12.30-2.45pm & 7.30-10.30pm Tue-Sat, 12.30-2.45pm Sun Sep-Jun) Wigi's is the Malti pronunciation of 'Luigi's'. This much appreciated, family-run Italian restaurant offers views over the bay through its large plate-glass windows. It proffers delicious steaks, calamari and pork, among other delights; desserts include pear and ricotta cheesecake or date pudding.

La Cucina del Sole ITALIAN €€
(☑2060 3434; lacucinadelsole.com.mt; Tigné Point; mains €7.90-25; ⊙7-10.30pm daily, 12.30-3pm Sat & Sun) If you've found yourself sucked into Malta's biggest mall at the Point, this is a bright and breezy place to head to eat tasty pizzas, fresh fish and meat dishes. There's a sunny terrace with great views across to Valletta and Manoel Island.

★ Electro Lobster Project SEAFOOD €€€
(Pjazza Balluta; mains €17-25; ⊙11am-11pm Tue-Sun ☑) This is a bar-club-restaurant with outside seating in a lovely spot overlooking Balluta Bay. There's nowhere like this on Malta, with a bar and restaurant upstairs, and a small club/venue downstairs with live gigs. And there's lobster! Anyway you like it! Cuisine is Sicilian with a healthy modern twist; there's a separate vegetarian menu.

Barracuda MEDITERRANEAN €€€
(☑2133 1817; 195 Triq il-Kbira; mains €20-22; ⊙7-11pm) This is a traditional, elegant restaurant set in the drawing room of an early-18th-century seaside villa on the edge of the water. There are brilliant blue sea views framed in the windows, a sunshaded terrace and a menu of carefully prepared Italian and Mediterranean dishes. The service receives mixed reports, however.

MALTA'S WATCHTOWERS

The Knights of St John concentrated their defences on the Three Cities and Valletta. Up to the 19th century, only the two old capitals – Mdina on Malta and Victoria on Gozo – were fortified, and even their defences were not particularly robust. Farmers on the outskirts of the capitals could shelter within the cities, but villages elsewhere were left to fend for themselves.

Malta had long had watchtowers, but Grand Master Juan de Lascaris-Castellar of the Knights of Malta commissioned five towers from 1637 to 1640; another knight, Grand Master Martin de Redin, subsequently built a string of 13 towers around the perimeters of the islands from 1658 to 1659. These were strong enough to withstand a small attack, but not a long siege. They were positioned so Gozo and Malta could signal to each other – with fire, gunfire and flags – if Turkish invaders were sighted off the coast. The towers still stand today, and range from simple, small watchtowers, to larger mini-fortresses.

🍷 Drinking & Nightlife

★**Electro Lobster Project**   BAR
(Pjazza Balluta; ⊙ 11am-late Tue-Sun) The Electro Lobster is a cool hybrid bar-restaurant-club in the Gothic-tinged art deco Balluta building. There are regular live gigs in the downstairs bar, or you can drink outside, with sofas, chairs and tables out on the picturesque Balluta Bay. Cocktails are made from fresh ingredients (no syrups), and you've got a wide choice of whisky, vodka and tequila.

City of London   PUB
(☑ 2133 1706; 193 Triq il-Kbira; ⊙ 11am-late Mon-Sat, from 10am Sun) This tiny pub, almost in St Julian's, has been open since 1914. It's packed at weekends and there's a great party atmosphere, plus outside seating. It's popular in the gay scene, but everyone is welcome; there's a nicely mixed crowd of expats, locals and students.

🛍 Shopping

Sliema's Triq ix-Xatt and Triq it-Torri together comprise Malta's prime shopping area. There are some decent shoe shops and clothing labels, including the big British and European high-street labels. The shopping mall at Tigné Point (p67), on the tip of the peninsula, dwarfs all the other competition, with big-name chains such as Debenhams, Guess and Adidas.

ℹ Information

Mater Dei Hospital (☑ 2545 0000, emergency 112; www.ehealth.gov.mt; Tal-Qroqq) Malta's main general hospital is 2km southwest of Sliema, and 3km west of Valletta, near the University of Malta. Staff at the hospital can be contacted for any diving incidents requiring medical attention on ☑ 2545 5269 or via the emergency number ☑ 112.

The hospital can be accessed by numerous buses, including 31 and 37 from Valletta, 202 and 203 from St Julian's, or X3 from Buġibba.
Police Station (☑ 2133 2282; cnr Triq Manwel Dimech & Triq Rudolfu)
Post Office (118 Triq Manwel Dimech; ⊙ 7.45am-12.45pm Mon-Sat)
Western Union Business Solutions (☑ 2132 2747; Il-Piazzetta; ⊙ 8am-1pm & 2-5pm Mon-Fri)

ℹ Getting There & Away

BUS
Buses 202, 203 and 13 (10 minutes, half-hourly) run to St Julian's and Paceville. Buses include:

12/13 Valletta
202/203 Ta'Qali Crafts Village, Rabat and Mdina
12 Buġibba
222 Ċirkewwa (for Gozo ferries), via Buġibba
Night buses, running between midnight and 3am or 4am on Friday and Saturday nights, include:
N3 Three Cities
N11 Buġibba, Mellieħa and Ċirkewwa (for Gozo ferries)
N13 Valletta

BOAT
Valletta Ferry Services – Sliema (☑ 2346 3862; www.vallettaferryservices.com; single/return adult €1.50/2.80, child €0.50/0.90; ⊙ 7am-7pm Oct-May, to 12.15am Jun-Sep) Operates ferries to Valletta's Marsamxett Harbour, which take around five minutes.

ST JULIAN'S & PACEVILLE

St Julian's, on a prong of peninsula just north of Sliema, is as frenetic as it gets in Malta, a hubbub of restaurants, bars and language schools (many overseas students come here to learn English). Glitzy developments, such as Portomaso Marina, are ideal settings for cocktails with a view, and the area has Malta's highest concentration of five-star hotels. More rough and ready is Paceville, a few streets to the west of St Julian's – it's full of pubs, clubs and 'gentlemen's clubs', where a young party-loving crowd see it out till dawn.

◉ Sights & Activities

Portomaso Apartment & Marina Complex   AREA
The glitzy development of Portomaso is overlooked by the towering Hilton Hotel, and centres on a marina ringed by restaurants and bars. It's a popular place to hang out, drink and dine while watching the sun bounce off the yachts and the water.

St George's Bay   BEACH
Most of the beaches around St Julian's are of the bare rock or private lido variety (the five-star hotels offer beach clubs and watersports), but at the head of St George's Bay there's a small, sandy beach.

Palazzo Spinola
HISTORIC BUILDING

(Triq il-Knisja) Once St Julian's was rural, with just a few grand houses, of which this was one, built for the Italian knight Rafael Spinola. It is surrounded by a walled garden and is home to the Parliamentary Assembly of the Mediterranean.

Villa Dragonara
HISTORIC BUILDING

Villa Dragonara, an aristocratic residence that became the Dragonara Casino in 1964, is dramatically set on the rocky southern headland of St George's Bay. It was built in 1870 as the summer residence of the Marquis Scicluna, a wealthy banker.

Divewise
DIVING

(☑ 2135 6441; www.divewise.com.mt; Westin Dragonara Resort) Respected dive school with a great team of instructors, including one Japanese speaker.

Yellow Fun Watersports
WATERSPORTS

(☑ 2135 0025; www.yellowfunwatersports.com; Portomaso) Yellow Fun Watersports operates from the Portomaso marina in St Julian's, under the Hilton Hotel, and offers a huge menu of activities including jet-ski rental, yacht charter, self-driven boats, water taxis to Sliema, Valletta or Vittoriosa, and trips to Gozo and Comino.

✖ Eating

RiverReno
ICE CREAM €

(Triq Ross; cone/cup from €3; ⊙ 10am-midnight Sun-Thu, to 12.30am Fri & Sat) This bright gelateria in the centre of St Julian's offers fantastic Italian ice cream in many different, delicious flavours using the best natural ingredients.

Badass Burgers
BURGERS €€

(Badass Burgers; ☑ 2138 4066; www.badassburgers.eu; 1 La Spinola; burgers €10-16; ⊙ 6-11pm Mon-Thu, noon-midnight Fri-Sun) Badass offers Malta's finest burgers. Besides 100% gourmet beef, the menu includes 'Off the Hook' burgers with prawn and haddock, and the 'Maltese' with rabbit and sausage. All are tasty and top quality, and the setting is in a historic building on the waterfront.

Gululu
MALTESE €€

(☑ 2133 3431; 133 Ix-Xatt ta'Spinola; mains €15-20; ⊙ noon-11pm) Offering water's-edge dining, this place has balconies overlooking Spinola Bay, where you can enjoy Maltese homestyle favourites such as *aljotta* (fish soup) and *torta al-fenek* (rabbit pie). It's packed with Maltese families on Sundays.

Lulu
MEDITERRANEAN €€

(☑ 2137 7211; 31 Triq il-Knisja; 3-course set menu €29.50; ⊙ 7-11pm Mon-Sat) Lulu's, set on a quiet side street close to the Portomaso complex, is informal yet sophisticated. It is prettily decorated in ochre, white and green, with a small terrace. Expect friendly service and a modern Med menu, from which you can choose any three dishes – the set menu is not a fixed menu.

Cuba
MEDITERRANEAN €€

(☑ 2010 2323; Triq San Ġorġ; mains €11-25; ⊙ 9am-late; ☑) Always busy and lively, the sunny terrace here is a prime people-watching spot, almost jutting over the water, with a fantastic view of Spinola Bay. There's a wide-ranging, crowd-pleasing menu, with breakfast eggs, pizza, pasta and more.

Avenue
MEDITERRANEAN €€

(☑ 2131 1753; Triq Gort; mains €6.70-30; ⊙ 12.30-2.30pm & 6-11.30pm) Enduringly popular Avenue now takes up a sizeable stretch of the street. Despite its size, it's always bustling – families, students and groups of friends keep coming for its lively atmosphere and huge portions of good-value meat and fish, pizza and pasta. The interior combines bright colours and stained glass; there are also tables outside along the stepped narrow street.

★ Sciacca
ITALIAN €€€

(Triq Santu Wistin; mains €19-28; ⊙ noon-11.30pm Tue-Sun, 7-11.30pm Mon) On the outskirts of Paceville lies this serene restaurant offering sophisticated Sicilian cooking, with ingredients imported from Malta's nearby neighbour. Dishes include fettucine with sea urchins, and *orecchiette* with calamari. The style is chic and contemporary, with leather-look chairs and wooden tables.

Zest
FUSION €€€

(☑ 2138 7600; Hotel Juliani; mains €15-27; ⊙ 7-11pm Mon-Sat) To see and be seen, head to Zest, in the stand-out boutique Hotel Juliani (p140). Locals love this fusion restaurant, which offers a mix of Japanese, Thai, Indonesian and European flavours. Book ahead and specify an outside table if you want a bay view.

SLIEMA, ST JULIAN'S & PACEVILLE ST JULIAN'S & PACEVILLE

St Julian's & Paceville

0 — 200 m
0 — 0.09 miles

Corinthia Hotel
St George's Bay
(350m)

St George's Bay

Triq ix-Xatt
Ta San Gorg

Triq id-Dragunara

Il-Qaliet

Triq Santu Wistin

Triq San Gorg

Triq Elija Zammit

Triq Andrija

Triq Ball

Triq il-Wilga

Taxi Rank

Triq
Schreiber

PACEVILLE

Triq Paceville

Triq 9
Dobbie

Triq il-Knisja

Millenium
Chapel

PORTOMASO

Triq Gort

Hilton
Hotel

Triq Ivo Muscat Azzopardi

The
Gardens

Triq Ross
Wembleys

Triq Mikiel Anton

Portomaso Marina

Triq Il-Qaliet

ST JULIAN'S

Triq San Gorg

Triq Spinola

Triq Forrest

Malta Water
Taxis – St
Julian's

Spinola
Bay

Triq Gorg Borg Olivier

Triq Il-kbira

Hostel Malti
(450m)

City of London (250m);
Wigi's (350m)

🍷 Drinking & Nightlife

Level 22
BAR

(☎2310 2222; www.22.com.mt; Level 22, Portomaso Tower; ⏱9.30am-4am Jun-Aug, Wed-Sun only Sep-May) Sleek and glitzily chic, lounge-bar Level 22 is ideal if you're in the mood for cocktails with a touch of swank. Situated on the 22nd floor of Portomaso Tower, the bar has square-cornered sofas and an amazing view over the lights of Portomaso and St Julian's and out to sea. It turns into a club on Friday and Saturday nights. Cocktails cost between €6.50 and €13.

Shadow Lounge
BAR

(☎7909 8181; http://shadowloungemalta.com; ⏱8pm-late) On the 2nd floor above Hugo's Lounge, this place is more sophisticated than many of Paceville's other operations, and attracts an older crowd who are in their 20s rather than their teens. The music policy is house and the vibe is laid-back.

Bedouin Bar
BAR

(St George's Bay; ⏱10pm-4am Fri) This waterside chill-out space, at the Westin Dragonara, is all white curtains and sofas, and has sparkling views over to St Julian's. It's popular with a mix of locals and tourists, and

St Julian's & Paceville

is a great place to hang out on a summer night over a cocktail listening to loungey DJ sounds.

Hugo's Lounge   LOUNGE
(☏ 2138 2264; Triq San Ġorġ; ◷ noon-1am) Hugo's, amid of one of Paceville's main drags, is a lively alfresco, sleek-looking bar, and the nicest of the many 'Hugo' options in the area. It's great for cocktails and lounging on sofas, and you can soak up the booze with a menu of well-executed Asian food – sushi, curries, noodles, stir-fries and Thai soups (mains €13 to €18).

Ryan's Pub   IRISH PUB
(☏ 2135 0680; ◷ 11.30am-1am Mon-Thu, to 4am Fri & Sat, 1-4pm Sun) Lively pub action can be found at Ryan's Irish Pub, perched high up overlooking the action on Spinola Bay. It's a popular stop-off – crowded, lively, friendly and well-stocked with cold Guinness, and offers some great pub grub, including gourmet burgers and delicious ribs, as well as screening football games. It becomes clubbier later, with regular DJs getting the crowd going.

Native Bar   BAR
(St Rita's Steps; ◷ noon-late) This Latino-flavoured bar on Paceville's party street is always buzzing and has some of the longest hours on the strip. Its indoor and outdoor areas are generally packed out with cocktail- and beer-slurping hedonists. In case the flirtatious action inside and out gets tiresome, there is also live sport on TV.

Nordic   BAR
(☏ 2138 2264; St Rita's Steps; ◷ 6pm-late) This popular Scandinavian-style bar is in the thick of Paceville's party strip, has wood-lined walls, and like most it has TV screens showing live sport.

Fuego   CLUB
(www.fuego.com.mt; Triq Santu Wistin; ◷ 8pm-late) Get hot and sweaty dancing up a storm at this very popular indoor/outdoor salsa bar. The open terraces (covered and heated in winter) are full of people checking each other out – there's something of a meat-market atmosphere, but it's friendly, fun and not too sleazy. There are free dance classes from 8.30pm Monday to Wednesday so get your dancing shoes on.

Havana   CLUB
(☏ 2137 4500; 82 Triq San Ġorġ; ◷ 8pm-4am) A mixed menu of R&B, soul, hip hop and commercial favourites keep the crowds happy here, and there are two clubs within: Cabanas, a popular place for mainstream pop and R&B, and the rockier, more retro Flashback.

☆ Entertainment

Eden Century Cinemas   CINEMA
(☑2371 0400; www.edencinemas.com.mt; Triq Santu Wistin) This large complex has 17 screens (on both sides of the road) showing first-run films. Adult tickets cost from €5.50, and all films are in English, or in their original language with English subtitles. See the website or local newspapers for screening times.

🛍 Shopping

St Julian's has several worth-a-browse small malls, selling clothes, swimwear and accessories, as well as foodstuffs, including the **Bay Street Complex** (www.baystreet.com.mt; Triq Santu Wistin; ⊙10am-10pm) and the **Portomaso Shopping Complex** (Triq il-Knisja; ⊙8am-10pm).

ℹ Information

Be aware that there are occasional outbreaks of drink-fuelled violence in Paceville late at night. The nightlife zone is also noisy, so you may prefer to seek accommodation elsewhere.

Police Station (☑2133 2196; Triq San Ġorġ)
Post Office (Lombard Bank, Triq Paceville; ⊙8am-1pm Mon-Fri mid-Jun–Sep, 8.30am-2.30pm Mon-Fri Oct–mid-Jun)

ℹ Getting There & Away

BUS

Buses 202, 203 and 13 (10 minutes, half-hourly) run from Sliema to St Julian's and Paceville.

Direct bus services to/from St Julian's and Paceville include the 202/203 to Ta'Qali Crafts Village, Rabat and Mdina; bus 12 along the coast to Buġibba; bus 222 to Ċirkewwa (for Gozo ferries) via Buġibba; bus 205 for Naxxar, Mosta, Attard and Rabat; and bus X2 to the airport.

Night buses, running between midnight and 3am or 4am on Friday and Saturday nights, include the N3 for the Three Cities; the N11 for Buġibba, Mellieħa and Ċirkewwa (for Gozo ferries); the N13 for Valletta; the N52 to/from Rabat; and the N71 and N81 to/from the airport.

BOAT

Malta Water Taxis – St Julian's (☑9993 9443; www.maltawatertaxis.com.mt; per person Valletta–St Julian's €12, per person harbour cruise €30) Malta Water Taxis operates between Valletta and St Julian's, but you need to call ahead to book. It also offers harbour cruises in a *dgħajsa* (traditional rowing boat or water taxi; pronounced 'die-sa').

ℹ Getting Around

Wembleys (p180) provides a reliable 24-hour radio taxi service. There's also a busy taxi rank close to the intersection of Triq San Ġorġ and Triq il-Wilga in Paceville.

Northwest Malta

Includes ➡

Best Places to Eat

➡ Tarragon (p88)

➡ Giuseppe's Restaurant & Wine Bar (p81)

➡ Rebekah's (p82)

➡ Baia Beach Club (p84)

Best for Views

➡ Ras il-Qammieħ (p82)

➡ Malta National Aquarium's promenade (p85)

➡ Victoria Lines (p89)

➡ Sweethaven (p82)

Why Go?

Balmy sandy beaches, watersports, boat trips, birdwatching, horse riding, and walks along the dramatic coastline – Malta's northwest beckons as a prime location for laid-back holiday fun.

Buġibba and Qawra form Malta's largest resort area, with facilities galore, and the area now has the added attractions of the fabulous new Malta National Aquarium set on the beautifully landscaped Qawra promenade, with stunning views.

Beaches on the northwest coast range from the wonderfully accessible Mellieħa Bay, a long stretch of white sand speckled by sunbeds, kiosks and watersports, to the more remote Għajn Tuffieħa Bay, less crowded because of its steeply stepped approach. You can go off the beaten track here too, in search of Selmun Bay, the wildest beach and a well-kept locals' secret, or roam to discover splendid views from the cliffs at Ras il-Qammieħ, Malta's westernmost point.

When to Go

➡ Malta's major beach zone gets busy over July and August. Schools are out, prices are higher, and the weather is at its hottest. If you're after a party scene, it's at its height during this time.

➡ If you're looking for sunshine and off-season bargains, travel in April, May, September and October (it'll only be hot enough to swim in May and September).

Northwest Malta Highlights

1 Explore the dramatic underwater seascape while scuba-diving off the **Marfa Peninsula** (p82).

2 Exult in vast coastal views from the wild headland of **Ras il-Qammieħ** (p82).

3 Make the long climb down to the near-empty **Għajn Tuffieħa Bay** (p78) on a quiet spring day.

4 Enjoy the setting on the Qawra promenade and the fabulous underwater inhabitants of the **Malta National Aquarium** (p85).

5 Take a speedboat trip across navy-blue waters, launching off from lovely **Golden Bay** (p78).

Golden Bay & Għajn Tuffieħa

The fertile Pwales Valley stretches 4km from the head of St Paul's Bay to Għajn Tuffieħa. Here, two of Malta's best sandy beaches draw crowds of sun-worshippers.

👁 Sights & Activities

Golden Bay   BEACH
The lovely sandy arc of Golden Bay has a beautiful setting, and is a popular place to hang out, with a few cafes, watersports and boat trips available. It's not too built up; there's just one mammoth five-star hotel rising above the shoreline.

Għajn Tuffieħa Bay   BEACH
Għajn Tuffieħa Bay (ayn too-*fee*-ha, meaning 'Spring of the Apples') is even lovelier than neighbouring Golden Bay, with no buildings overlooking it, and less busy, as it's reached via a long flight of 186 steps from the nearby car park. It's a 250m strip of red-brown sand, backed by slopes covered in acacia and tamarisk trees, and guarded by a 17th-century watchtower. Sun lounges can be hired here.

Park tal-Majjistral   NATURE RESERVE
(📞 2152 1291; www.majjistral.org; 🚌 44 Valletta-Tuffieħa) The area between Golden Bay and Anchor Bay was once earmarked for a new golf course, but opposition from environmental groups led to the creation instead of Park tal-Majjistral. Information boards show waymarked walking trails; the park arranges regular guided walks (usually adult/child €5/3) from October to April, generally on Sundays, including many sunset walks. Also available from July to September are 2½-hour snorkelling trips (adult/child €12/10; over 9s only).

Bus 44 runs here from Valletta, calling on the way to Għajn Tuffieħa.

Check the website for upcoming events, and book via email (walks@majjistral.org).

The park protects a region of wild sea cliffs and limestone boulder scree, home to plants such as euphorbia, Maltese rock centaury and golden samphire, and wildlife including Mediterranean chameleons.

⭐ Charlie's Discovery
Speedboat Trips   BOAT TOUR
(📞 9940 0019; adult/child €12/9; Comino trip €18/12; ☉ coastal trip noon & 2.30pm, Comino

trip 4pm) Charlie is a knowledgable, award-winning guide. He'll take you on an exhilarating speedboat trip to view cliffs, bays and grottoes, including Għajn Tuffieħa, Ġnejna and Fomm ir-Riħ, and you'll get a chance to swim in Smurf-blue waters. Look out for Charlie, in his red hat and yellow T-shirt, on the Golden Bay beach.

From April to October Charlie also operates a daily trip, which includes a 1½-hour swim, to Comino's Blue Lagoon – a wonderful chance to visit once the crowds have left.

Borg Watersports   WATERSPORTS
(📞 2157 3272; ahoj@maltanet.net; Golden Bay; ☉ Mar-Nov) On the shoreline of Golden Bay, Borg Watersports has a range of activities: SUPs (stand-up paddle boards; €10 per hour), one-/two-person canoes (€10/14 per hour), powerboats (€200 per hour), sailboats (€30 per hour), jet skis (€60 per 20 minutes) and pedaloes (€15 per hour). It also operates trips to the Blue Lagoon.

Orangeshark H2O   DIVING
(📞 2356 1950; www.orangeshark.eu; Radisson Blu Resort & Spa, Golden Bay) This five-star PADI centre is attached to the five-star Radisson on Golden Bay.

Golden Bay Horse Riding   HORSE RIDING
(📞 2157 3360; www.goldenbayhorseriding.com; 1hr ride/90min sunset ride €20/30) This horse riding centre, signposted from Golden Bay, offers enjoyable rides on fields overlooking the northwest beaches for all levels of experience. Book ahead.

🍴 Eating

Your best bet for a meal is to brush the sand off your toes and head to one of the upmarket options at the 10-storey Radisson Blu Resort & Spa (p140).

Pebbles   CAFE €€
(📞 2356 1000; Radisson Blu Resort & Spa, Golden Bay; mains €9-14; ☉ 9am-11pm) The fab outdoor terrace of Pebbles is perfect for coffee, cake, platters, light meals or a cocktail (€7 to €12).

Agliolio   MEDITERRANEAN €€
(📞 2356 1000; Radisson Blu Resort & Spa, Golden Bay; mains €8-24.50; ☉ noon-4pm & 6.30-10pm) Cheery, noisy and aqua-coloured Agliolio has an appealing Med-flavoured menu heavy on pizza, pasta and salads; nab a table outside overlooking the beach.

Essence
MEDITERRANEAN €€€

(✆2356 1111; Radisson Blu Resort & Spa, Golden Bay; mains €20-27; ⊗7-10pm Tue-Sat) Romantic Essence is this area's number one pick for a fancy-pants dinner with beautiful sea views. Cooking is sophisticated, with Chef Andrew Valla conjuring up delicious, surprising combinations of flavours using seasonal ingredients. Bookings are recommended.

ⓘ Getting There & Away

Bus 223 serves Buġibba (25 minutes, hourly) via St Paul's Bay (10 minutes). Bus 225 runs to/from Sliema and St Julian's (50 to 70 minutes, half-hourly). Bus 44 goes to/from Valletta (one hour, hourly), while buses 101/102 run between here, Mellieħa and Ċirkewwa every two hours.

Mġarr & Around

The village of Mġarr (mm-*jarr*), 2km to the southeast of Għajn Tuffieħa (not to be confused with Mġarr on Gozo), is dominated by the dome of the famous **Egg Church**. The Church of the Assumption was built in the 1930s with money raised by local parishioners, largely from the sale of local eggs.

A minor road leads west from Mġarr past the ornate early-19th-century manor house **Zammitello Palace**, now a wedding and function hall, to Ġnejna Bay.

◉ Sights

Ġnejna Bay
BEACH

This gentle red-sand beach is backed by terraced hillsides and has boathouses built into the rocks to one side. The Lippija Tower on the northern skyline makes a good target for a short walk.

Mġarr Shelter
HISTORIC SITE

(✆2157 3235; Triq il-Kbira; adult/child €3/1.50; ⊗9.30am-noon Tue-Sat, 10-11am Sun) The Mġarr Shelter was used by locals during the WWII bombings of Malta (enter through Il-Barri restaurant). You can only imagine the long, uncomfortable hours spent down here in the humidity, 12m underground, but to show that life went on under such tough conditions there are rooms on display that served as classrooms and hospitals.

Skorba Temples
ARCHAEOLOGICAL SITE

(✆2158 0590; heritagemalta.org/museums-sites/skorba/; Triq Sant'Anna; adult/child €3.50/2.50; ⊗9am-4.30pm Tue, Thu & Sat) The excavation of the Skorba Temples, in the neighbouring

village of Żebbiegħ, exposed two temples and some habitations dating to the temple builders' phase, and some even predating this, which are thus the oldest prehistoric structures discovered on the islands.

Ta'Ħaġrat Temple
ARCHAEOLOGICAL SITE

(✆2123 9545; Triq San Pietru; adult/child €3.50/2.50; ⊗9am-4.30pm Tue, Thu & Sat) The site of the Ta'Ħaġrat Temple, dating from around 3600 to 3300 BC, is concealed down a side street off Triq Fisher. There's not that much to see, except a few tumbled stones, but they represent some of the earliest temple building in Malta.

✖ Eating

Il-Barri
MALTESE €€

(✆2157 3235; Triq il-Kbira; mains €6-17; ⊗noon-3pm Tue-Sun, 7-10pm daily) Run by the same family since 1940, Il-Barri is on the Mġarr village square. The slick interior is a surprise, with its monochrome and wavy ceiling. It's a favourite local venue for a *fenkata* (rabbit casserole), and other Maltese-as-they-come local favourites such as *aljotta* (fish broth), quail and horsemeat, plus pizzas in the evening. Expect monster portions.

Mellieħa

POP 10,090

The small town of Mellieħa (mell-*ee*-ha) perches picturesquely atop the ridge between St Paul's Bay and Mellieħa Bay. It's a popular resort, but hasn't been over-developed due to its distance from the beach, and outside the centre, the town has a laid-back, local feel. There are numerous large hotels in town, but Mellieħa retains a certain elegance, and is home to some excellent restaurants. A 15-minute walk leads down the steep hill to Mellieħa Bay (also known as Għadira Bay), the longest and most popular sandy beach in the Maltese Islands, with white sands, clear water, watersports, sunbeds and ice creams.

◉ Sights & Activities

Church of Our Lady of Victory
CHURCH

(⊗6.30am-noon & 5-7.30pm) The Church of Our Lady of Victory sits prominently on a rocky spur overlooking Mellieħa Bay. It's attached to the Sanctuary of Our Lady of Mellieħa, which has been a place of pilgrimage since medieval times – it is believed to have been blessed by St Paul himself. Its walls are

Mellieħa

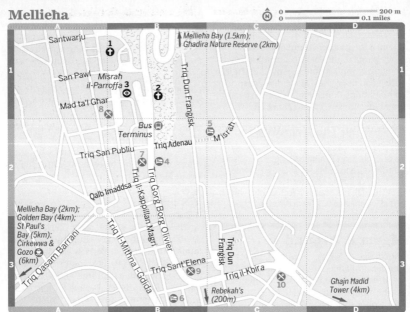

Mellieħa

covered with votive offerings – baby clothes and plaster casts. The fresco of the Madonna above the altar is said to have been painted by St Luke.

Grotto of the Madonna   CHURCH

(◷8am-6pm Sep-May, to 7pm Jun-Aug) Across the main street from the shrine, a gate in the wall and a flight of steps lead down to the Grotto of the Madonna, a shrine dedicated to the Virgin. It is set deep in a cave lit by flickering candles, beside a spring with waters that are reputed to heal sick children. Baby clothes hung on the walls are

votive offerings given in thanks for successful cures.

Mellieħa Air-Raid Shelters   HISTORIC SITE

(☑ 7952 1970; Triq il-Madonna tal-Għar; adult/child €2.40/0.70; ◷9am-3.30pm Mon-Sat) The Mellieħa air-raid shelters were dug by hand to shelter the town's population from WWII bombs. It's one of the largest underground shelters in Malta, with a depth of 12m and a length of around 500m, and gives a haunting sense of what it was like to shelter down here. Spooky mannequins and some furnishings bring home the cramped, damp environment, where each person was allotted 0.6 sq metres of space.

Mellieħa Bay   BEACH

The warm, shallow waters and soft white sand of Mellieħa Bay are easily accessible (via bus or you can park on the road that backs the beach), safe for kids and great for swimming. Add the water-skiers, rental canoes, banana rides, parasailing boats, and the fact that the reliable northeasterly breeze blowing into the bay in summer makes it ideal for windsurfing, and you'll begin to realise that Mellieħa Bay is not the place to get away from it all.

Still, there are good summertime facilities, including sunbeds, umbrellas and windsurfing and kite-surfing gear for hire, and numerous kiosks serving drinks and snacks.

Għadira Nature Reserve   NATURE RESERVE
([☎] 2134 7645, 2134 7644; www.birdlifemalta.org; Triq Il-Marfa; donations welcome; ⊙ 10am-4pm Sat & Sun Nov-May) **[FREE]** Close to Mellieħa Bay, Malta's busiest beach, is the Għadira Nature Reserve, managed by BirdLife Malta volunteers. This area of shallow, reedy ponds surrounded by scrub is an important resting area for migrating birds (over 200 species have been recorded here). The name, pronounced aa-*dee*-ra, means 'marsh'. To reach it, walk past the Mellieħa Holiday Centre on your left, and past the roundabout; the entrance is close to the bus stop marked 'Għadira' (routes 37, 41, 42, 221, 222 and X1).

Tunny Net Complex   WATERSPORTS
At the southern edge of Mellieħa Bay is the Tunny Net Complex, with restaurants and a few shops, as well as boat trips, a lido and a watersports operator open from April to October (parasailing, ringo rides on rubber tubes, jet skis, canoes and paddle boats etc). There's also a diving operator, **Sea Shell Dive Centre** ([☎] 2152 2595; www.seashell-divecove.com; Tunny Net Complex, Mellieħa Bay).

✖ Eating & Drinking

Għaqda Band Club   PUB FOOD €
(Misraħ il-Parroffa; mains €4-13; ⊙ 6am-10pm) A great choice for a cheap meal is this local band club, a high-ceilinged hall with snooker tables at the back. There are some outdoor chairs and tables overlooking the large yet quiet square, which is away from the main tourist drag. A *ftira* (tuna or ham and cheese sandwich in traditional bread) costs €1.50.

Giuseppe's Restaurant & Wine Bar   MEDITERRANEAN €€
([☎] 2157 4882; cnr Triq Ġorġ Borg Olivier & Triq Sant'Elena; mains €13.50-23; ⊙ 7.30-10.30pm Mon-Sat) Giuseppe's, run by Malta's favourite TV chef, Michael Diacono, is full of charm. Its walls are hung with paintings, and it has a relaxed atmosphere and a stand-out menu of creative treats – such as stuffed cuttlefish – that changes regularly according to seasonal produce. The fresh fish is reliably good, and regulars recommend the king prawns. Bookings are advised.

Il-Mitħna   MALTESE €€
([☎] 2152 0404; 45 Triq il-Kbira; mains €18-25; ⊙ 6-11pm Mon-Sat) This is a lovely place to dine – the restaurant is housed in a 400-year-old windmill, the only survivor of three that once sat atop Mellieħa Ridge. There are

NORTHWEST MALTA MELLIEĦA

ⓘ CATCHING THE FERRY FROM ĊIRKEWWA

Ċirkewwa is the port for car and passenger ferries to Gozo. Boats also leave from here to Comino.

By car, you can make the trip to/from Valletta in about 45 minutes. A taxi from Malta International Airport to Ċirkewwa costs €32.

Buses running from here to various destinations include:

➡ **41 & 42** Valletta (1¼ hours, every 20 minutes)

➡ **X1** Airport (one hour 10 minutes, hourly)

➡ **221** Buġibba (40 minutes, half-hourly)

➡ **221** Mellieħa (12 to 20 minutes, half-hourly)

➡ **222** Sliema & St Julian's (one hour, hourly)

Gozo Channel ([☎] 2155 6114; www.gozochannel.com; foot passenger day/night €4.65/4.05, child €1.15, car & driver day/night €15.70/12.80) Operates the passenger and car ferry that shuttles between Malta's Ċirkewwa and Gozo's Mġarr. You pay on the return journey.

United Comino Ferries ([☎] 9940 6529; www.unitedcominoferries.com; adult/child return €9/4.50; ⊙ from Ċirkewwa & Marfa 8.30am-3pm, to 4pm in summer) Serves Comino island from Ċirkewwa and the Marfa jetty. Services take 35 minutes, and leave half-hourly in summer (hourly the rest of the year).

Ebsons Comino Ferries ([☎] 2155 4991; www.cominoferryservice.com; adult/child €10/5; ⊙ 8.30am-3.40pm) Operates ferries from Ċirkewwa and Marfa, as well as between Mġarr and Comino.

NORTHWEST MALTA AROUND MELLIEĦA

DIVING OFF THE MARFA PENINSULA

Some of Malta's most spectacular dive sites lie off the Marfa Peninsula coast, including Marfa Point, Tugboat Rozi and Ċirkewwa Arch. Local dive schools include:

➡ **Sea Shell Dive Centre** (p81)

➡ **Dive Deep Blue** (p87)

➡ **Subway Dive Centre** (p87)

➡ **Buddies Dive Cove** (p87)

outdoor tables in a pretty courtyard, and a menu of local dishes with a creative twist, such as sea bass topped with an almond, mint and parmeggiano crust.

The set menu (€19.50) served between 6pm and 7.30pm is a bargain.

Rebekah's   MEDITERRANEAN €€€
(12 Triq It-Tgham; mains €17-25; ⏱7-10.30pm Mon-Sat Nov-May, daily Jun-Oct) 🌿 Rebekah's is tucked away in Mellieħa's backstreets, but it's worth seeking out (head south to the end of Triq Dun Franġisk, then take a right). Located in a 300-year-old house with flagstone walls and a nice little courtyard, it serves up delicious, spectacular food. The menu ranges from melt-in-the-mouth scallops to slow-roasted rabbit.

Arches   MEDITERRANEAN €€€
(✆2152 3460; 113 Triq Ġorġ Borg Olivier; mains €25-27.50; ⏱7-11pm Mon-Sat) This acclaimed restaurant is large, elegant and stately, and decorated in white set against terracotta walls; the menu, prices and service all befit the chic decor and formality. The food is accomplished, delicious and adventurous, featuring dishes such as venison cooked in Valrhona chocolate. Book ahead.

❶ Getting There & Away

Buses 37, 41 and 42 from Valletta pass through Mellieħa (one hour). Buses 41 and 42 go on to Ċirkewwa (20 minutes) for the Gozo ferry. Bus 221 connects with Ċirkewwa too, as well as with Buġibba. Buses 101 and 102 go to Golden Bay and Għajn Tuffieħa and also serve Ċirkewwa.

Around Mellieħa

The crest of Mellieħa Ridge offers some good walking to the southeast and south-west of the town. Take a left before you reach Selmun Palace and you'll reach lovely, secluded Selmun (Imġiebaħ) Bay, around 2km away. A right turn just before you get to the palace leads in just over 1km to the derelict **Fort Campbell**, an abandoned coastal defence built by the British between WWI and WWII. The headland commands a fine view over St Paul's Islands, and you can hike down to the coastal salt pans of Blata il-Bajda and around to Mistra Bay, or westwards along the clifftop to the ruined **Għajn Ħadid tower** above the little beach at Mġieba Bay.

A left turn at the foot of the hill leading down to Mellieħa Bay puts you on the road to Anchor Bay, about 1.5km away on the west coast. Beyond Anchor Bay lies the **Marfa Peninsula**.

◉ Sights & Activities

Red (St Agatha's) Tower   FORTRESS
(✆2122 0358; dinlarthelwa.org; adult/child €2/free; ⏱10am-1pm & 3-6pm) The chess-piece-like Red Tower was built in 1649 for Grand Master Lascaris, as part of the chain of signal towers that linked Valletta and Gozo; the view from its flat roof is stunning. This simple fortress is one of the more elaborate towers – it once housed a garrison of up to 49 men, and the walls are 4.5m thick. The plaque above the entrance indicates that this is not a place of sanctuary, despite containing a chapel. It's staffed by volunteers so is occasionally closed.

Ras il-Qammieħ   AREA
The western headland, 129m at its highest point, commands fantastic views and feels like the end of the world. It's home to an old radar station.

Sweethaven   AMUSEMENT PARK
(Anchor Bay; ✆2152 4782; www.popeyemalta.com; adult/child €14.50/11.50, discounts in low season; ⏱9.30am-5.30pm Mar-Jul, Sep & Oct, to 7pm Aug, to 4.30pm Nov-Feb) Steep-sided, pretty little Anchor Bay was named after the many Roman anchors that were found on the seabed by divers, some of which can be seen in the Maritime Museum (p62) at Vittoriosa. In 1979 Anchor Bay was transformed into the ramshackle fishing village of Sweethaven, the set for the 1980 Hollywood musical *Popeye*, starring Robin Williams. The vintage set still stands and houses an old-fashioned theme park; it's great fun for kids.

Admission includes animation shows, splash pools and a 15-minute boat ride.

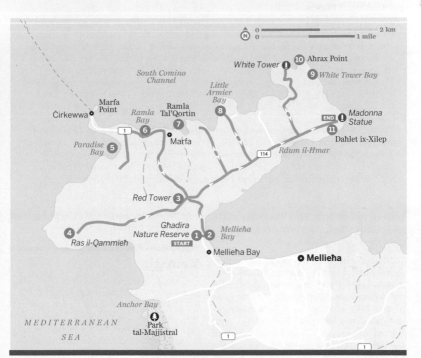

Driving Tour
Malta's Wildest Corner: The Marfa Peninsula

START GĦADIRA NATURE RESERVE
END DAĦLET IX-XILEP
LENGTH 22KM; 1½–TWO HOURS

Take an atmospheric spin around the Marfa Peninsula, the island's final flourish before dipping beneath the waters of the Comino Channel. This trip encompasses a nature reserve, an impressive tower, windswept coastal walks and some favourite local beaches.

Driving onto the peninsula, you'll pass the ① **Għadira Nature Reserve** on your left, with ② **Mellieħa Bay** on your right. When you reach the next junction, turn left, and aim uphill to the ③ **Red Tower** and its dizzying views. From here the road gets bumpier. Drive until you reach the wild headland of ④ **Ras il-Qammieħ**, with more incredible views north to Gozo and south along Malta's western sea cliffs.

Next, return to the main road, following it down towards Ċirkewwa, the Gozo ferry terminal. Take the left turn before you reach the Paradise Bay Resort Hotel. This lane

leads to ⑤ **Paradise Bay**, a picturesque but narrow patch of sand backed by cliffs.

To access the rest of the peninsula, you'll need to drive back to the main road that runs along its spine. From here you can visit the area's little bays. First stop is ⑥ **Ramla Bay**, its small, sandy beach monopolised by the resort of the same name; just east is ⑦ **Ramla Tal'Qortin**, which has no sand and is surrounded by an unsightly sprawl of Maltese holiday huts.

Drive back to the main road, and you could take the second left down to ⑧ **Little Armier Bay**, to hang out, eat and drink at the lovely Baia Beach Club. The fourth road leads to ⑨ **White Tower Bay**, which has another seaweed-stained patch of sand and a rash of holiday huts combining to form a small shanty town. A track continues past the tower to the low cliffs of ⑩ **Aħrax Point**, from which a pleasant coastal walk leads 1km south to a statue of the Madonna on ⑪ **Daħlet ix-Xilep**. You can also reach the Madonna statue and a small chapel by following the main road east across the Marfa Peninsula.

SHARK'S TEETH

The cliffs around the Marfa Peninsula and Ċirkewwa are dotted with fossils. Keep an eye out and you may even spot sharks' teeth, for which Malta is particularly famous. 'Stony tongues' *(glossopetrae)* were collected by visitors to Malta from the earliest times. These were gleamingly polished, triangular objects, and were once thought to be related to the shipwrecking of St Paul in AD 60. According to legend, he was bitten by a snake, and he cursed it, banishing it from the island. The only remnant of the reptile was its petrified tooth.

In the 16th century, the German Conrad Gesner pointed out the similarity of *glosso-petrae* to the tooth of the dogfish. In 1666 a Danish doctor, Nikolaus Stensius, dissected a shark that had washed up locally and was able to prove the real origin of the stony tongues. It's now forbidden to collect fossils, but if you don't spot any on the cliffs, you can see the impressive teeth at either Malta or Gozo's Natural History Museums.

You can pay extra for the chance to make a movie (€6), which is particularly good fun.

Selmun Palace   PALACE
To the east of Mellieħa Ridge, the ornate fortress-like Selmun Palace, which now houses a hotel and restaurant, dominates the skyline above St Paul's Bay. It was built in the 18th century for a charitable or-der called the Monte di Redenzione degli Schiavi (Mountain of the Redemption of the Slaves), whose business was to ransom Christians who had been taken into slavery on the Barbary Coast.

Selmun (Imgiebah) Bay   BEACH
Secluded Selmun Bay is an adventure to find, and a great place to escape the crowds; bring refreshments and sunshades. Take the road to Selmun Palace from Mellieħa, but turn left at Selmun chapel, before the palace. Follow the track for 1.75km, whereupon the road will bend to the right and you'll reach a crossroads. Take a left towards the coast and drive 200m, where you'll find a parking spot; you can walk to the beach from there.

Baia Beach Club   BEACH
(www.baiabeachclub.com; Little Armier) With a beautiful setting on Little Armier beach, this is a lido where you could go and hang out for a few hours or a day, with sunbeds to hire and beachside service, as well as a lovely restaurant with views upstairs offer-ing Sicilian cooking and specialising in fresh fish and pasta.

① Getting There & Away
Bus 42 runs through this area to/from Valletta. Other services are bus 221 to/from St Paul's Bay; 222 to/from Sliema/St Julian's; and X1 to/

from the airport. There's also a shuttle bus from the Tunny Net Complex (p81) in Mellieħa.

Xemxija

The small, south-facing village of Xemxija (shem-*shee*-ya), on the north side of St Paul's Bay, takes its name from *xemx*, meaning 'sun' in Malti; it overlooks a lovely loop of bay, but is decked with low-rise custard-coloured apartment blocks that don't do a lot for the view. There are a couple of private lidos along the waterfront, but Pwales Beach at the head of St Paul's Bay is just a narrow strip of gravelly sand.

◉ Sights & Activities

Is-Simar Nature Reserve   NATURE RESERVE
(☑2134 7646; www.birdlifemalta.org; donations welcome; ◷10am-4pm Sun Nov-May) FREE
Is-Simar was opened in 1995 on a marshy patch of neglected land and is managed by BirdLife Malta (p30) volunteers on be-half of the government. Over 180 bird spe-cies have been recorded at the site. As with the Għadira Nature Reserve (p81), it's wonderful to see a commitment to Malta's natural assets with an area where local and migratory bird life is protected from hunt-ers. The entrance is on the side street Triq Il-Pwales.

Xemxija Heritage Trail   WALKING
Starting at Triq Raddet ir-Roti there is a lovely waymarked Heritage Trail that leads up the hill behind Xemxija. This former Roman road leads to Bajda ridge, passing ancient cave dwellings, Punic-Roman-era apiaries, and pilgrims' graffiti on what was a former pilgrimage trail, which takes from an hour to several hours to walk. A booklet

describing the trail is available from tourist offices.

✖ Eating

Porto del Sol   MEDITERRANEAN €
(☑ 2157 3970; www.portodelsolmalta.com; It Telegha tax-Xemxija; mains €9.50-11.50; ☺ noon-3pm & 7-10.30pm Mon-Sat) Porto del Sol is a family-run restaurant with views of the bay from its large picture windows, and a sun-shaded outdoor terrace. It's popular with locals for its fresh seafood and local dishes.

Buġibba, Qawra & St Paul's Bay

St Paul's Bay is named after the saint who was shipwrecked here in AD 60. Despite being a built-up area, there's a scenic view across the bobbing boats of the harbour. Although there are hotel developments, the promenade along the Qawra part of the coast is stunningly pretty, and has the fantastic Malta National Aquarium at its tip, as well as panoramic views and some scenic rocks from which to swim. The Buġibba area is the most built up, entirely devoted to tourism, and with the most facilities.

This is the heartland of the island's cheap-and-cheerful package-holiday trade, and it's mobbed and lively in summer. It's full of hotels, bars and restaurants – the perfect base for a spell of inexpensive, sun-filled hedonism.

◉ Sights & Activities

There's plenty to do along this bit of the coast, with the €15.6 million Malta National Aquarium, close to Qawra Tower, providing state-of-the-art wonder and a great new focus for family fun. There are various diving and boating operators based in Buġibba, plus the new free Buġibba water park, and a number of private lidos lining the waterfront, many offering sun lounges, watersports, swimming pools and cafe-bars.

★ Malta National Aquarium   AQUARIUM
(☑ 2258 8100; www.aquarium.com.mt; Triq it-Trunċiera; adult/child €12.90/6; ☺ 10am-6pm) Opened in 2013, this glass and metal starfish-shaped building perches in a sublime position on the Qawra headland, with endless-blue views. It's great fun, with huge tanks showing environments that mimic the waters around the islands (for example, there's a replica of the bronze submerged

Christ of the Abyss statue), as well as those further afield. There's a 12m underwater tunnel that allows visitors to walk through a huge tank, as well as another smaller tunnel to crawl through. The complex includes a fabulous playground (free of charge) and stunning views from its Le Nave restaurant and outdoor cafe.

Buġibba Water Park   AMUSEMENT PARK
(☺ 9am-5pm Jun-Sep) **FREE** This is a fun, small, supervised (and free!) water park that kids will love, and includes various loopy colourful fountains that are perfect for kids running around on a hot day. There are different sections for different ages (divided by height), and chairs so adults can relax (hopefully) around the edge.

Malta Classic Car Collection   MUSEUM
(☑ 2157 8885; www.classiccarsmalta.com; Triq it-Turisti; adult/child €8.50/4.50; ☺ 9am-6pm Mon-Fri, 9am-1pm Sat) Housed in a purpose-built 3000-sq-metre premises, the Malta Classic Car Collection is a tribute to Carol Galea's love of cars. The privately owned collection of mint-condition vehicles (cars and motorbikes) includes plenty of 1950s and '60s British- and Italian-made classics, plus vintage jukeboxes and memorabilia from these eras to get you in the mood.

Wignacourt Tower   FORTRESS
(☑ 2122 0358; dinlarthelwa.org; Triq it-Torri; adult/child €2/free; ☺ 10am-1pm Mon-Wed, Fri, Sat & 1st Sun of month, 4-6pm Thu) Built in 1609, the Wignacourt Tower was the first of the towers built by Grand Master Wignacourt. It guards the point to the west of the church, and houses a tiny museum with exhibits on local fortress history, including a small selection of guns and armour. There are stupendous views from here.

Church of St Paul's Bonfire   CHURCH
The old fishing village of St Paul's Bay, now merged with Buġibba, has retained something of its traditional Maltese character and has a few historical sights. The 17th-century Church of St Paul's Bonfire stands on the waterfront to the south of Plajja Tal'Bognor, supposedly on the spot where the saint first scrambled ashore. A bonfire is lit outside the church during the Festival of St Paul's Shipwreck (10 February).

Għajn Rasul   FOUNTAIN
To the west of Buġibba, near the fishing-boat harbour at the head of the bay, is Għajn

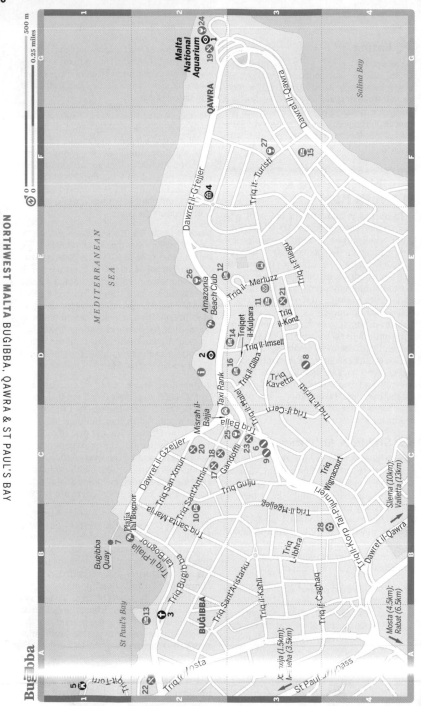

Buġibba

Malta National Aquarium

QAWRA

Salina Bay

MEDITERRANEAN SEA

Amazonia Beach Club

St Paul's Bay

Bugibba Quay

Plajja Tal-Bognor

BUĠIBBA

Taxi Rank

Triq il-Ħalel

Triq il-Ballja

Gandolfli

Misraħ il-Ballja

Dawret il-Gżejjer

Triq San Xmun

Triq Sant'Anton

Triq Gulju

Trriq Santa Marija

Triq il-Plajja

Tal-Bognor

Triq Buġibba

Triq Sant'Aristarku

Triq il-Kaħli

Triq il-Ħġejjeġ

Triq L-Libħra

Triq Wignacourt

Triq Kavetta

Triq il-Cern

Triq il-Konz

Triq il-Kulpara

Triq il-Imsell

Triq il-Ġilba

Trejqet il-Imsell

Triq il-Merluzz

Triq il-Fliegu

Dawret il-Gżejjer

Triq it-Turisti

Dawret il-Qawra

Triq it-Turisti

Triq Ħorb Tal-Pulinjieri

Triq il-Caghaq

Triq f'Mosta

Triq Tat-Torri

St Paul's Bypass

Mosta (4.5km); Rabat (6.5km)

Sliema (10km); Valletta (13km)

Dawret il-Qawra

Xemxija (1.5km); Mellieħa (3.5km)

500 m
0.25 miles

Buġibba

◉ **Top Sights**
1 Malta National Aquarium G2

◉ **Sights**
2 Buġibba Water Park D2
3 Church of St Paul's Bonfire A2
4 Malta Classic Car Collection F2
5 Wignacourt Tower A1

◉ **Activities, Courses & Tours**
6 Buddies Dive Cove C3
7 Captain Morgan Cruises B1
8 Dive Deep Blue D3
9 Subway Dive Centre C3
Yellow Fun Watersports.............(see 26)

◉ **Sleeping**
10 Buccaneers Guesthouse B2
11 db San Antonio Hotel & Spa............... E3
12 Dolmen Resort Hotel...........................E2
13 Gillieru Harbour Hotel A2
14 Sea View Hotel D3
15 Seashells Resort at Suncrest............. F3
16 Sunseeker Holiday Complex D3

◉ **Eating**
17 Acqua Marina C2
18 Capuvino C2
19 Le Nave.. G2
20 Malét C2
21 Ta'Pawla E3
22 Tarragon A2
23 Venus..C3

◉ **Drinking & Nightlife**
24 Cafe del Mar G2
25 Fat Harry's C3
26 Mynt Club..E2
27 Simon's Pub.. F3

◉ **Entertainment**
28 Empire Cinema Complex B4

Rasul (Apostle's Fountain), where St Paul is said to have baptised the first Maltese convert to Christianity.

Boat Trips & Watersports

Plenty of smaller operators offer tours from the jetty at Plajja Tal'Bognor. As well as shorter trips around St Paul's Bay, some operators offer trips to Comino for around €20.

Hornblower Cruises · BOAT TOUR
(www.hornblowerboat.com; ⊙ Apr-Oct) Family-run Hornblower offers day trips either to the Blue Lagoon and Comino via some of their caves (adult/child €20/10), which includes a 4¼-hour stop on Comino, or another that

stops for three hours on Gozo and an hour on Comino (€25/15).

Captain Morgan Cruises · BOAT TOUR
(☎ 2346 3333; www.captainmorgan.com.mt) Most Captain Morgan Cruises operate out of Sliema, but there are Buġibba departures for an hour-long 'underwater safari' in a glass-bottomed boat that explores the marine life around St Paul's Islands. Underwater safaris depart from Plajja Tal'Bognor three times a day Monday to Saturday from June to September, and Monday to Friday during April, May and October (€17/11 per adult/child).

Yellow Fun Watersports · WATERSPORTS
(☎ 2355 2570; www.yellowfunwatersports.com; Dawret il-Gżejjer) Offers powerboat trips to the Blue Lagoon on Comino. Trips leave daily at 10.30am, returning at 3.30pm (€20 per person). Yellow Fun can also arrange boat charters, sea-taxi services, fishing trips and showers of watersports fun, such as water-skiing, jet-skiing, canoeing, windsurfing and paragliding.

Diving

There are several dive operators in Buġibba that can help you explore the excellent nearby dive sites or those around the Maltese Islands.

Buddies Dive Cove · DIVING
(☎ 2157 6266; www.buddiesmalta.com; 24/2 Triq il-Korp Tal-Pijunieri) Popular and well-regarded family-run dive centre.

Dive Deep Blue · DIVING
(☎ 2158 3946; www.divedeepblue.com; 100 Triq Ananija) Well-regarded dive centre for all levels, run by an experienced team.

Subway Dive Centre · DIVING
(☎ 2157 0354; www.subwayscuba.com; Triq il-Korp Tal-Pijunieri) Respected dive centre and PADI five-star instructor development centre.

✖️ Eating

Buġibba is awash with eating places, with everything from cheap-and-cheery fish and chips to upmarket creative cuisine for dressed-up, blow-out nights on the town.

Capuvino · MEDITERRANEAN €
(www.capuvino.com; Triq Sant'Antnin; snacks €3-8; ⊙ 10am-11pm) Capuvino is near Bugibba's centre but feels slightly removed; the restaurant is shaded by tall palms and features chequered tablecloths and a few outside

SHARKLAB

If you visit the **Malta National Aquarium** (p85), you'll see some fascinating, alien-looking egg cases suspended in one of the tanks. These are shark eggs, rescued from the Pixxkerija (fish market), and some have been successfully hatched, helping to discover more about the development of oviparous (egg-laying) sharks.

Sharks tend to get bad press, but there is an organisation in Malta on their side. The NGO responsible is **Sharklab** (www.sharklab-malta.org), which is devoted to protecting elasmobranch species, namely sharks, rays and skates. Its activities include elasmobranch-spotting snorkelling trips, visits to the fish market to rescue eggs, and shark releases. If you want to protect one of the world's most misunderstood creatures, you can take part, or otherwise help by registering sightings on its website.

tables on a pedestrianised section of street. Food includes *ftira* sandwiches and pasta, and a cocktail costs €5.50.

★ Acqua Marina
ITALIAN €€

(✆2703 4933; 160 Triq Sant'Antnin; mains €9-15; ☺noon-3pm & 7pm-midnight) A tiny Italian restaurant that stands out for its attention to detail. It's a cut above, from the sea-hued decor and careful table decorations to the warm welcome, and the simple yet delicious Italian cooking and daily fresh fish specials.

Le Nave
BISTRO €€

(Malta National Aquarium; mains €8.75-25; ☺12.30-3pm & 7-10.30pm) With floor-to-ceiling windows, Le Nave has a stylish pared-down decor that lets the sea views sing, though it has the noisy clatter of a museum cafe. Considering it's above the Malta National Aquarium, you may feel uncomfortable about the amount of fish on the menu, but if not, dig in, you're in for a feast. There are burgers and pizzas too.

Venus
MEDITERRANEAN €€

(✆2157 1604; cnr Triq Bajja & Gandoffli; mains €17.50-25; ☺6.30-11pm) Venus is where to go in Buġibba for a touch of romance and fine dining. There's a bright and sophisticated interior and the modern fusion menu adds an imaginative twist to traditional ingredients. The three-course set menu is a snip at €25.

Ta'Pawla
MALTESE €€

(✆2157 6039; Triq it-Turisti; mains €7.50-22; ☺6.30-10.30pm) You can get a taste of good, authentic Maltese cuisine in the cute gingham-clad interior of this busy little place, which is fronted by a small glass-covered terrace. The menu includes local classics like rabbit in garlic and octopus stew, but there's also standard pizza, pasta and steak.

Maħi I

(✆2758 1023; Triq San Xmun; mains €10-22; ☺6-10.30pm) This popular traditional Maltese

restaurant, just off the promenade, has an intimate feel, white linen tablecloths, and rabbit on the menu as well as fillet of beef.

★ Tarragon
MEDITERRANEAN €€€

(✆2157 3759; Triq il-Knisja; mains €15-30; ☺6.30-11.30pm Mon-Sat, noon-6pm Sun) Tucked above the harbour at St Paul's Bay, Tarragon is a haven of sophistication with sea views to soothe the soul, a Mediterranean/fusion menu to satisfy the taste buds, and a white-tablecloth, wooden-floorboard style that's upmarket yet informal. The speciality is fresh fish (landed earlier that day at the quay below the restaurant) baked in salt (or cooked whichever way you want).

🍷 Drinking & Nightlife

Take your pick from the dozens of bars along Triq it-Turisti and the streets around Misrah il-Bajja (particularly Triq Sant'Antnin) – they're mainly traditional British-style pubs or buzzing bars.

★ Cafe del Mar
BAR

(Triq Trunciera; ordinary sunbed €10-15, VIP sunbed €20-30, gazebo €75-100; ☺10am-late) Part of the Cafe del Mar empire, this glamorous open-air haunt alongside Malta's new aquarium feels very Ibiza-esque, with its fantastic sea views, infinity pools and white sunshades. It's more than just a bar – you can spend the day here – and sunbed hire is worth it to revel in some luxury. Look out for regular club nights.

Simon's Pub
BAR

(✆2157 7566; simonselvisbar.com; Triq it-Turisti; ☺6pm-2am) **FREE** Simon is clearly a huge fan of the King, and his pub is a two-room shrine to Elvis. There's live entertainment every night – stop in on Monday or Friday for the highlight, the Elvis tribute. Cheesy fun, thankyouverymuch.

Fat Harry's
PUB
(☑ 2158 1298; Triq Bajja; ⊙ 11am-11.30pm) Fat Harry's is an English-style pub doing all-day traditional pub grub such as fish and chips, and offering plenty of draught beer, outdoor tables, live sports on the big screen and live entertainment.

Mynt Club
CLUB
(☑ 2355 2410; Dawret il-Gżejjer; ⊙ 9pm-4am Jun-Sep, Fri-Sun only Oct-May) This pumping summer club, at the lido opposite the Dolmen Resort Hotel, is popular with tourists and locals happy to carry on all night to cool tunes in a lush waterfront setting.

☆ Entertainment

Empire Cinema Complex
CINEMA
(☑ 2158 1787; www.empirecinema.com.mt; Triq il-Korp Tal-Pijunieri) Seven-screen multiplex showing new movies. Tickets cost €6/3.50 per adult/child (€5 for adults before 5pm on weekdays).

ℹ Information

Buġibba Tourist Information (☑ 2141 9176; ⊙ 9am-5.30pm Mon-Sat, 9am-1pm Sun) Helpful new information office.

HSBC Bank (Misraħ il-Bajja) Has an ATM.

Police Station (☑ 2157 1174, 2157 6737; Triq it-Turisti)

ℹ Getting There & Away

There is a taxi rank on Misraħ il-Bajja in Buġibba.

Buġibba bus station is on Triq it-Turisti near the Dolmen Resort Hotel. Bus 12 runs to/from Valletta (every 10 minutes, one hour), via Sliema (25 minutes) and St Julian's (40 minutes). Bus 31 also runs between Buġibba and Valletta (every 20 minutes), via Naxxar (30 minutes) and Mosta (40 minutes). Bus 223 goes from Buġibba to Għajn Tuffieħa Bay (25 minutes, hourly)

via St Paul's Bay (10 minutes). Bus 223 heads to Ċirkewwa for ferries to Gozo (40 minutes, half-hourly), via Mellieħa (30 minutes) and St Paul's Bay (15 minutes).

Baħar iċ-Ċagħaq

Baħar iċ-Ċagħaq (*ba*-har eetch *cha*-ag; also known as White Rocks) lies halfway between Sliema and Buġibba. It has a scruffy rock beach and a hugely popular water park.

◉ Sights

Splash & Fun Park
AMUSEMENT PARK
(☑ 2137 4283; www.splashandfun.com.mt; adult/child €22/12, after 3pm Jul–mid-Sep & after 1pm mid-May–Jun & mid-Sep–early Oct €15/8, advance family ticket €52; ⊙ 9.30am-6pm mid-May–Jun & late Sep–early Oct, 9am-9pm Jul–early Sep) This huge, if tired-looking, wave park is a fun place for a day out. Kids will love it, though be warned it's fresher and cleaner earlier in the season. That said, the wave pool constantly pumps 1.5m artificial waves; there are plenty of tunnels and spray jets; fibreglass waterslides; the 'Black Hole'; and a 240m-long 'lazy river' you can coast down on a rubber tube. Note that food can't be brought into the park.

Qalet Marku Tower
FORTRESS
Qalet Marku Tower, on Qrejten Point, west of Baħar iċ-Ċagħaq Bay, was built in a frenzy of fortified development ordered by Grand Master de Redin, which saw 13 such watchtowers constructed in a year along this coastline.

ℹ Getting There & Away

To get to Baħar iċ-Ċagħaq, take bus 12 from Valletta (50 minutes, every 20 minutes), which travels via Sliema (25 minutes) and St Julian's (10 minutes).

THE VICTORIA LINES

The Victoria Lines were built by the British in the late 19th century. They were intended to protect the main part of the island from potential invaders landing on the northern beaches, but never saw any military action. The fortifications were named after Queen Victoria's Diamond Jubilee in 1897. The lines run about 12km along a steep limestone escarpment that stretches from Fomm ir-Riħ in the west to Baħar iċ-Ċagħaq in the east and are excellent places for a walk, affording magnificent views. If you're interested in doing some independent exploration, try to get hold of *The Victoria Lines*, edited by Ray Cachia Zammit. This guide to the site includes a foldout map and is available in the better bookshops in Valletta. For more information as well as walking tours, see www.victorialinesmalta.com. Three forts – Madliena Fort, Mosta Fort and Binġemma Fort – are linked by a series of walls, entrenchments and gun batteries. The best-preserved section, the Dwejra Lines, lies north of Mdina.

Central Malta

Best Places to Eat

➡ Medina (p95)

➡ Crystal Palace (p98)

➡ Diar il-Bniet (p100)

➡ Fontanella Tea Gardens &
Vinum Wine Bar (p94)

➡ Rickshaw (p103)

Best Places to Stay

➡ Xara Palace (p142)

➡ Knights in Malta (p142)

➡ Chapel 5 Suites (p143)

➡ Maple Farm Bed &
Breakfast (p142)

Why Go?

Central Malta combines beautiful historic centres with some of the island's most spectacular scenery. Here, you can explore Mdina, Malta's atmospheric ancient walled capital perched on a hilltop with stupendous views over the hills and out to sea, visit remarkable medieval frescoes in ancient catacombs, marvel at one of Europe's largest church domes, and spend the night worshipping the dance gods at some of Malta's best nightclubs. Natural attractions include stark cliffs (the perfect place to watch a sunset), and a scenic bay ideal for swimming (if only you can find it). There are sleeping and eating options ranging from luxurious five-star hotels to rustic village restaurants where locals come for their weekend feasts of rabbit.

If you're after traditional Maltese traditional culture and a tranquil holiday that's a little off the well-worn path, this is the perfect base.

When to Go

➡ Spring (April to June) and autumn (September and October) are the best times to visit this region.

➡ If you're coming in early spring, you can see the pageantry of Holy Week and catch the Mdina Medieval Festival in mid-April.

Mdina & Rabat

Mdina is the hilltop walled medieval city, packed with the historic mansions of Maltese nobility. Outside the city walls, Rabat is a separate, yet adjoining town, with some superb sights of its own.

Just inside Mdina's main gate is a helpful **Tourist Information Centre** (☑ 2145 4480; Torre dello Stendardo; ⊙ 9am-5.30pm Mon-Sat, 9am-1pm Sun Apr-Sep, 10am-4pm Oct-Mar).

You'll find banks and ATMs in Rabat opposite the bus stop, and an ATM on Pjazza tas-Sur. There are public toilets outside the main gate. Point de Vue (p95) has wi-fi.

A ride in a *karrozzin* (traditional horse–drawn carriage), departing from Mdina's main gate, costs €35 for a circuit around Mdina and Rabat; you'll soak up more atmosphere on foot.

❶ Getting There & Away

The local bus terminus is in Rabat on Is-Saqqajja, 200m south of Mdina's main gate.

From Valletta, take bus 50, 51, 52 or 53 (30 minutes, every 10 minutes). Bus 52 goes on to Dingli. Buses 202 and 203 travel to/from Sliema (50 minutes, half-hourly) and St Julian's (one hour), going on to Dingli. The X3 express bus travels between here and Buġibba (25 minutes, half-hourly) as well as the airport (55 minutes).

Mdina

POP 290

The mysterious golden-stone Arabic walled city of Mdina crowns the hilltop, and is a world apart from modern Malta. Its hidden lanes offer exquisite architectural detail and respite from the day-tripping crowds, who largely stick to the main street.

The citadel of Mdina was fortified from as long ago as 1000 BC when the Phoenicians built a protective wall and called their settlement Malet, meaning 'place of shelter'. The Romans built a large town here and called it Melita. It was given its present name when the Arabs arrived in the 9th century – *medina* is Arabic for 'walled city'. They built strong walls and dug a deep moat between Mdina and its surrounding suburbs (*rabat* in Arabic). The moat has recently been landscaped to become a garden with surreally neat lawns; it's a pleasant place for a stroll and a venue for regular festivals.

In medieval times Mdina was called Città Notabile – the Noble City. It was the favoured residence of the Maltese aristocracy and the

MDINA CATHEDRAL CONTEMPORARY ART BIENNALE

The first **Mdina Cathedral Contemporary Art Biennale** (mdinabiennale.org) is scheduled to run from 13 November 2015 to 7 January 2016, and between 2017 and 2018, the latter edition to coincide with Valletta as European Capital of Culture for 2018. It will see many historic locations, such as Palazzo de Piro, St Paul's Cathedral and the cathedral's subterranean vaults, turned into exhibition spaces for artists from all over the world.

seat of the *universitá* (governing council). The Knights of St John, who were largely a sea-based force, made Grand Harbour and Valletta their centre of activity, and Mdina sank into the background as a holiday destination for the nobility. Today, with its massive walls and peaceful, shady streets, it is often referred to as the Silent City, a nickname that becomes appropriate after dark.

◉ Sights & Activities

★ **St Paul's Cathedral**   CHURCH
(Pjazza San Pawl; adult/child €5/free incl Cathedral Museum; ⊙ 9.30am-4.45pm Mon-Sat, 3-4.45pm Sun) The cathedral is said to be built on the site of the villa belonging to Publius, the Roman governor of Malta who welcomed St Paul in AD 60.

The original Norman church was destroyed by an earthquake, and the restrained baroque edifice you see today was built between 1697 and 1702 by Lorenzo Gafa, who was influenced by the Italian master Borromini. Note the fire and serpent motifs atop the twin bell towers, symbolising the saint's first miracle in Malta.

Echoing St John's Co-Cathedral in Valletta, the floor of St Paul's is covered in the polychrome marble tombstones of Maltese nobles and important clergymen, while the vault is painted with scenes from the life of St Paul. The altar painting, *The Conversion of St Paul* by Mattia Preti, survived the earthquake; so too did the beautifully carved oak doors to the sacristy on the north side, and the apse above the altar, featuring the fresco *St Paul's Shipwreck*.

Central Malta Highlights

1 Enjoy the haunting silence of the walled city of **Mdina** (p91) after dark.

2 Absorb the local vibe of Rabat before going underground to admire the frescoes of **St Agatha's Catacombs** (p95).

3 Lunch at farmhouse restaurant **Diar il-Bniet** (p100), followed by a stroll along the top of the **Dingli Cliffs** (p100).

4 Chill out at remote **Fomm ir-Riħ Bay** (p102).

5 Question divine intervention while marvelling at the unexploded bomb in the **Mosta Dome** (p100).

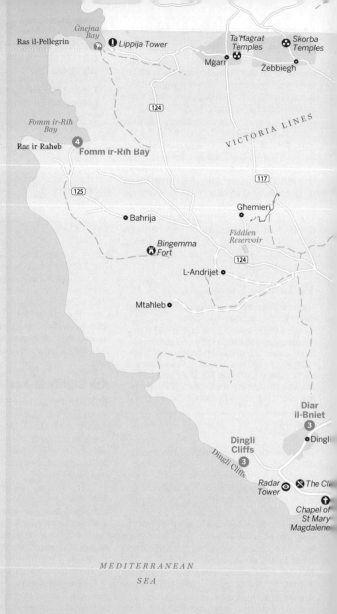

MDINA DITCH GARDEN

Mdina's ditch – the sunken area around the city walls – was an important element of its fortifications. It was first created in the 15th century, but the Knights of St John's military architect Charles François de Mondion widened it and added to the surrounding fortifications. More recently, the Mdina city walls had become overgrown with ivy and vegetation, and the ditch was filled by 273 citrus and seven olive trees, a wild and beautiful jumble, that hid somewhere among it a football pitch and tennis court.

In a regeneration project to create the **Mdina Ditch Garden**, completed in 2015, the trees were removed or moved, and the bastions restored. The citrus grove has been replaced by a severe mix of lawn, stone paving and saplings in pots. The landscaping has proved controversial, with an outcry over the removal of the mature citrus trees, the lack of shade and the stark aesthetic. However, the restored bastions now gleam splendidly and are much more visible, and the gardens are far more accessible – there's even a lift leading down to them from near Mdina's car park. The ditch now forms a space for festivals such as food fairs and concerts. Enquire at the tourist office about forthcoming events.

Cathedral Museum
MUSEUM
(☑ 2145 4697; Pjazza San Pawl; adult/child €5/free incl St Paul's Cathedral; ⊙ 9.30am-4.30pm Mon-Fri, to 3.30pm Sat) The Cathedral Museum's outstanding highlight is a series of woodcut and copperplate prints and lithographs by the German Renaissance artist Albrecht Dürer. However, there are other items of interest, including Egyptian amulets dating from the 5th century BC and a remarkable coin collection, which includes Carthaginian and Romana-Maltese examples. The museum is housed in a baroque 18th-century palace originally used as a seminary.

Palazzo Falson
HISTORIC BUILDING
(☑ 2145 4512; www.palazzofalson.com; Triq Villegaignon; adult/child €10/free; ⊙ 10am-5pm Tue-Sun, last admission 4pm) The magnificent Palazzo Falson is a beautifully preserved medieval mansion. Formerly the home of artist and philanthropist Olof Gollcher (1889–1962), the palace offers a rare glimpse into the sumptuous private world behind Mdina's anonymous aristocratic walls. A self-guided audiotour leads you from the beautiful stone courtyard through Gollcher's kitchen, studio, 4500-volume library, bedroom and chapel – all decorated with his impressive collections of art, documents, silver, weapons and rare rugs from Azerbaijan and Kazakhstan. Under 5s not admitted.

There's a rooftop cafe with wi-fi and views.

National Museum of Natural History
MUSEUM
(☑ 2145 5951; Piazza San Publiju; adult/child €5/2.50; ⊙ 9am-5pm) Housed in the elegant Palazzo de Vilhena is an interesting – if old-

school fusty – array of displays. Of particular note is the geology section, which explains the origins of Malta's landscape and displays the wide range of local fossils. The tooth belonging to the ancient shark *Carcharodon megalodon* is food for thought – measuring 18cm on the edge, it belonged to a 25m monster that prowled the Miocene seas 30 million years ago.

The skeletal anatomy room is also interesting, and includes the delicate filigree bones of a snake.

✗ Eating

★ Fontanella Tea Gardens & Vinum Wine Bar
CAFE €
(☑ 2145 4264; Triq is-Sur; mains €5-9.50; ⊙ 10am-late) Fontanella – a Maltese institution – has a wonderful setting atop the city walls, with sweeping views. It serves delicious homebaked cakes, *pastizzi* (filled pastries), sandwiches, pizzas and light meals, including particularly tasty *ftira* (traditional Maltese bread sandwiches). It also has an intimate wine bar, with flagstone walls and views from the ramparts.

Ciapetti
MEDITERRANEAN €€
(☑ 2145 9987; 5 Wesgħa Ta'Sant'Agata; mains €15.60-21; ⊙ noon-3pm daily, 7-10pm Tue-Sun) Ciapetti attracts a mix of locals and tourists with its Mediterranean menu that ranges from traditional rabbit stew to pan-fried calamari with marjoram and lemon thyme (from the restaurant's own herb garden). You can eat in the art-filled dining room, the small vine-draped courtyards or out on the terrace atop the city walls.

Point de Vue Guesthouse & Restaurants
MEDITERRANEAN €€

(⌨ 2145 4117; www.pointdevuemalta.com; 5 Is-Saqqajja; mains €10-23; ⊙8am-10pm; ≋) Point de Vue, just outside Mdina's city walls, is popular with locals for its tasty pizzas, traditional dishes and impressive selection of steaks and ribs. It overlooks the not-so-scenic Mdina's car park from the front, but at the rear there's a rather better 'point of view' across the local countryside.

Trattoria AD 1530
MEDITERRANEAN €€

(⌨ 2145 0560; Misrah il-Kunsill; mains €8-30; ⊙12.30-3pm & 7-10.30pm) Part of boutique hotel Xara Palace (p142), this stylishly casual trattoria offers outdoor seating on the pretty square. The food is nothing special, but the location is great on a sunny day; there's a kids menu, and the grown-ups can choose from pizza and pasta choices, plus more substantial mains of fish and meat.

The outdoor seating on the square is great for kids as they can get up and run around once they've eaten.

★ Medina
MEDITERRANEAN €€€

(⌨ 2145 4004; 7 Triq is-Salib Imqaddes; mains €8.50-26; ⊙7pm-late Mon-Sat) Medina won best overall restaurant for 2015 in the *Definitive(ly) Good Guide to Restaurants in Malta & Gozo,* and is a pretty-as-a-picture romantic venue – a medieval townhouse with vaulted ceilings and fireplaces, a leafy garden-courtyard for alfresco dining and sophisticated, artfully presented Maltese, Italian and French dishes.

De Mondion
MEDITERRANEAN €€€

(⌨ 2145 0560; www.xarapalace.com.mt; Misrah il-Kunsill; mains €32-40; ⊙7.30-10.30pm Mon-Sat) Romantic enough to provoke proposals, this place is set on the 17th-century rooftop of one of the island's loveliest hotels, Xara Palace (p142). The French-inspired menu is seasonal, but expect esoteric delights like foie gras and truffles.

Rabat

POP 11,500

Rabat, sprawled to the south of Mdina, is a charming town in its own right, with narrow streets and wooden *galerijas* (Maltese balconies). It feels resolutely local, particularly in the evening when the day trippers have ebbed away.

◉ Sights

St Agatha's Crypt & Catacombs
CATACOMBS

(⌨ 2145 4503; Triq Sant'Agata; adult/child €5/2; ⊙9am-5pm Mon-Fri, to 1pm Sat) These catacombs contain a series of remarkable frescoes dating from the 12th to 15th centuries. According to legend, this was the hiding place of St Agatha when she fled Sicily. Back at ground level is a quirky little museum containing everything from fossils and minerals to coins, church vestments and Etruscan, Roman and Egyptian artefacts. Regular tours are available of the crypt and catacombs.

St Paul's Catacombs
CATACOMBS

(⌨ 2145 4562; Triq Sant'Agata; adult/child €5/1.50; ⊙9am-5pm) St Paul's Catacombs (so-named for their proximity to the church) date from the 3rd century AD and were used for burial for around 500 years. Worship took place here in the Middle Ages, but later the complex was used as an agricultural store. It's an atmospheric labyrinth of rock-cut tombs, narrow stairs and passages. Admission includes a self-guided, 45-minute audiotour, and a new visitors centre and children's pavilion are being added.

Casa Bernard
HISTORIC BUILDING

(⌨ 2145 1888; 46 Triq San Pawl; adult/child €8/4; ⊙10am-4pm Mon-Sat) FREE You'll be personally guided through this privately owned 16th-century palace by one of the home's charming owners, who will explain the history of the mansion and the impressive personal collection of art, objets d'art, furniture, silver and china. Tours last 40 to 50 minutes and take place on the hour, with the last one at 4pm.

THE TRAGEDY OF ST AGATHA

St Agatha was a 3rd-century Christian martyr from Sicily – Catania and Palermo both claim to be her birthplace – who fled to Malta to escape the amorous advances of a Sicilian governor. On returning to Sicily she was imprisoned and tortured, her breasts were cut off with shears, and she was burnt at the stake. In Rabat there's a church, **St Agatha's Chapel**, dedicated to her, near the **catacombs** that are said to have been her hiding place in Malta.

Mdina & Rabat

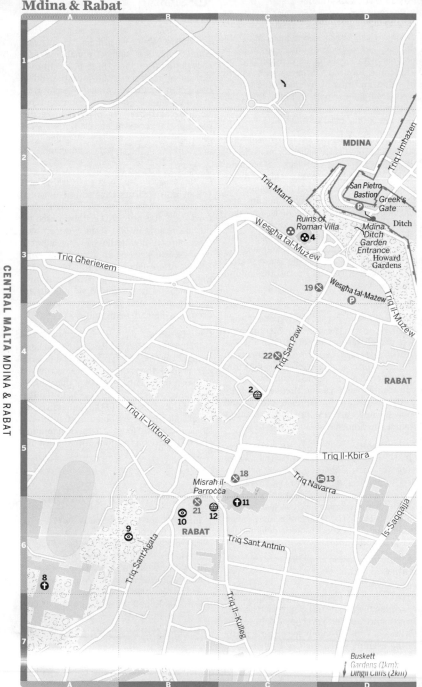

MDINA

Triq l-Imtaħleb

Triq Mtarfa

San Pietro
Bastion

Greek's
Gate

Ditch

Wesgħa tal-Mużew

Ruins of
Roman Villa

Mdina
Ditch
Garden
Entrance
Howard
Gardens

Triq Għeriexem

Wesgħa tal-Mażew

Triq il-Mużew

Triq San Pawl

RABAT

Triq il-Vittoria

Triq Il-Kbira

Triq Navarra

Is-Saqqajja

Misraħ il-
Parroċċa

RABAT

Triq Sant'Agata

Triq Sant Antnin

Triq Il-Kulleġ

Buskett
Gardens (1km);
Dingli Cliffs (2km)

CENTRAL MALTA MDINA & RABAT

Domus Romana   ARCHAEOLOGICAL SITE

(☎ 2145 4125; Wesgħa tal-Mużew; adult/child €6/3; ☺ 9am-5pm) The Roman House was built in the 1920s to incorporate the excavated remains of a large 1st-century-BC townhouse. There's a small but fascinating museum, which includes Roman glass perfume bottles and bone hairpins, as well as a display on the 11th-century Islamic cemetery that overlaid the villa. There are also some beautiful mosaics. At the centre of the original peristyle court there is a depiction of the *Drinking Doves of Sosos*, a fashionable Roman motif.

St Paul's Church & the Grotto of St Paul   CHURCH

(Misraħ il-Parroċċa; adult/child €5/2.50, incl Wignacourt Museum; ☺ 9.30am-5pm Mon-Sat) St Paul's Church was built in 1675. Beside it, stairs lead down into the mystical Grotto of St Paul, a cave where the saint is said to have preached during his Malta stay. The statue of St Paul was gifted by the Knights in 1748, while the silver ship to its left was added in 1960 to commemorate the 1900th anniversary of the saint's shipwreck. Come in the early morning or late afternoon to avoid the tour groups that congest the narrow space.

Wignacourt Museum MUSEUM
(☑2749 4905; Triq il-Kulleg; adult/child €5/2.50, incl Grotto of St Paul, audioguide €2; ⊙9.30am-5pm) This recently refurbished museum has a gloriously hotchpotch collection that encompasses 4th-century Christian catacombs, a WWII air-raid shelter, a baroque chapel, religious icons and vestments, and paintings including Mattia Preti's *The Penitent St Peter*.

✖ Eating

★**Crystal Palace** PASTRIES €
(pastizzi €0.30; ⊙3am-11pm) Spot it by the hoards outside; this hole-in-the-wall *pastizzerija* close to Mdina's city walls is renowned as one of Malta's best, as it freshly bakes the little moreish pastry parcels throughout the night.

Parruċċan Confectionery SWEETS €
(Misraħ il-Parroċċa; sweets from €1; ⊙9.30am-5pm) Here you can pick up samples of Maltese specialities like nougat, delicious nut brittle and fig rolls.

San Andrea MEDITERRANEAN €€
(☑2145 2562; Triq San Pawl; mains €15.50-27.50; ⊙noon-3.30pm Sun, 7-10.30pm Tue-Sat) Palazzo Castelletti, formerly used by the Knights of St John, has been converted into the appropriately grand restaurant San Andrea, with pale limestone walls, a lovely courtyard and complex cooking such as duck breast with teriyaki jus. On the rooftop is **RedWhite** (mains €8-18.50; ⊙6-11pm), a more casual restaurant serving pasta and gourmet burgers.

Cosmana Navarra ITALIAN €€
(☑2145 0638; Triq San Pawl; mains €8-20; ⊙noon-4pm daily & 6.30-10.30pm Wed-Sun) Cosmana Navarra was the Maltese aristocrat who paid for St Paul's Church, and this restaurant is housed in her former home. It's a lovely old building that preserves many original features, and a good family choice, predominantly serving pizza and pasta but with *fenkata* (rabbit stew) too. The pick of

the desserts is the *mqarets* (fried date pastries) with ice cream.

🍷 Drinking & Nightlife

Gianpula CLUB
(☑9947 2133; www.gianpula.com; ⊙Groove Gardens 11pm-4am Sat, Marrakech 10pm-4am Sat & Sun, Phoenix 11pm-4am Fri & Sat) The open-air Gianpula Complex, just east of Rabat, is more of a village than a club. Areas include 'Groove Gardens', with an underground vibe; 'Marrakech', with a sophisticated 'VIP' look and R&B; newly added house venue 'Phoenix', with appropriately flaming torches; and a recently added rooftop club. It hosts big-name events showcasing top international DJs and the occasional festival.

Club Numero Uno CLUB
(☑2141 5241; www.clubnumerouno.com; Ta'Qali Crafts Village; ⊙11pm-4am Fri & Sat Jun-Sep) In Ta'Qali Crafts Village, this popular open-air local club hauls in Malta's beautiful crowd on Saturday and Sunday nights in summer, shaking it to house and R&B.

Around Mdina & Rabat

◉ Sights & Activities

Ta'Qali Crafts Village VILLAGE
(⊙9am-4pm Mon-Fri, 9am-noon Sat & Sun; 🚍Buġibba-Mdina X3, Valletta-Mdina 51, 52, 53, Dingli-Mdina-Mosta 201, 202, 203) Arts and crafts workshops at Ta'Qali are housed in the old Nissen huts on this WWII Royal Air Force (RAF) airfield, and have a slightly shanty-town look, but are well worth a look. You can watch glass-blowers at work, and shop for gold, silver and filigree jewellery, paintings by local artists, leather goods, Maltese lace, furniture, ceramics and ornamental glass.

It's about 2km from the bus terminus in Rabat to the village.

To reach here, take the X3 from Buġibba or Mdina, or the 51, 52 or 53 from Valletta or Mdina. The 201, 202 and 203 run between here, Mosta, Mdina and Dingli.

Ta'Qali is also used for occasional music festivals.

Malta Aviation Museum MUSEUM
(☑2141 6095; www.maltaaviationmuseum.com; adult/child €7/2; ⊙9am-5pm Sep-May, 9am-5pm Mon-Sat, 9am-1pm Sun Jun-Aug) This is aircraft enthusiast heaven, located on the

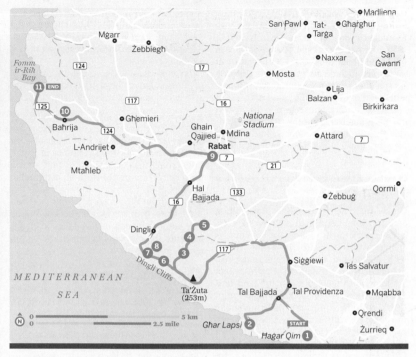

Driving Tour
Temples, Sea Cliffs & Gardens

START ḤAĠAR QIM & MNAJDRA
FINISH FOMM IR-RIḤ
LENGTH APPROX 15KM; ONE HOUR

In this remarkably small area you can experience some of Malta's finest prehistoric temples, some breathtaking stretches of coast, grand palaces and mysterious cart ruts, on a trip around the island's most traditional region.

Start your tour at the megalithic temples of **1 Ħaġar Qim & Mnajdra**, with sweeping views over the coast. From here, drive down to **2 Għar Lapsi**, then take the road inland through the Girgenti Valley. Next, veer towards the coast again, along the southern end of Dingli Cliffs. After about a kilometre, turn inland to visit the **3 Cart Ruts** – mysterious prehistoric tracks – at Clapham Junction. From here it's a short drive to **4 Buskett Gardens** (from the Italian *boschetto*, meaning 'little wood'), Malta's only extensive woodland area. The gardens were planted by the Knights as a hunting ground; today they

are a hugely popular outing for the Maltese, and the groves of Aleppo pine, oak, olive and orange trees provide shady picnic sites in summer and orange-scented walks in winter. Close by you'll see **5 Verdala Palace**, which was built in 1586 as a summer residence for Grand Master Hugues Loubeux de Verdalle. It was designed in the form of a square castle with towers at each corner, but only for show – it was intended to be a hunting retreat. Next, double back to the cliffs to rejoin the panoramic road, passing the **6 Chapel of St Mary Magdalene**. After travelling a short distance to the north you'll see the outlandish **7 Radar Tower** perched on the edge of the cliffs; right by here is **8 The Cliffs**, for some lunch.

After lunch, drive inland to **9 Rabat**, from where you can take Triq Għajn Qajjet westwards towards the village of **10 Baħrija**. Where the village's road splits, take the right-hand fork and follow the road towards the coast. When the road forks, turn right; this will lead you down to a viewpoint over **11 Fomm ir-Riħ Bay**.

former site of the RAF station, with stars of the show including a WWII Spitfire Mk IX and a Hawker Hurricane IIa, salvaged in 1995 after 54 years at the bottom of the sea off Malta's southwest coast. Other aircraft on display include a vintage Flying Flea, a De Havilland Vampire T11, a Fiat G91R and a battered old Douglas Dakota DC-3.

There's a CitySightseeing Malta (p177) open-top bus tour stop (North Route) outside the museum. Buses 51, 52 and 53 stop here on their routes between Rabat and Valletta.

Dingli Cliffs

Dingli was named after either the Maltese architect Tommaso Dingli (1591–1666) or his 16th-century English namesake Sir Thomas Dingley, who lived nearby. It's a quiet village with not much to it, apart from a new, recommended farm restaurant. But less than a kilometre to the southwest the land falls away at the spectacular 220m-high **Dingli Cliffs**. A potholed tarmac road runs along the top of the cliffs, and it's well worth heading here for some great walks south, past the incongruous radar tower to the lonely little 17th-century **Chapel of St Mary Magdalene** and onwards to Ta'Żuta (253m), the highest point on the Maltese Islands. Here you'll enjoy excellent views along the coast to the tiny island of Filfla.

✖ Eating

★ Diar il-Bniet   MALTESE €€
(☑2762 0727; www.diarilbniet.com; Main St, Ħad-Dingli; mains €8.25-20; ⊙noon-3pm daily & 6.30-9pm Mon-Sat) With all produce sourced from 'the house of the girls', their farm around 200m away, or other local producers, this lovely family-run farmhouse restaurant is something special, located in a historic farmhouse in the centre of Dingli village. Dishes include deliciously stuffed aubergines or courgettes, homemade pies and fried rabbit, followed by desserts worth leaving space for, such as date and anisette tart.

★ The Cliffs   MALTESE €€
(☑2145 5470; www.thecliffs.com.mt; mains €7.50-19.50; ⊙10.30am-4pm & 7-10.30pm Fri & Sat Oct-May, 10.30am-4pm & 7-10.30pm Wed-Mon Jun-Sep; ⊙) Close to Dingli's radar tower, on the cliffs, this place is run by two local brothers and is an attractive, contemporary, brasserie-style restaurant with a narrow, glass-framed terrace running around it. It specialises in local food using local produce, such as wild asparagus and garlic, local cheeses and honey, and Maltese wines.

It's more than just a restaurant, with lots of information on the area's topography, and also sells quince, chutney and jam.

Bobbyland Restaurant   MALTESE €€
(☑2145 2895; mains €9-20; ⊙12.30-3pm Tue-Sun Oct-May, 12.30-3pm Tue-Sun & 7-10pm Tue-Sat Jun-Sep) At the northwest end of the Dingli Cliffs you'll find Bobbyland, a fine setting for a drink or a meal before a postprandial clifftop stroll. This rustic former Nissen hut is 500m from the Dingli junction; food and service are distinctly average at best, but its airy outdoor seating makes it a good choice for kids. Specialities include fried rabbit, and there's also pizza.

❶ Getting There & Away

Bus 52 runs from Valletta (45 minutes, at least hourly). Bus 201 connects Dingli with Rabat (15 minutes, hourly) and, in the other direction, runs along the coast to Ħaġar Qim (20 minutes), the Blue Grotto and the airport (45 minutes). Bus 202 runs between Dingli, Rabat, Mosta (35 minutes, hourly), Sliema (1 hour 10 minutes) and St Julian's.

Clapham Junction

Continue past the entrance to Buskett Gardens and follow the signs to reach a rough track signposted 'Cart Tracks'. To the right (west) of this track is a large area of sloping limestone pavement, scored with several sets of intersecting prehistoric 'cart ruts'. The name Clapham Junction – a notoriously complicated railway junction in London – was given to the site by British visitors.

Mosta

POP 20, 240

Mosta is a busy and prosperous town spread across a level plateau, famous for its splendid domed church. It's also an ideal starting point for exploring the **Victoria Lines** (p89).

◉ Sights & Activities

Mosta Dome   CHURCH
(☑2143 3826; Pjazza Rotunda; donations welcome, ⊙9-11.10am & 4pm) Mosta's parish Church of Santa Maria, better known as the

CART RUTS

One of the biggest mysteries of Malta's prehistoric period is the abundance of so-called 'cart ruts' throughout the islands. In places where bare limestone is exposed, it is often scored with a series of deep parallel grooves, looking for all the world like ruts worn by cartwheels. But the spacing of the ruts varies, and their depth – up to 60cm – means that wheeled carts would probably get jammed if they tried to use them.

A more likely explanation is that the grooves were created by a travois – a sort of sled formed from two parallel poles joined by a frame and dragged behind a beast of burden, similar to that used by Native Americans of the Great Plains of North America. The occurrence of the ruts correlates quite closely to the distribution of Bronze Age villages in Malta.

This still leaves the question of what was being transported. Suggestions have included salt and building stone, but it has been argued that whatever the cargo was, it must have been abundant, heavy and well worth the effort involved in moving it. The best suggestion to date is that the mystery substance was topsoil – it was carted from low-lying areas to hillside terraces to increase the area of cultivable land, and so provide food for a growing population.

In some places the ruts are seen to disappear into the sea on one side of a bay, only to re-emerge on the far side. In other spots they seem to disappear off the edge of a cliff. These instances have given rise to all sorts of weird theories, but they are most convincingly explained as the results of long-term erosion and sea-level changes due to earthquakes – the central Mediterranean is a seismically active area and Malta is riddled with geological faults.

Good places to see the ruts and come up with your own theories include Clapham Junction near Buskett Gardens and the top of the Ta'Ċenċ cliffs on **Gozo** (p122).

Rotunda or Mosta Dome, was designed by the Maltese architect Giorgio Grognet de Vassé and built (1833–60) using funds raised by the local people. It has a stunning blue, gold and white interior, where you can also see the bomb that fell through it in 1942 as around 300 parishioners waited to hear Mass. Miraculously, the bomb failed to detonate – a replica is to the left of the altar in the sacristy. The church's circular design with a six-columned portico was closely based on the Pantheon in Rome, and the great dome – a prominent landmark (its external height is 61m) – is visible from most parts of Malta. With a diameter of 39.6m, it's one of the world's largest domes, though dome comparison is a tricky business: the parishioners of Xewkija on Gozo claim that their church has a bigger dome than Mosta's – although the Gozitan Rotunda has a smaller diameter (25m), it is higher and has a larger volumetric capacity. So there!

Bidnija Horse Riding School HORSE RIDING
(☑ 7999 2326; www.bidnijahorseriding.com; Bidnija; ☺ 9am-dusk) Just northwest of Mosta, on the road to St Paul's Bay, Bidnija offers horse rides from one to seven hours, accompanied by qualified instructors.

Eating

Pjazza Café CAFE €
(☑ 2141 3379; 1st level, Pjazza Rotunda; mains €7-17; ☺ 9am-11pm) At the elevated Pjazza Café you can enjoy great views of the dome from a table by the window, while downing a light lunch or snack, pizza or pasta.

Ta'Marija Restaurant MALTESE €€
(☑ 2143 4444; www.tamarija.com; Triq il-Kostituzz-joni; mains €8.50-30; ☺ noon-2.30pm Tue-Sun, 6.30-11pm daily) Ta'Marija Restaurant is one of Malta's most highly rated restaurants in terms of authentic Maltese cuisine, with a traditional *kenura* (stone) stove used to heat side dishes. It's a great choice if you don't mind a bit of (dare we say?) cheesy entertainment with your meal, as there's regular folkloric entertainment and traditional Maltese folk music.

Getting There & Away

Numerous buses pass through Mosta. From Valletta take bus 41, 42 or 44 (30 minutes). Buses 41 and 42 go on to St Paul's Bay (25 minutes), Mellieħa (40 minutes) and then Ċirkewwa (for Gozo; 55 minutes). Bus 31 connects with Buġibba, and bus 205 with St Julian's. Buses stop by the Rotonda.

WORTH A TRIP

ГOMM IR-RIĦ: SECRET SWIMMING SPOT

Fomm ir-Riħ (meaning 'mouth of the wind') is Malta's most remote and difficult-to-reach bay. During rough weather, the grey clay slopes and limestone crags merge with the grey clouds and the wave-muddied waters. But on a calm summer's day it's a beautiful spot, with good swimming and snorkelling in the clear blue waters off the southern cliffs, and few other people to disturb the peace.

Locals will marvel at any nonlocals who manage to find it! You'll need your own transport. Head to the village of Baħrija, and after passing through, take the right fork next to the children's playground.

About 1.2km from Baħrija's town square the road drops down to the left into a valley; drive down the road until you reach a junction with 'RTO' (reservato) painted on the wall. Turn right and follow this road down to a small parking area.

To reach the head of the bay, you need to follow a precarious footpath across a stream bed and along a ledge in the cliffs. Locals say that former Maltese Prime Minister Dom Mintoff used to ride his horse along this path – today posts have been cemented in place to prevent horses and bicycles using it.

If you fancy participating in the Maltese Sunday lunch ritual of dining on authentic dishes (including horse meat and rabbit), there are a handful of unassuming options on Baħrija's square, such as **Ta'Gagin** (☑2145 0825; Triq Patri Tumas Xerri; mains €15-22; ☺5-11pm Mon-Sat, 11am-3pm Sun) and **North Country Bar & Restaurant** (☑2145 6688; Triq Is-Sajf Ta' San Martin; mains €15; ☺6pm-midnight Tue-Sat, noon-midnight Sun).

Naxxar

POP 13,445

Naxxar, a couple of kilometres northeast of Mosta (so close the towns almost merge), is a graceful, stately town that is off the tourist trail and has a few important historic sights.

◉ Sights

Palazzo Parisio　　　　　　HISTORIC BUILDING
(☑2141 2461; www.palazzoparisio.com; Pjazza Vittorja; adult/child €12/5 incl audioguide, garden free; ☺9am-6pm) The glorious Palazzo Parisio was originally built in 1733 by Grand Master Antonio Manoel de Vilhena, then acquired and refurbished by a Maltese noble family in the late 19th century. The magnificent interior (in particular the gilded ballroom) and baroque gardens resemble a miniature Versailles. You can also eat at Luna restaurant, and tea in the gardens is particularly lovely.

Parish Church of Our Lady　　　　CHURCH
The Parish Church of Our Lady is one of the tallest baroque edifices in Malta. Construction was started in the early years of the 16th century, according to the designs of Vittorio Cassar (son of the more famous Gerolamo Cassar, who designed Verdala Palace).

✕ Eating

Luna　　　　　　　　　　　CAFE €€
(☑2141 2461; Pjazza Vittorja; mains €11-28; ☺9.30-11.45am & noon-2.45pm, tea 3-6pm) In the aristocratic surroundings of Palazzo Parisio you'll find the excellent Luna restaurant, patrolled by gracious, white-clad staff serving superb coffee, luscious cakes, tempting lunch specials, elegant afternoon teas, and dinner. You can also eat out in the gardens. Childen are welcome during the day.

❶ Getting There & Away

To get to Naxxar, take bus 31 or 37 from Valletta, or bus 225 from St Julian's, which goes on to Golden Bay, via Mosta.

Birkirkara & the Three Villages

The main road from Valletta to Mosta passes through the town of Birkirkara (population 22,245), one of the biggest population centres on the island and part of the huge conurbation that encircles Valletta and the Three Cities.

Just west of Birkirkara is an upmarket suburban area known as the Three Villages, centred on the medieval settlements of Attard, Balzan and Lija. Although modern development has fused the three into a continuous urban sprawl, the old village centres still retain their parish churches and narrow streets, and there are some interesting sites here, particularly Attard's grand mansions and gardens.

Triq il-Mdina, the main road that skirts the southern edge of Attard, follows the line of the Wignacourt Aqueduct, built between 1610 and 1614 to improve the water supply to Valletta. Substantial lengths of the ancient structure still stand beside the road.

◎ Sights

San Anton Palace & Gardens   GARDENS
(Triq Birkirkara; ⊙7am-6pm) The early-17th-century San Anton Palace in Attard was the country mansion of Grand Master Antoine de Paule. It served as the official residence of the British Governor of Malta, and now is that of the Maltese president. You can visit the lovely walled gardens, which contain groves of citrus and avocado, as well as a bird aviary. The Eagle Fountain, just inside the main gate, dates from the 1620s.

Villa Bologna   HISTORIC BUILDING
(☑2141 7973; www.villabologna.com; Triq Sant'Antnin; adult/child €6/free; ⊙9am-5pm Mon-Fri, 9am-1pm Sat) This baroque 18th-century mansion in Attard, still owned by and inhabited by the same family who built it, has wonderful gardens whose greenery is like balm to the eyes; there were some lovely features added in the 1920s such as the sunken pond and the dolphin garden. The villa also contains the marvellous Ceramika Maltija pottery, producing handmade ceramics made to traditional designs.

Church of St Helen   CHURCH
(Is-Santwarju; ⊙6am-7pm) Birkirkara's Church of St Helen is probably the most ornate of Malta's churches, a late flowering of baroque exuberance built in the mid-18th century. On the strength of his performance here, the designer, Domenico Cachia, was given the job of remodelling the facade of the Auberge de Castile in Valletta.

Maria Rosa Winery   WINERY
(☑7900 4330; mariarosawineestate.com; Sqaq Il-Ħofra; wine & food pairing €25; ⊙9am-4pm Mon-Fri) The small, family-run Maria Rosa estate just south of Attard stands on 4.2 hectares of agricultural land, which produce three varieties of grape: cabernet sauvignon, Syrah and Sirakuzan. The winery runs regular tours and tastings; call for details.

Church of St Mary   CHURCH
(Pjazza Tommaso Dingli; ⊙7am-6pm) The Church of St Mary in Attard, designed by Tommaso Dingli and built between 1613 and 1616, is one of the finest Renaissance churches in Malta.

Church of St Saviour   CHURCH
(Misraħ it-Trasfigurazzjoni; ⊙7am-7pm) Lija's Church of St Saviour, designed in 1694, has one of Malta' earliest domes. It's the focus of the Feast of the Transfiguration of Our Lord, a lively festa (feast day), famed for its spectacular fireworks, held on 6 August.

✖ Eating

There's plenty of choice at the gracious Corinthia Palace Hotel in Attard – the elegant **Villa Corinthia** (☑2144 0301; Vjal de Paule; mains €16-28; ⊙7-10pm) for fine dining; **Rickshaw** (☑2544 2190; Vjal de Paule; mains €12-30; ⊙7-11pm Tue-Sat) offering pan-Asian cuisine; and the **Summer Kitchen** (Vjal de Paule; mains €8-10; ⊙11am-4pm & 7-11pm May-Oct), a seasonal alfresco pizza-and-pasta eatery that's good for families.

Melita Gardens   MEDITERRANEAN €
(☑2147 0663; Triq id-Dmejda; mains €7-22; ⊙10am-11pm; 🐾) By the entrance to the San Anton Gardens in Attard; its outdoor seating is particularly balmy, with sunshades, wrought-iron chairs and tables, and greenery. The menu ticks the pizza, pasta and posh burger boxes, the atmosphere is noisy, and it's a great choice for families.

ℹ Getting There & Away

Buses 51, 52 and 53 travel between Valletta and Attard, going on to Mdina and Rabat, and bus 52 goes on to Dingli. The X3 travels here from the airport, via Paola.

CENTRAL MALTA BIRKIRKARA & THE THREE VILLAGES

Southeast Malta

Best Places to Eat

➡ Tartarun (p105)

➡ Ir-Rizzu (p105)

➡ La Campana (p108)

➡ Tal-Familja (p109)

Best Off the Beaten Track

➡ St Peter's Pool (p105)

➡ Għar Dalam Cave & Museum (p108)

➡ Delimara Point (p105)

Why Go?

Several of Malta's most extraordinary historical sites lie in the less visited southeast of the country, including its most breathtakingly located prehistoric temples (Ħaġar Qim and Mnajdra) dating back over 5000 years, and the Għar Dalam cave, full of fossilised remains of prehistoric animals. There's splendid coastal scenery, too, boat trips to visit grottoes, and some fabulous swimming spots off the tourist trail. It's also the base of much of the country's heavy industry, which means tourism is less developed here, though many locals head to the southeast to eat out at the weekend. In fact, the world and his wife descend on the sometime fishing village of Marsaxlokk for its Sunday fish market and to eat seafood at the small town's many restaurants, fronted by a harbour full of bobbing, colourful boats.

When to Go

➡ Late spring and early autumn (May, June and September) are ideal months to be in this part of the country, while high summer will see the area at its busiest.

➡ Avoid the Blue Grotto and Għar Lapsi on public holidays as they'll be packed.

Marsaxlokk

POP 3535

The ancient fishing village of Marsaxlokk (marsa-shlock; from *marsa sirocco*, meaning 'southeasterly harbour') at the head of Marsaxlokk Bay remains resolutely a slice of real Maltese life, despite the encroachment of industry and the descent of hundreds of tourists every Sunday for its weekly fish and souvenir market.

Old low-rise houses ring the waterfront, and a photogenic fleet of brightly coloured *luzzu* (fishing boats) dance in the harbour. Men with weathered faces sit by the waterside mending nets and grumbling about the tax on diesel, while others scrape, paint and saw as they ready their boats for the sea. The town is home to around 70% of the Maltese fishing fleet, and is – not surprisingly – renowned for its top-notch seafood restaurants, making it a magnet for long-lunching locals and bus loads of day trippers.

Marsaxlokk makes for a relaxed base once the Sunday hoards have left. If you're after nightlife into the wee small hours you'll be disappointed, but if you're looking to chill out (and regularly tuck into all manner of fishy morsels), you'll be happy.

History

Marsaxlokk Bay is Malta's second natural harbour. It was here that the Turkish fleet was moored during the Great Siege of 1565, and Napoleon's army landed here during the French invasion of 1798. In the 1930s the calm waters of the bay were used as a staging post by the huge, four-engined Short C-Class flying boats of Britain's Imperial Airways as they pioneered long-distance air travel to the far-flung corners of the Empire. During WWII Marsaxlokk Bay was the base for the Fleet Air Arm, and in 1989 the famous summit meeting between Soviet and US leaders Mikhail Gorbachev and George Bush (senior) was held on board a warship anchored in the bay. Today the harbour is framed by the fuel tanks and chimney of a power station and the huge cranes of the Kalafrana Container Terminal – eyesores that dominate this once entirely scenic part of the Maltese coast.

◎ Sights & Activities

Sunday Fish Market   MARKET

At Marsaxlokk's colourful, packed-to-the-gills Sunday Fish Market, you can admire the riches of the Med before they're whisked off to Malta's top hotels and restaurants. The market starts early in the morning and the best stuff is long gone by afternoon.

★ St Peter's Pool   BAY

St Peter's Pool is a fantastic swimming spot, a natural lido in the rocks with large areas of flat slab for sunbathing between swims. Follow the narrow road out towards Delimara Lighthouse until you are just past the power station chimney (about 1.5km from the main road), and you'll see a low building on the left with 'Peter's Pool' signposted on it.

A rough track leads down to a small parking area – if you meet a car coming the other way it'll be a face-off over who'll back up. Don't leave valuables in your car.

Delimara Point   AREA

Delimara Point, southeast of Marsaxlokk, is blighted by a huge power station whose chimney can be seen for miles around, but there are a few good swimming places on the eastern side of the peninsula, where the power station isn't in view, and this is a pleasant place to walk. You can access St Peter's Pool from here, and walk on to a large scoop of bay called Hofra Iz-Zghira, which has some salt pans.

Waterfront Market   MARKET

The Sunday fish stalls are far outnumbered by the stalls of this daily market that mainly sells kitsch aimed at tour groups visiting the town.

✕ Eating

It's all about the seafood in Marsaxlokk. Restaurants ranging from casual to smart line the harbour, most offering alfresco dining. Booking is advised.

★ Tartarun   SEAFOOD €€

(☑ 2165 8089; www.tartarun.com; Xatt is-Sajjieda; mains €10.50-26.50; ⊙ noon-3.30pm Tue-Sun, 7.30-10.30pm Tue-Sat) Locals love upmarket Tartarun, which offers a more sophisticated take on all things fishy. Dishes such as sea bream, roasted prawn and cherry tomatoes are perfectly executed. There are a few outside tables, though they're somewhat traffic-plagued on Sunday.

Ir-Rizzu   SEAFOOD €€

(☑ 2165 1569; 52 Xatt Is-Sajjieda; mains €8.50-18.50; ⊙ 11.30am-3pm daily, 6-10pm Mon-Sat) Ir-Rizzu was opened by a fisherman nearly 30 years ago and is now run by his sons. It

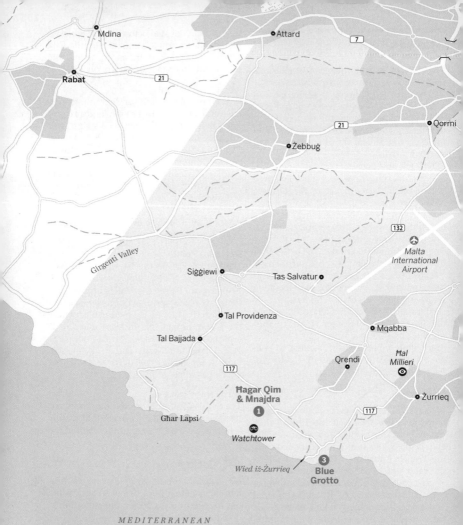

Southeast Malta Highlights

1 Question who, when, how and why, while drinking in the scenery at the mysterious temples of **Ħagar Qim and Mnajdra** (p110).

2 Leap into the glittering royal blue waters of **St Peter's Pool** (p105).

3 Take a mid-morning boat trip to marvel at the **Blue Grotto** (p110).

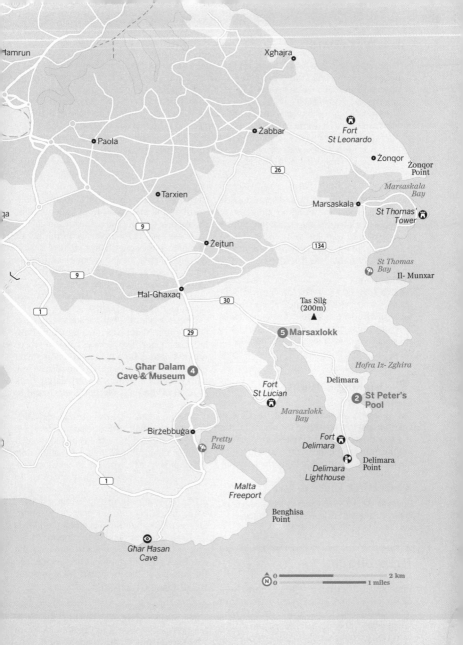

Xghajra

Ħamrun

Paola

Żabbar

Fort St Leonardo

Żonqor

Żonqor Point

Marsaskala Bay

Tarxien

26

Marsaskala

St Thomas' Tower

9

Żejtun

134

St Thomas Bay

Il- Munxar

Hal-Għaxaq

30

Tas Silġ (200m)

29

5 Marsaxlokk

Hofra Iz- Zghira

Għar Dalam Cave & Museum 4

Delimara

Fort St Lucian

2 St Peter's Pool

Birżebbuġa

Pretty Bay

Marsaxlokk Bay

Fort Delimara

Delimara Point

Delimara Lighthouse

1

Malta Freeport

Benghisa Point

Għar Ħasan Cave

N

0   2 km

0   1 miles

4 Explore the mysterious underworld of **Għar Dalam Cave & Museum** (p108).

5 Devour seafood with a view of bobbing fishing boats in **Marsaxlokk** (p105).

MALTESE BOATS

The brightly coloured fishing boats that crowd the harbours around the coast have become one of Malta's national symbols. Painted boldly in blue, red and yellow, with the watchful 'Eyes of Osiris' on the bows to ward off evil spirits, the *luzzu* (*loots*-zoo) is a large double-ended fishing boat (for nonsailors, that means it's pointed at both ends). The *kajjik* (*ka*-yik) is similar in appearance, but has a square transom (it's pointed at the front end only). The *dgħajsa* (*dye*-sa) is a smaller and racier-looking boat, with a very high stem and stern-posts – a bit like a Maltese gondola. These are not solid, seaworthy fishing boats, but sleek water taxis. They were once all powered by oars, but today's *dgħajsas* generally carry an outboard engine.

has a bustling dining room, and some outside tables. Check out the mind-boggling list of local piscatorial specimens, with everything from *lampuka* (dolphin fish) and delicious octopus salad to king prawns or a hearty bowl of *aljotta* (Maltese fish soup).

La Campana　　　　　　SEAFOOD €€
(☑ 2165 7755; 60 Xatt is-Sajjieda; mains €16.50-18.50; ☺ noon-3pm & 7-10.30pm Tue-Sun) This little local favourite is famous for its delicious fish and some serious eating goes on here. It's packed out with locals – reserve ahead, especially if you'd like one of the few outside tables.

🍸 Drinking & Nightlife

Southport Villa　　　　　　BAR
(Xatt is-Sajjieda; ☺ Vino Lounge 7pm-late, Concept Cafe 9am-late) In a converted historic villa, this is a restaurant-bar-cafe complex, with seating out the front and on the terrace, both of which are ideal for a drink overlooking the harbour.

❶ Getting There & Away

Buses 81, 82 and 85 run from Valletta to Marsaxlokk regularly, via Paola. The 119 runs between here and Marsaskala (20 minutes).

Birżebbuġa

POP 9735

Birżebbuġa (beer-zeb-*boo*-ja, meaning 'well of the olives') lies on the western shore of Marsaxlokk Bay. It began life as a fishing village, but today it's a dormitory town for workers from the nearby Malta Freeport.

◉ Sights

⭐ **Għar Dalam Cave & Museum**　　　ARCHAEOLOGICAL SITE
(☑ 2165 7419; adult/child €5/2.50; ☺ 9am-5pm)
The reason to head to Birżebbuġa is to see the Għar Dalam Cave and Museum, 500m north on the main road from Valletta. Għar Dalam (aar-da-lam; the name means 'cave of darkness') is a 145m-long cave in the Lower Coralline Limestone. It has yielded a magnificent harvest of fossil bones and teeth. The lowermost layers of the cavern, over 500,000 years old, yielded remains belonging to dwarf elephants, hippopotamuses, micro-mammals and birds.

The animals are all of European type, suggesting that Malta was once joined to Italy, but not to northern Africa. It's also where the first signs of human habitation on Malta, from 7400 years ago, have been discovered, with remains including pottery dating back to 5200 BC and neanderthal teeth found in the top layer.

The museum at the entrance contains an exhibition hall with displays on how the cave was formed, how the remains of such animals came to be found here, and their development in response to local conditions, as they evolved in different ways to such creatures elsewhere. In the older part of the museum are display cases mounted with thousands and thousands of bones and teeth. Beyond the museum a path leads down through gardens to the mouth of the cave, where a walkway leads 50m into the cavern. A pillar of sediment has been left in the middle of the excavated floor to show the stratigraphic sequence.

Għar Ħasan Cave　　　　　　CAVE
Għar Ħasan Cave lies within the cliff-bound coastline south of Birżebbuġa. From Birżebbuġa follow the road towards Żurrieq, then turn left on the minor road at the top of the hill to reach a clifftop parking area just before an industrial estate; the cave entrance is down some steps in the cliff face to the left. (At the time of research, the access to the cave was fenced

off for safety reasons – check with the tourist office in Valletta (p57) to see if it has reopened.)

The 'Cave of Hasan' is supposed to have been used as a hideout by a 12th-century Saracen rebel. With a torch you can follow a passage off to the right to a 'window' in the cliff face.

❶ Getting There & Away

To get to Għar Dalam and Birżebbuġa, take regular bus 82 or 85 from Valletta, which run via Paola. The cave museum is on the right-hand side of the road at a small, semicircular parking area 500m short of Birżebbuġa. There is no public transport to Għar Ħasan – it's a 2.5km walk south of Birżebbuġa.

Marsaskala

POP 12,135

Marsaskala (also spelt Marsascala), gathered around the head of a long, narrow bay, was originally a Sicilian fishing community: the name means 'Sicilian Harbour'. Today it is an increasingly popular residential area and seaside resort among the Maltese. It appeals because of its great restaurants, bustling little harbour with its bobbing boats, and local feel.

◉ Sights & Activities

St Thomas Bay   BEACH
St Thomas Bay is a deeply indented bay to the south of Marsaskala, lined with concrete and breeze-block huts and a potholed road, and surrounded by apartments. It has a sandy beach, and the place is popular with local people and windsurfers. It's about a 10-minute walk from Marsaskala along Triq Tal-Gardiel. From St Thomas Bay you can continue walking along the coast to Marsaxlokk (about 4km).

St Thomas' Tower   FORTRESS
This small 17th-century fortress lies at the northern point of St Thomas Bay. It was built by the Knights of St John after a Turkish raiding party landed in Marsaskala Bay in 1614 and plundered the nearby village of Żejtun.

✖ Eating

Locals travel across Malta to enjoy the many restaurants of Marsaskala. The town is particularly famed for its seafood.

La Favorita   SEAFOOD €€
(☑2163 4113; Triq Tal-Gardiel; mains €8-22; ☉noon-2.30pm Tue-Sun & 7-10.30pm Mon-Sat) This long-standing family-run restaurant is popular with locals for its delicious fresh fish. Head here for a long lazy lunch or dinner.

Ta'Grabiel   MEDITERRANEAN €€
(☑2163 4194; Pjazza Mifsud Bonnici; mains €9-30; ☉12.30-3pm & 7-10.30pm Mon-Sat) Elegant Ta'Grabiel combines an upmarket seafood restaurant with a terrace kiosk-style cafe, which has less interesting food at cheaper prices (eg omelettes, pasta or roast chicken priced from €5 to €10).

Tal-Familja   SEAFOOD €€
(☑2163 2161; Triq Tal-Gardiel; mains €8-22; ☉noon-11pm Tue-Sun) A local favourite, with a huge menu and daily specials, at the heart of which are fresh seafood and classic Maltese cuisine.

❶ Getting There & Away

Buses 91, 92 and 93 run regularly from Valletta to Marsaskala and bus X5 runs to the airport. The bus terminus is on Triq Sant'Antnin at the southern end of the waterfront promenade.

Żurrieq

POP 10,820

The village of Żurrieq sprawls across a hillside on the south coast, in a sort of no man's land to the south of the airport. This part of Malta feels cut off from the rest of the island, and although it's only 10km from Valletta as the crow flies, it seems much further. Signage from Żurrieq to neighbouring towns is poor, but this region is small and it shouldn't take long to find the direction you need (ask locals for guidance if you get stuck).

◉ Sights & Activities

Parish Church of St Catherine   CHURCH
The Parish Church of St Catherine was built in the 1630s and houses a fine altarpiece of St Catherine – painted by Mattia Preti in 1675, when the artist took refuge here during a plague epidemic – and there are several 17th- and 18th-century windmills dotted about the village.

Chapel of the Annunciation CHURCH

(☑ 2122 5952; www.dinlarthelwa.org; ⊕ 9am-noon 1st Sun of month) On a minor road between Żurrieq and Mqabba is the Chapel of the Annunciation in the deserted medieval settlement of Ħal Millieri. This tiny church, set in a pretty garden, dates from the mid-15th century and contains important 15th-century frescoes – the only surviving examples of medieval religious art in Malta.

Wied iż-Żurrieq BOAT TOUR

(☑ 2164 0058, 9945 5347; adult/child €8/4; ⊕ 9am-5pm) About 2km west of Żurrieq lies the tiny harbour of Wied iż-Żurrieq, set in a narrow inlet in the cliffs and guarded by a watchtower. Here, boats depart, weather permitting, for enjoyable 30-minute cruises to the Blue Grotto, a huge natural arch in the sea cliffs 400m to the east.

The boat trips also take in seven caves, including the Honeymoon Cave, Reflection Cave and Cat's Cave.

The best time is before mid-morning, when the sun is shining into the grotto. If there is any doubt about the weather or sea conditions, call to check.

You can see the Blue Grotto without a boat from a viewing platform beside the main road, just east of the turn-off to Wied iż-Żurrieq.

✖️ Eating & Drinking

Step In SEAFOOD €€

(☑ 2168 3104; Triq Wied Hoxt; mains €6.50-22; ⊕ 10.30am-5pm Tue-Sun) There is a cluster of restaurants around the launching point for Blue Grotto trips, and Step In is the pick of the bunch, as it wins hands down for its setting, with a fantastic terrace offering views out to sea and over to the little island of Filfla. It's very informal and a great place for a drink with a view.

❶ Getting There & Away

Bus 201 runs hourly from Rabat to Wied iż-Żurrieq via Dingli Cliffs, Għar Lapsi and Ħaġar Qim, and goes on to the airport, via Żurrieq. Bus 71 connects Żurrieq (which is about 1.5km from the Blue Grotto harbour) with Valletta every 20 to 30 minutes daily. The Blue Grotto harbour is also a stop on the south route of the CitySightseeing Malta (p177) hop-on, hop-off bus.

Ħaġar Qim & Mnajdra

Ħaġar Qim & Mnajdra ARCHAEOLOGICAL SITE

(☑ 2142 4231; heritagemalta.org; Triq Ħaġar Qim; adult/child €10/5.50; ⊕ 9am-6pm Apr-Sep, 9am-5pm Oct-Mar) The megalithic temples of Ħaġar Qim (adge-ar eem; 'standing stones') and Mnajdra (mm-nigh-dra) are the best

---

MEGA-ATTRACTIONS

The megalithic temples of Malta, which date mainly from the period 3600 to 3000 BC, are among the oldest free-standing stone structures in the world. They pre-date the pyramids of Egypt by more than 500 years.

The oldest surviving temples are thought to be those of Ta'Ħaġrat and Skorba near the village of Mġarr (p79) on Malta. Ġgantija (p128) on Gozo and Ħaġar Qim and Mnajdra (p110) on Malta are among the best preserved. Tarxien (p64) is the most developed, its last phase dating from 3000 to 2500 BC. The subterranean tombs of the Hypogeum (p64) date from the same period as the temples and mimic many of their architectural features below ground.

The purpose of these mysterious structures is the subject of much debate. They all share certain features in common – a site on a southeasterly slope, near to caves; a spring and fertile farmland; a trefoil or cloverleaf plan with three or five rounded chambers (apses) opening off the central axis, which usually faces between south and east; megalithic construction, using blocks of stone weighing up to 20 tonnes; and holes and sockets drilled into the stones, perhaps to hold wooden doors or curtains made from animal hide. Most temple sites have also revealed spherical stones, about the size of cannonballs – it has been suggested that these were used like ball bearings to move the heavy megaliths more easily over the ground.

No burials have been found in any of the temples, but most have yielded statues and figurines of so-called 'fat ladies' – possibly fertility goddesses. Most have some form of decoration on the stone, ranging from simple pitting to the elaborate spirals and carved animals seen at Tarxien. There are also 'oracle holes' in some of the inner chamber walls which may have been used by priests or priestesses to issue divinations.

Ħaġar Qim Temple

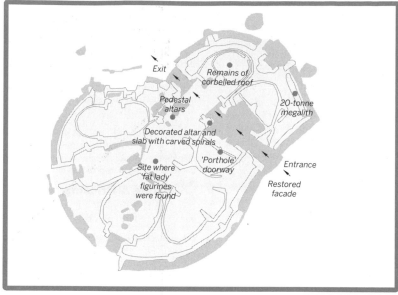

Exit

Remains of
corbelled roof

Pedestal
altars

20-tonne
megalith

Decorated altar and
slab with carved spirals

Site where
'fat lady'
figurines
were found

'Porthole'
doorway

Entrance

Restored
facade

preserved, most evocative of Malta's prehistoric sites, with an unparalleled location atop sea cliffs. Permanent tentlike canopies have been erected over the temples to protect them from the elements.

There's an informative hands-on visitors centre to explain the background to the structures, a children's room where kids can build a temple out of blocks, and an atmospheric if not all that informative 4D film introduction.

Ħaġar Qim is the first temple you reach after the visitors centre. The facade, with its trilithon entrance, has been restored, and gives an idea of what it may once have looked like. The temples were originally roofed over, probably with corbelled stone vaults, but these have long since collapsed.

Before going in, look round the corner to the right – the megalith here is the largest in the temple, weighing over 20 tonnes. The temple consists of a series of interconnected, oval chambers with no uniform arrangement, and differs from other Maltese temples in lacking a regular trefoil plan. In the first chamber on the left is a little altar post decorated with plant motifs, and in the second there are a couple of pedestal altars. The 'fat lady' statuettes and the 'Venus de Malta' figurine that were found here are on

display in the National Museum of Archaeology (p44) in Valletta.

Mnajdra, a 700m walk downhill from Ħaġar Qim, is more elaborate. There are three temples side by side, each with a trefoil plan and a different orientation. The oldest temple is the small one on the right, aligned towards the southwest and Filfla Island. The central temple, pointing towards the southeast, is the youngest. All date from between 3600 and 3000 BC.

In the right-hand apse there is a separate chamber entered through a small doorway, with an 'oracle hole' to its left. The function of this is unknown.

It has been claimed that the southern temple is full of significant solar alignments. At sunrise during the winter solstice, a beam of sunlight illuminates the altar to the right of the inner doorway. At sunrise during the summer solstice, a sunbeam penetrates the window in the back of the left-hand apse to the pedestal altar in the left rear chamber. Around the summer (June) and winter (December) solstices, Heritage Malta (www.heritagemalta.org) organises special guided tours to experience these alignments (€25 per person; book well in advance).

THE ISLET OF FILFLA

Filfla is the smallest of Malta's archipelago of five islands. It's 5km off the south coast of Malta, and was separated from the mainland as the result of the geological Magħlaq Fault. Its name probably comes from the Arabic *filfel*, which means chilli or pepper, and it was possibly so-named because of its shape. It suffered the ignominy of being used for target practice by the British armed forces until it was declared a nature reserve in 1970. The islet supports important breeding colonies of seabirds, including an estimated 5000 to 8000 pairs of storm petrels, as well as two species of lizard and snail not found elsewhere. It's also off limits due to unexploded shells lying in the surrounding waters.

There are some waymarked nature trails in the area surrounding the temples, which allow for splendid views out to sea.

On the clifftop to the southeast of Mnajdra is a 17th-century watchtower and a memorial to Sir Walter Congreve (Governor of Malta 1924–27), who was buried at sea off this point. You can hike west along the cliffs to Għar Lapsi. The tiny uninhabited island Filfla, 5km offshore, is clearly visible.

✕ Eating

Ħaġar Qim Restaurant MALTESE €€
(☏ 2142 4116; mains €6-20; ◷ 10am-4pm & 7-10.30pm Tue-Sun, 10am-4pm Mon Jun-Sep, 10am-4pm Tue-Sun, 7-10.30pm Sat & Sun Oct-May) This pleasingly spacious restaurant, just above the Ħaġar Qim and Mnajdra car park, has a large open-air terrace shaded by a bamboo-slatted canopy, a cheesy music soundtrack and some classical statuary. It serves excellent beef, rabbit and fish dishes plus the usual suspects (pizza and pasta).

ⓘ Getting There & Away

Bus 201 runs hourly Monday to Saturday from Rabat to Ħaġar Qim via Dingli Cliffs and Wied iż-Żurrieq, going on to the airport. Ħaġar Qim is also a stop on the south route of the CitySightseeing Malta (p177) hop-on, hop-off bus.

Għar Lapsi

On the road west of the Ħaġar Qim and Mnajdra temples is a turn-off (signposted) to Għar Lapsi. The name means 'Cave of the Ascension', and there was once a fishermen's shrine here. The road winds steeply to the coast and ends at a car park beside a couple of restaurants and boathouses. The main attraction here is the swimming – a little cove in the low limestone cliffs has been converted into a natural lido, with stone steps and iron ladders giving access to the limpid blue water. It's a popular spot for bathing and picnicking among locals, and is well frequented by divers and fishermen.

✕ Eating & Drinking

If swimming has given you an appetite, try one of the restaurants above the cove.

Carmen's Bar & Restaurant MEDITERRANEAN €
(☏ 2146 7305; mains €8-15; ◷ 11am-10pm) This tiny bar-restaurant is set in a fisherman's boat hut, among fishing boats, just above the Għar Lapsi swimming hole, and is a splendid, simple place to sit and have a drink or tuck into some fresh fish.

Blue Creek MEDITERRANEAN €€
(☏ 2146 2786; mains €7-28; ◷ noon-3pm & 7-10.30pm Wed-Mon) Blue Creek's best tables are the hotly contested ones on the sunny outdoor terrace (directly above the water). The menu has something for all: snacks, sandwiches, pasta or seafood, including octopus stewed in red wine, and a shellfish platter of steamed mussels, clams, razor clams and prawns. Come for lunch rather than dinner, and enjoy the setting.

Ta'Rita Lapsi View MALTESE €€
(☏ 2164 0608; mains €6-19; ◷ 11am-3pm & 6.30-10.30pm Tue-Sun) This 1950s-style restaurant has the look of a '50s municipal swimming pool, with a slightly crumbling exterior fronted by trestle tables, but inside is a taste of retro-Malta, an echoing place with high ceilings. As you'd expect, old-fashioned home-cooking is the order of the day, with burgers, rabbit, steak, *lampuka* and stewed octopus. There's pizza in the evening.

ⓘ Getting There & Away

Bus 201 runs from Rabat along Dingli Cliffs, via Ħaġar Qim and to the Blue Grotto, then on to Żurrieq and the airport. Otherwise bus 71 runs from Valletta to Żurrieq in 45 mins.

Gozo & Comino

Why Go?

Gozo, called Għawdex (*aow*-desh) in Malti, is a gloriously pretty island, with what the 19th-century nonsense poet Edward Lear called a 'pomskizillious and gromphibberous' landscape. He coined the words especially, looking for a way to describe the island's fairy-tale hillocks topped by enormous churches, its hidden, glittering coves, and its sculptured coastal cliffs. Gozo moves at a much slower pace than its bigger, busier neighbour. Although it is more than one-third the size of Malta, it has less than one-tenth of the population – only about 30,000 Gozitans live here (and they are Gozitans first, Maltese second). People leave their front doors unlocked; only one car has apparently ever been stolen, and the perpetrators were arrested before they reached the ferry.

This is a lovely place to kick back, with sandy beaches, rocky coves, excellent scuba diving and snorkelling, plus history in the form of megalithic temples and medieval citadels.

Best Places to Eat

➡ Rew Rew (p122)
➡ Tmun Mġarr (p121)
➡ Boat House (p123)
➡ Oleander (p130)

Best Places to Stay

➡ Gozitan farmhouses (p144)
➡ Hotel Ta'Ċenċ (p144)
➡ Thirtyseven (p144)
➡ Quaint Boutique Hotel (p146)
➡ Mia Casa (p143)

When to Go

➡ Gozo and Comino are at their loveliest in spring and autumn, when the crowds have ebbed away.

➡ If you want to visit Comino's famous Blue Lagoon, it's much easier to enjoy its charms outside the summer months.

➡ Still, high summer is a great time for clubbing at the island's outdoor venues.

➡ It's also worthwhile being here during Carnival (February), Easter and Christmas to bask in local colour.

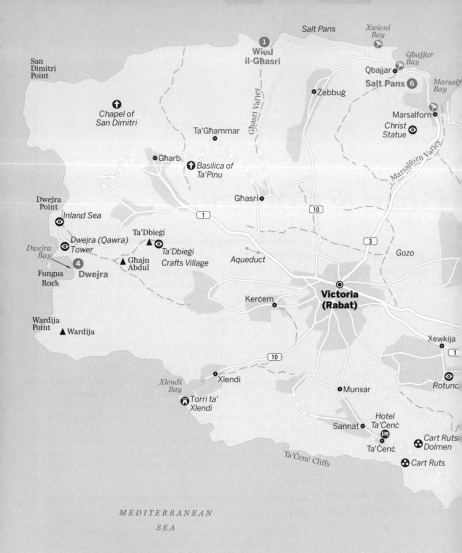

Gozo & Comino Highlights

1 Swim in azure coves such as **Wied il-Għasri** (p127).

2 Get red sand in your shorts at lovely **San Blas Bay** (p132).

3 Take in the incredible 360-degree views from tiny **Comino** (p132).

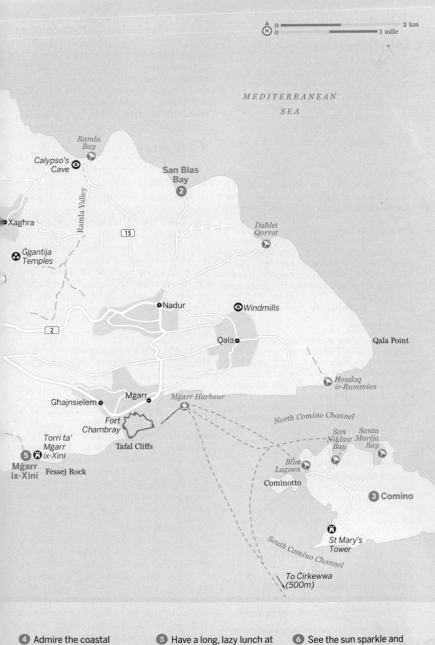

MEDITERRANEAN SEA

Ramla Bay

Calypso's Cave

San Blas Bay 2

Xaghra

Dahlet Qorrot

Ġgantija Temples

Ramla Valley

15

Nadur

Windmills

2

Qala

Qala Point

Hondoq ir-Rummien

Ghajnsielem

Mġarr

Mġarr Harbour

North Comino Channel

Fort Chambray

San Niklaw Bay

Santa Marija Bay

Torri ta' Mġarr ix-Xini

Tafal Cliffs

Blue Lagoon

5 Mġarr ix-Xini

Fessej Rock

Cominotto

3 **Comino**

South Comino Channel

St Mary's Tower

To Ċirkewwa (500m)

4 Admire the coastal moonscape of **Dwejra** (p125).

5 Have a long, lazy lunch at **Mġarr ix-Xini** (p122), ideally having arrived in style by boat.

6 See the sun sparkle and waves crash at the **salt pans** (p126) outside Marsalforn.

GOZO

ℹ Getting There & Away

Gozo Channel (p181) runs the car and foot passenger ferry connecting Ċirkewwa in Malta and Gozo's Mġarr (every 45 minutes from 6am to 10.30pm, and roughly every 1½ hours overnight). You pay for your ticket in Mġarr on the return trip, not on the way out.

ℹ Getting Around

BUS

Buses tend to run daily, about hourly, and most pass through Victoria. You can buy your ticket aboard the bus, or at the ticket machines at the Victoria bus station, which is close to the town centre. A two-hour ticket costs €2 between July and September (€1.50 between October and June); a block of 12 tickets costs €15, and a seven-day Explorer pass €21. **City Sightseeing Gozo** (www.city-sightseeing.com; adult/child €18/10; ⊙ every 45min 9.45am-6.30pm) and **Malta Sightseeing Gozo** (www.maltasightseeing.com; adult/child €20/13; ⊙ every 45min 9.40am-3pm) offer hop-on, hop-off bus tours.

CAR & BICYCLE

If you want to see as much of the island as possible, then it makes sense to rent a car. It's also even cheaper than in Malta, though in high season you'll need to book ahead as supply is limited. Cycling is also a great option on Gozo as the roads are mostly quiet. If you need help on the hills, electric bikes are ideal, but at the time of research these were only available on Malta, so you can rent them there and bring them over.
Mayjo Car Rentals (☑ 2155 6678; www.mayjo-carhire.com; Triq Fortunato Mizzi, Victoria; per day €28) A large range of cars at good rates.
Victoria Garage (☑ 2155 6414; www.victoriagaragegozo.com; Triq Putirjal, Victoria; bicycle per day from €5, car per day €21) Victoria Garage, opposite the bus station, rents out bicycles (including locks) and cars.

TAXI

Approximate taxi fares from Victoria include: €10 to Marsalforn or Mġarr €10; €12 to Xagħra; and €15 to Xlendi. To book a taxi, call Belmont Garage (p181) or **Mario's Taxis** (☑ 2155 7242). Otherwise, there's a taxi rank near Victoria's bus station and at Pjazza Indipendenza.

Victoria (Rabat)

POP 6900

Victoria, the chief town of Gozo, sits in the centre of the island, 9km from the ferry terminal at Mġarr and 3.5km from the resort town of Marsalforn. It's crowned by the tiny citadel Il-Kastell, which appears to grow out of its rocky outcrop. The small walled city houses numerous interesting museums.

Gozo's capital is the island's main hub of shops and services. Named for the Diamond Jubilee of Queen Victoria in 1897, it was originally known as Rabat, and is still called that by many of the islanders (and on several road signs).

⊙ Sights

⊙ Il-Kastell

While the walls surrounding Il-Kastell date from the 15th century, there have been fortifications atop this flat-topped hill since the Bronze Age: it developed under the Phoenicians and later became a Roman town. After some terrible raids on Gozo by the Turks, it became customary for all the island's families to stay within Il-Kastell overnight, a practice that lasted into the 17th century. You can walk almost all the way around the city walls, for astounding views over Gozo and as far as the sea.

Cathedral of the Assumption   CHURCH
(Map p117; Misraħ il-Katidral; adult/child €3.50/free, incl museum; ⊙10am-5pm Mon-Sat) Built between 1697 and 1711 to replace a church destroyed by a 1693 earthquake (which was in southern Italy but caused damage as far away as here), the cathedral was designed by Lorenzo Gafa, also responsible for St Paul's Cathedral (p91) at Mdina. The elegant facade is adorned with the escutcheons of Grand Master Ramon de Perellos and Bishop Palmieri. Due to a lack of funds the dome was never finished, but a trompe l'œil painting makes it look as if it were.

Cathedral Museum   MUSEUM
(Map p117; ☑ 2155 6087; Triq il-Fossos; adult/child €3.50/free, incl cathedral; ⊙9am-5pm Mon-Sat) This jumble of objects within the Cathedral Museum includes a *zucchetto* (skull cap) worn by Pope Francis, church gold and silver, some religious art (including a disturbing 19th-century painting depicting the martyrdom of St Agatha), and a 19th-century bishop's carriage.

Archaeology Museum   MUSEUM
(Map p117; ☑ 2155 6144; Triq Bieb il-Mdina; adult/child €3/1.50, incl 2 museums €5/2.50; ⊙9am-5pm) Victoria's Archaeology Museum houses some incredible finds. There are some 'fat

Il-Kastell

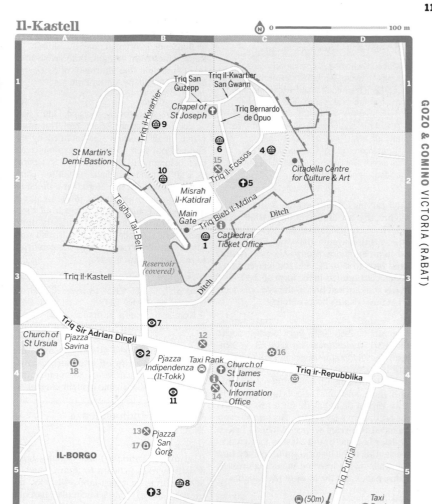

Il-Kastell

ℹ️ VICTORIA'S MUSEUM PASSES

Museum aficionados can purchase a ticket to two of Victoria's museums (€5/2.50 per adult/child, excluding the Cathedral Museum). For the really dedicated there's the Citadel Day Ticket (€8/4 per adult/child), allowing entry to all four. If you have a Malta Pass (maltapass.com.mt), of course, all entry is covered; otherwise passes can be purchased at each museum.

lady' carvings from Ġgantija Temples and Xagħra, that are around 3000 to 4000 years old. There are also Roman anchors, a 3rd- to 5th-century skeleton that was found buried in an amphora, Bronze Age jugs dating from 2400 to 1500 BC, and some fascinating Phoenician amulets in the form of the Eye of Osiris – an ancient link to the symbols seen on Maltese fishing boats of today.

Old Prison HISTORIC BUILDING

(Map p117; ☑2156 5988; Triq il-Kwartier; adult/child €3/1.50, incl 2 museums €5/2.50; ☺9am-5pm) The Old Prison served as a jail from the late 1500s to 1904, and proved particularly useful for locking up hot-tempered Knights until they cooled off. The cells here once held Jean Parisot de la Valette for a few months for beating up a lay person. His punishment included two years service in Tripoli before he later became Grand Master. Particularly fascinating is the historic graffiti etched into the walls by the inmates, including crosses, ships, hands and the cross of the Knights.

Folklore Museum MUSEUM

(Map p117; ☑2156 2034; Triq Bernardo de Opuo; adult/child €3/1.50, incl 2 museums €5/2.50; ☺9am-5pm) The Folklore Museum is a lovely maze of stairs, rooms and courtyards: the fine rambling old building itself, dating to 1500, houses a collection of domestic, trade and farming implements that give an insight into rural life on Gozo.

Natural Science Museum MUSEUM

(Map p117; ☑2155 6153; Triq il-Kwartier; adult/child €3/1.50, incl 2 museums €5/2.50; ☺9am-5pm) This gracious old building houses a series of low-key exhibits explaining the geology of the island and its water supply. There are some interesting fossils on display, including huge megalodon shark teeth.

Basilica of St George CHURCH

(Map p117; ☑2155 6377; Pjazza San Ġorġ) The well-attended original parish church of Rabat dates from 1678, and the lavish interior contains a fine altarpiece of *St George and the Dragon* by Mattia Preti.

Heart of Gozo MUSEUM

(Map p117; www.heartofgozo.org.mt; Triq il-Karita; donations welcome; ☺9am-5pm) This innovative small museum was founded by the Fondazzjoni Belt Victoria to exhibit treasures belonging to the Basilica of St George as well as other artefacts, including coins and lamps from the Herod era in Israel and scrap silver amounting to the weight of a shekel. A column runs through all three floors showing the island's history from prehistoric Ġgantija through to British rule. There's an audio room, where you can listen to traditional local music.

Gozo 360° AUDIOVISUAL

(Map p117; ☑2155 9955; www.gozo360.com.mt; entrance on Telgħa Tal-Belt; adult/child €7/3; ☺10am-3pm Mon-Fri, 10am-1pm Sat) Gozo 360°, at the Citadel Cinema, is a 30-minute audiovisual show that gives a good, basic introduction to the island's history and sights before veering off into tourist board–style fluff. Shows are every 30 minutes, and commentary is available in eight languages.

◉ Pjazza Indipendenza & Around

Pjazza Indipendenza PIAZZA

(Map p117) Victoria's main square hosts a daily market (6.30am to 2pm), which is known throughout the island as It-Tokk (the meeting place). The semicircular baroque building at the western end of the square is the **Banca Giuratale** (Map p117; Pjazza Indipendenza), built in 1733 to house the city council; today it contains government offices.

Il-Borgo AREA

The old town, known as Il-Borgo, is a maze of narrow, meandering alleys around Pjazza San Ġorġ. It's a beguiling place to wander.

Rundle Gardens GARDENS

(Map p119; ☺6am-8pm Jun-Sep, 7am-6pm Oct-May) The Rundle Gardens, south of Triq ir-Repubblika, were laid out around 1914 by General Sir Leslie Rundle (Governor of Malta 1909–15), and are pleasant and shady for walking around.

Victoria

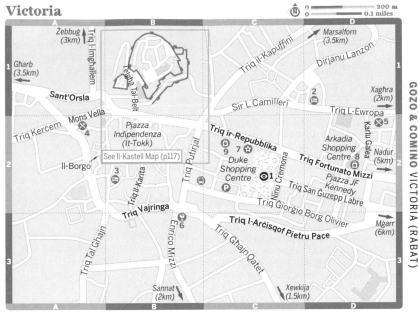

✖ Eating

★ Ta'Rikardu
GOZITAN €

(Map p117; ☑ 2155 5953; 4 Triq il-Fossos; mains €7.50-10.75; ⊗ 10am-8pm) An institution in Victoria and the only place to eat in Il-Kastell, Ta'Rikardu sells excellent local produce – honey, cheese and wine (with particularly good rosé) – along with souvenirs and paintings. Take a seat and order a cheap, delicious platter, which includes cheese, bread, tomatoes, capers and olives. Vegie soup or homemade ravioli is also available; wash it all down with the owners' Gozitan wine.

Grapes Wine Bar
GOZITAN €

(Map p117; ☑ 7947 3503; Pjazza San Ġorġ; mains €6-15; ⊗ 9am-10pm) For a memorable Gozitan experience, settle down in this piazza with views of the basilica, choose a good local or international wine or the local Lord Chambray craft beer, and graze on a platter of regional cheese/sausage/seafood, *ftira* (traditional Maltese bread), and rabbit or pizza.

Café Jubilee
CAFE €

(Map p117; ☑ 2155 8921; Pjazza Indipendenza; mains €5.75-16.75; ⊗ 8am-10.30pm; 🛜) This cafe-bar has a nice atmosphere, with its marble counter, brass rails, lots of dark wood and vintage ads on the walls, and has

Victoria

◉ Sights
1 Rundle Gardens C2

🛏 Sleeping
2 Downtown Hotel D1
3 Mia Casa...B2

✖ Eating
4 Maldonado Bistro A2
5 Patrick's D2

🍷 Drinking & Nightlife
6 Tapies Bar..B3

✪ Entertainment
7 Aurora Opera House C2

🛍 Shopping
8 Arkadia Supermarket........................D2
9 Bookworm C2

a couple of outside tables on the square. In the evening it becomes a popular wine bar and serves good local drops, and also offers local dishes such as rabbit, as well as other snacks.

It-Tokk
GOZITAN €€

(Map p117; ☑ 2155 1213; Pjazza Indipendenza; mains around €20) It-Tokk is a cosy restaurant with flagstone walls and an arched, bamboo-shaded 1st-floor terrace overlooking the square. Come here for traditional Maltese dishes such as rabbit stew and *braġioli* (a beef dish), though they also serve pasta, steaks and so on.

Maldonado Bistro
BISTRO €€

(Map p119; ☑9901 9270; 18 Triq Mons; mains €8-20; ☺7pm-late Mon & Wed-Sun) This cellar bistro is a fun place for an *aperitivo* or dinner – intimate and welcoming – and popular with locals and tourists in the know for its delicious Italian cooking, including handmade pasta, and good accompanying wines.

Patrick's
MEDITERRANEAN €€€

(Map p119; ☑2156 6667; www.patrickstmun. com; Triq l-Ewropa; mains €16.90-32.50; ☺6.30-10.30pm Mon-Sat Jul-Oct, 6.30-10.30pm Tue-Sat, noon-2.30pm Sun Nov-Jun; ☎) Patrick's (named after and run by the son of the restaurateurs at Tmun Mġarr; p121), is polished and professional, from the linen-covered tables to the extensive wine list and menu of complex fusion dishes. Asian influences, New Zealand beef and fresh local fish come together wonderfully in a nautical yet elegant blue-and-white dining room.

Drinking & Nightlife

Tapies Bar
BAR

(Map p119; Triq Enrico Mizzi; ☺5am-11pm) Tapies is an old-fashioned bar with outside tables. It's always busy from morning to night, with a sociable mix of Gozitans, expats and tourists enjoying the insomniac-friendly opening hours, laid-back always-the-same atmosphere and cheap beer (€1.50).

Entertainment

Despite its diminutive size, Victoria has two theatres compared to Valletta's one.

★ Aurora Opera House
THEATRE

(Map p119; ☑2156 2974; www.teatruaurora. com; Triq ir-Repubblika) The Aurora Opera House stages opera, ballet, comedy, drama, cabaret, pantomime, celebrity concerts and exhibitions.

Astra Theatre
THEATRE

(Map p117; ☑2155 0985; www.lastella.com. mt; Triq ir-Repubblika) Astra Theatre is the 19th-century home of Soċjetà Filarmonika La Stella, and stages predominantly opera, music and ballet.

Shopping

Pio's Antiques
ANTIQUES

(Map p117; ☑9906 6101; Pjazza Savina; ☺8am-12.30pm) An Aladdin's cave of Gozitan and Maltese bric-a-brac, including candlesticks and tradtional door knockers.

Bookworm
BOOKS

(Map p119; ☑2155 6215; 105 Triq ir-Repubblika; ☺7.30am-7pm Mon-Fri, 7.30am-1pm Sat) Well-stocked shop with a good range of fiction and guidebooks, plus local and British newspapers.

Arkadia Supermarket
FOOD & DRINK

(Map p119; Triq Fortunato Mizzi; ☺7am-8pm) Gozo's best supermarket, with some Waitrose products.

Organika
FOOD

(Map p117; ☑2701 3548; 13 Pjazza San Ġorġ; ☺10am-6pm Mon-Fri, 10am-4pm Sat) Locally grown organic produce.

Information

Aurora (Opera House, Triq ir-Repubblika; ☺7am-midnight; ☎) There is free wi-fi offered at the Aurora cafe in the Opera House.

Bank of Valletta (102 Triq ir-Repubblika; ☺8.30am-1.30pm Mon-Thu, to 4.30pm Fri, to 12.30pm Sat)

General Hospital (☑2156 1600; Triq l-Arċisqof Pietru Pace)

Gozo Police Headquarters (☑2156 2040; Triq ir-Repubblika) Gozo's main police station is located near the corner of Triq ir-Repubblika and Triq Putirjal.

Post Office (Map p117; Triq ir-Repubblika; ☺8.15am-4.30pm Mon-Fri, 8.15am-12.30pm Sat)

Tourist Information Office (Map p117; ☑2291 5452; Tigrija Palazz, cnr Triq ir-Repubblika & Triq Putirjal; ☺9am-5.15pm Mon-Sat, 9am-12.15pm Sun & public holidays) A helpful office with maps and brochures.

SOUTHERN GOZO

Mġarr

Mġarr is Gozo's main harbour and the point of arrival for ferries from Malta. It's home to a cluster of restaurants and is a fun and scenic place to dine on fresh fish. There are also a few bars, including the characterful Gleneagles.

The hilltop above the town is capped by the ramparts of Fort Chambray, which was built by the Knights of St John in the early 18th century. It was originally intended to supplant Victoria's citadel as Gozo's main fortified town, and the area within the walls was laid out with a grid of streets similar to that of Valletta. But with the decline of the Order in the late 18th century, the plan came to naught. Instead, the fort served as a garrison and later as a mental hospital. Part of the complex has been converted into luxury apartments.

◎ Sights & Activities

Church of Our Lady of Lourdes   CHURCH
(🖉 2166 6537; Triq Lourdes) This 20th-century neo-Gothic church appears almost to hang over the village. Begun in 1924, a lack of funds meant that it was not completed until the 1970s.

Viewpoint   VIEWPOINT
Triq iż-Żewwiega leads to a stunning viewpoint just south of Qala. It's worth the effort to get here – 1.8km uphill from the harbour; once here you can enjoy the magnificent panorama over Gozo and out to sea.

Belvedere   VIEWPOINT
A right turn at the top of the harbour hill leads to a belvedere with a grand view over the harbour to Comino and northern Malta.

Bethlehem Village   AREA
(Għajnsielem) On the right after the first roundabout as you leave Mġarr is this life-size Bethlehem-style village, where 150 actors create a living nativity, which attracts thousands of people each year during the month of December. It's a fun place to explore even when it's not in use.

Boat Trips
You can arrange **boats to Comino** (around €10; ⏰10am-4pm) at stands along the kerb of the main road through town. For a small supplement most offer a quick trip to view some of Comino's caves.

Xlendi Pleasure Cruises   BOAT TOUR
(🖉 9911 1909; www.xlendicruises.com) This outfit offers boat trips around Gozo and/or Comino from April to October. A 4½-hour trip taking in Gozo and Comino costs €25/15 per adult/child, while an 8½-hour trip is €35/18 (with a buffet lunch for either costing €8/5). Private charters are €180 for three hours.

Trips depart from Mġarr Harbour, but transfers can be arranged.

You can book trips through most travel agents in the resort towns on Gozo.

✕ Eating & Drinking

Mġarr has become something of a foodie paradise in recent years, with some excellent restaurants within a short walk of the ferry terminal.

Bugeja Fish Market   MARKET €
(⏰8.30am-12.30pm & 4.30-7pm Mon-Sat) Head to Bugeja, just outside Mġarr, to purchase your fresh fish for a barbecue. It has a great range of local fish and seafood, and attracts queues of locals.

★ Tmun Mġarr   MEDITERRANEAN €€
(🖉 2156 6276; Triq Martino Garces; mains €11-22; ⏰noon-2.30pm & 6.30-10.30pm Wed-Mon; 🖉) Family-run Tmun Mġarr is considered to be Gozo's best restaurant, with a menu rich in dishes like bouillabaisse and fresh-from-the-sea fish. There are good vegetarian choices, too, and the desserts are delicious. Set behind the fishing boats at the water's edge, it has a laid-back feel and an outdoor terrace.

Sammy's – Il-Kcina Tal-Barrakka   SEAFOOD €€
(🖉 9921 3801; Triq Manoel de Vilhena; mains €8-25; ⏰5.30-11pm Mon, Tue & Thu-Sat, 11.30am-11pm Sun) In a great location by the harbour in a lively strip of restaurants, Sammy's is a popular family-run restaurant with a crammed and atmospheric outdoor terrace; indoors is cosy in winter. It's famous for its way with fresh fish and delicious fish soup. Service can be slow.

Gleneagles Bar   PUB
(🖉 2155 6543; Triq ix-Xatt; ⏰3pm-late Mon-Sat, noon-late Sun) This is the social hub of the village – if not the island – and a glorious place to head for a sundowner, with views over the harbour. It fills up in the early evening with a lively mix of locals, fishermen, yachties and tourists. It's named after the first ferry-service ship (1885).

❶ Information

Mġarr Harbour Info Booth (Ferry Terminal; ⏰9am-2pm) Helpful information office for when you arrive in Gozo.

Mġarr ix-Xini

The narrow, cliff-bound inlet of Mġarr ix-Xini (Port of the Galleys) was once used by the Knights of St John as their main harbour on Gozo. One of their watchtowers, **Torri ta'Mġarr ix-Xini**, still guards the entrance. The Turkish admiral Dragut Reis also found it handy, using it when he raided Gozo in 1551 and took most of the island's population into slavery. A more recent invasion was that of a film crew, when Brad Pitt and Angelina Jolie used this as the location to film *By the Sea* in 2014, building a hotel set on the cliffs and taking over the bay for five months.

There's a tiny shingle beach at the head of the inlet, and a paved area where tourists and locals stake out their sunbathing territories. It's a gorgeous place to swim and snorkel, and best on weekdays, when less people descend here. It's home to a classic Gozo restaurant, the marvellous **Rew Rew** (mains €20; ⊘ 11am-5pm Mar-Nov). This simple-looking place has a few chairs and tables next to a little cabin on the beach, and serves up fresh, delicious seafood to hungry punters. It was closed for a season while Brangelina filmed here, and appears as an old-fashioned grocery in their film. It's the perfect place for a long, lazy lunch looking out to sea. Book ahead.

Mġarr ix-Xini is accessed via a narrow winding road. It's well signposted, and perfectly accessible in a normal car. However, the loveliest way to arrive is by boat; charter one via your hotel, Xlendi or Mġarr.

Xewkija

POP 3300

The village of Xewkija – and most of southern Gozo – is dominated by the vast dome of the Parish Church of St John the Baptist, better known as the **Rotunda** (☑ 2155 6793; ⊘ 6am-noon & 3-8pm). Work on the church began in 1951 and was completed in 1971; it was built mainly with the volunteer labour of parishioners and paid for by local donations. The 74m-high dome is the third-largest in the world.

The church was built around the old 17th-century church, which was too small for the community's needs. There's no such risk with the rotunda, which can seat around three times the village's population. The interior is plain, but impresses through sheer size. Paintings of scenes from the life of St John the Baptist adorn the six side chapels. To the left of the altar is a museum displaying baroque sculptures and other relics salvaged from the old church. The wooden statue of St John was fashioned in 1845 by Maltese sculptor Paul Azzopardi. A small lift takes visitors up to the gallery surrounding the dome, for great panoramas.

Ta'Ċenċ

The quiet village of Sannat, once famed for its lace-making, lies 2km south of Victoria, and gives access to the Ta'Ċenċ plateau. Signs from the village square point the way to Hotel Ta'Ċenċ (p144), one of Gozo's finest; its bar is a great place for a sundowner. You can rent sunbeds or eat at its gorgeously set **Il-Kantra Lido Bar & Restaurant** (Hotel Ta'Ċenċ; mains €20; ⊘ 10am-6pm), with incredible views over towards the inlet of Mġarr ix-Xini. The track to the left of the entrance to the walled hotel grounds leads to the high plateau of Ta'Ċenċ – the **views** north to Victoria, Xewkija and Xagħra are good, especially towards sunset. Wander off to the left of the track, near the edge of the limestone crag, and you will find a prehistoric **dolmen** – a large slab propped up on three smaller stones like a table. Keep your eyes peeled – the dolmen is not signposted and is a little tricky to spot.

The best walking is off to the right, along the top of the huge Ta'Ċenċ **sea cliffs**. These spectacular limestone crags, more than 130m high, were once the breeding ground of the Maltese peregrine falcon. Near the cliff top you can see traces of prehistoric **cart ruts**, origins unknown.

Bus 305 runs between Victoria and Ta'Ċenċ (10 minutes).

Xlendi

The sometime fishing village of Xlendi is now a small, popular resort town. The cluster of hotels are low-rise and unobtrusive, and it's a beautiful bay. It's a favourite place for weekending Maltese and tourists to chill out by the sea, with good swimming, snorkelling and diving, and plenty of rocks for sunbathing. In the 19th century, this was known as 'women's harbour', as it was reserved for women-only bathing.

There's an ATM by the bus stop and car park, a block back from the waterfront.

LOCAL KNOWLEDGE

CLIMBING GOZO

The British Army first pursued climbing on Gozo and Comino in the 1950s and '60s, even producing a guidebook of the islands' routes. After independence, it was subsequently forgotten as a local sport, but in recent years has been rediscovered. There are now over 300 climbs in 12 locations across the island in amazingly dramatic yet easy to approach locations. Dwejra has good-quality rock and some incredible climbs, although climbers have to be aware of not disturbing nesting sea birds in spring. Another important area is between Xlendi and Munxar, with 21 bolted new routes in a coastal gorge. You can learn to climb here, or there are multiple climbs at grades 7 to 8 for experts looking for a challenge. For more information see Gozo Climbing (www.gozo-climbing.com).

👁 Sights & Activities

At the head of the bay, steps lead over the cliff above the little fishing-boat harbour to a tiny cove in the rocks where you can swim. This was apparently once reserved for the local nuns. Alternatively, you can keep walking up the hillside above and then hike over to Wardija Point and Dwejra Bay. On the south side of Xlendi Bay, a footpath winds around to the 17th-century watchtower, Torri ta'Xlendi, on Ras il-Bajjada. Below here you can scramble down to some salt pans with fantastic, windswept views. From here you can hike east to the Sanap cliffs, and on towards Ta'Ċenċ.

Watersports

The local dive operators can help you explore the excellent nearby dive sites, offering 'taster' dives, beginners' courses and excursions for those who already know what they're doing.

Moby Dives   DIVING
(📞 2156 4429; www.mobydives.net; Triq il-Gostra) PADI five-star diving school.

St Andrews Divers Cove   DIVING
(📞 2155 1301; www.gozodive.com; Triq San Ximun) Long-standing, recommended PADI diving centre.

Xlendi Pleasure Cruises   BOAT TOUR
(📞 9911 1909; www.xlendicruises.com) Waterside Xlendi Pleasure Cruises offers motorboats, canoes and paddleboats for hire, as well as fishing trips (€45 per person), snorkelling and cave tours. The company also has a menu of cruises leaving from Mġarr Harbour and will provide transfers.

Xlendi Water Sports   WATERSPORTS
(📞 9942 7917; www.xlendicruises.com) Xlendi offers self-drive boats, jet skis (from €30 per 15 minutes), guided kayak tours (1½-hour trip €15 per person), hour-long trips along the coast to Dwejra (adult/child €15/7), and four-hour and longer trips to Comino and the Blue Lagoon (€19.50/9.75; an extra €8/4 for buffet lunch).

🍴 Eating

Ta'Nona   MEDITERRANEAN €
(mains €5.80-14.50, 2-course set menu €14.50; ⊙ noon-midnight) With tables so near the sea you may get splashed, this is a nice simple place to have a beer and pizza or *ftira*, and it offers more elaborate dishes as well.

★ Boat House   MEDITERRANEAN €€
(📞 2156 9153; mains €11.50-27; ⊙ noon-10.30pm) This is a highly rated restaurant where you can eat fresh fish with the sea almost lapping at your toes – there's a seafront, tented terrace. Seafood is the obvious choice, prices are reasonable and it's a great choice for families.

Ta' Karolina   MEDITERRANEAN €€
(📞 2155 9675; Triq Marina; mains €5-23; ⊙ 12.30-3pm & 6.30pm-late Tue-Sun Feb-Dec) This long-running seafront restaurant is a local favourite. It's named after the nun Karolina Cauchi, who raised money to have the steps cut into the cliffs at Xlendi in the 19th century. These days it features a covered terrace, and a great range of soups, pasta and Gozitan specialities.

Iċ-Ċima Restaurant   GOZITAN, ITALIAN €€
(📞 2155 8407; Triq San Xmun; mains €12.25-25; ⊙ noon-3pm & 6.30pm-late Wed-Mon) This friendly restaurant is situated a short walk uphill from the village and has an outstanding view over the bay and the coastal cliffs from its rooftop. It's an excellent choice, with the emphasis on seafood, plus dishes like *coniglio alla nonna* (rabbit grandma's way), plus pizzas.

🍸 Drinking & Nightlife

La Grotta
CLUB

(www.lagrottaleisure.com; Triq ix-Xlendi; admission varies; ⊘10pm-dawn Fri & Sat May-Oct) On the road to Victoria about 600m east of Xlendi, La Grotta has a unique setting with amazing views. It's housed in a limestone cave in the cliffs above the valley, with two large dance areas (indoors and out), and hosts big-party nights, DJs and live music (admission costs vary).

Ku Club
CLUB

(Triq Mro Giuseppe Giardini Vella; ⊘10pm-late Nov-Apr) Gozo's biggest club hauls in lots of international names in the winter months, and is the place to go to worship before godlike DJs, with hands-in-the-air trance and house.

❶ Getting There & Away

Buses 330 (13 minutes) and 306 (25 minutes) run between Xlendi and Victoria. By car, follow signs from the roundabout at the southern end of Triq Putirjal in Victoria. Or it's a 3km walk from Victoria bus station.

NORTHERN GOZO

Għarb & Around

POP 1540

The village of Għarb (pronounced aarb, meaning 'west') in the northwest of Gozo has one of the most beautiful churches on the Maltese Islands.

◉ Sights

Basilica of Ta'Pinu
CHURCH

(🕿2155 6187; www.tapinu.org; Triq ta'Pinu; ⊘6.45am-7pm Mon-Sat, 5.45am-12.15pm & 1.30-7pm Sun) The Basilica of Ta'Pinu, accessible via a short, scenic walk from Għarb, is an extraordinary sight – a huge, lone church on a Gozitan hillock, towering over the countryside. Malta's national shrine to the Virgin Mary is an important centre of pilgrimage. It was built in the 1920s on the site of a chapel where a local woman, Carmela Grima, claimed to have heard the Virgin speak to her in 1883.

Thereafter, numerous miracles were attributed to the intercession of Our Lady of Pinu, and it was decided to replace the old church with a grand new one.

Built in a Romanesque style, with an Italianate campanile, it has a tranquil interior of pale golden stone. Part of the original chapel, with Carmela Grima's tomb, is incorporated behind the altar. The rooms to either side of the altar are filled with votive offerings, including children's clothes, hoists and plaster casts. The basilica's name comes from Filippino Gauci, who used to tend the old church – Pinu is the Malti diminutive for Filippino. Visitors should dress appropriately.

It's well worth walking up the track leading to the top of the hill of Ta'Għammar opposite the church, which is punctuated by marble statues marking the Stations of the Cross.

Karmni Grima Museum
MUSEUM

(🕿2155 6187; admission €3; ⊘9am-4pm) In the former house of Carmela Grima, whose vision gave rise to the Ta'Pinu shrine, there's a small museum that gives an insight into rural 19th-century life.

Għarb Folklore Museum
MUSEUM

(🕿2156 1929; Triq il-Knisja; adult/child €5/free; ⊘9am-4pm Mon-Sat, 9am-1pm Sun) This 18th-century house, once the home of Frenc Mercieca, a local wise man who apparently was able to cure ailments, has 28 rooms crammed with a fascinating, lovely jumble of folk artefacts. The exhibits, assembled by the owner over the past 20 years, include a child's hearse, farming implements, fishing gear and jam-making equipment.

Church of the Visitation
CHURCH

Għarb's baroque Church of the Visitation was built between 1699 and 1729, with an elegant curved facade and twin bell towers. Three female figures adorn the front: Faith, above the door; Hope, with her anchor, to the right; and Charity. Inside, there is an altarpiece, *The Visitation of Our Lady to St Elizabeth,* which was gifted to the church by Grand Master de Vilhena.

Chapel of San Dimitri
CHURCH

A drive or pleasant walk of about 30 minutes (just over 2km) from Għarb leads to the tiny Chapel of San Dimitri (signposted on the road to the left of the church). This small, square church with its baroque cupola dates from the 15th century, though it was rebuilt in the 1730s. It stands in splendid isolation amid terraced fields. You can continue the walk down to the coast, and return via the Basilica of Ta'Pinu.

FUNGUS ROCK

Fungus Rock is known in Malti as 'Il-Ġebla tal-Ġeneral' (the General's Rock). Both its names derive from the fact that the Knights of St John used to collect a rare plant from the rock's summit. The plant *(Cynomorium coccineus)* is dark brown and club-shaped, and grows to about 18cm in height. It is parasitic and has no green leaves, which is why it was called a fungus or, in Malti, 'għerq tal-Ġeneral' (the General's root). It's native to North Africa, and Fungus Rock is the only place in Europe where it's found.

During the time of the Knights, extracts from the plant were believed to have powerful pharmaceutical qualities, and were said to stem bleeding and prevent infection when used to dress wounds. The miracle plant was also said to cure dysentery and ulcers, and was used to treat apoplexy and venereal diseases. It was long known to the Arabs as 'the treasure among drugs', and when a general of the Knights of St John discovered it growing on a rock on Gozo, he knew he had struck gold. A rope was strung between the mainland and the rock, and harvesters were shuttled back and forth in a tiny, one-man cable car. In 1637 the Knights built the fortress of **Dwejra (Qawra) Tower** (p126) from which to guard the precious resource, and they sheared the side of the rock to make it impossible to climb. As well as being much in demand in the Knights' hospitals, it was sold at a high price to the various courts of Europe. However, pharmacologists have since found it doesn't affect health in the ways it was thought, though it has been shown to lower blood pressure.

Eating

Jeffrey's Restaurant GOZITAN €€
(☑2156 1006; 10 Triq il-Għarb; mains €9-16; ⊙6-10.30pm Mon-Sat Apr-Oct) Where the road to Għarb from Victoria forks (400m after the turning to Ta'Pinu) you'll find Jeffrey's. Set in a converted farmhouse with a rustic interior, Jeffrey's is an intimate place with just a few tables, offering homestyle cooking that makes good use of local produce. Here you can sample Gozitan specialities including the highly rated rabbit in wine and garlic.

Getting There & Away

Bus 312 connects Għarb with San Lawrenz (six minutes) and Victoria (16 minutes, hourly), while the 308 runs between Victoria and Ta'Pinu (10 minutes, hourly).

San Lawrenz

POP 750

The charming village of San Lawrenz is where novelist Nicholas Monsarrat (1910–79) lived and worked for four years in the early 1970s. His love for the Maltese Islands is reflected in his novel *The Kappillan of Malta.*

Between San Lawrenz and Santa Luċija is the **Ta'Dbieġi Crafts Village** (⊙10am-4pm), selling handicrafts, lace, glass and pottery. You can often see artisans at work here, and it's a rewarding place to visit.

Eating

Tatita's MEDITERRANEAN €€
(☑2156 6482; Pjazza San Lawrenz; mains €9-34; ⊙12.30-3pm & 7-10.30pm Apr-Oct) Tatita's occupies what was once San Lawrenz police station; when it's warm you can dine alfresco on the postcard-perfect square. It's very welcoming – and family friendly, too, despite the formal look and snow-white tablecloths. The kitchen prepares local treats like grilled quail with Calvados and mushroom sauce; and calamari and king prawns.

Getting There & Away

Bus 312 connects San Lawrenz with Għarb (six minutes, hourly) and Victoria (15 minutes).

Dwejra

Geology and the sea have conspired to produce some of Gozo's most spectacular coastal scenery at Dwejra on the west coast. Two vast, underground caverns in the limestone have collapsed to create two circular depressions now occupied by Dwejra Bay and the Inland Sea. If this otherworldly scenery makes *Game of Thrones* spring to mind, you'd be right: the Azure Window was the backdrop for the Dothraki wedding in the TV show's first season.

☉ Sights & Activities

Dwejra Bay & Dwejra Point   AREA

The collapsed cavern of Dwejra Bay has been invaded by the sea, and is guarded by the brooding bulk of Fungus Rock. A path below Dwejra (Qawra) Tower leads to a flight of stairs cut into the rock, leading down to a little slipway on the edge of the bay. There is good swimming and sunbathing here, away from the crowds of day trippers who throng the rocks around the Azure Window.

For even more peace you can hike right around to the cliff top on the far side of the bay, for a view encompassing Fungus Rock and Dwejra Point and, between them, Crocodile Rock (seen from near Dwejra Tower it looks like a crocodile's head).

The broad horizontal shelf of rock to the south of Dwejra Point has been eroded along the geological boundary between the globigerina limestone and the lower coralline limestone – the boundary is marked by a layer of many thousands of fossilised scallop shells and sand dollars (a kind of flattened, disc-shaped sea urchin).

Blue Hole & the Azure Window   DIVE SITE

The Azure Window, a huge natural arch in the sea cliffs, is a breathtaking Gozitan view. In the rocks in front of it is another geological freak called the Blue Hole – a vertical chimney in the limestone, about 10m in diameter and 25m deep, that connects with the open sea through an underwater arch about 8m down. Scenes from *Game of Thrones* were filmed here in 2011, when the local production company ran into trouble for covering the area in construction sand.

Understandably, it's a very popular dive site and the snorkelling is excellent, too. Moby Dives (p123) and St Andrews Divers Cove (p123), both located in Xlendi, are available for lessons and equipment hire.

Inland Sea   LAGOON

The Inland Sea is a cliff-bound lagoon connected to the open sea by a tunnel that runs for 100m through the headland of Dwejra Point. The tunnel is big enough for small boats to sail through in calm weather, and the Inland Sea has been used as a fishermen's haven for centuries. Today, fishermen supplement their income by taking tourists on **boat trips** (per person 15 minutes €4) through the tunnel.

Dwejra (Qawra) Tower   CASTLE

(dinlarthelwa.org; adult/child €2/free; ⊘ 9am-3pm Mon-Sat, 10.30am-3pm Sun, or when flag is flying) Visit this restored tower for breathtaking views.

Chapel of St Anne   CHURCH

Between the Inland Sea and the Azure Window is the little Chapel of St Anne, built in 1963 on the site of a much older church.

❶ Getting There & Away

Bus 311 runs between Victoria and Dwejra (16 minutes, hourly). Alternatively, catch bus 312 to San Lawrenz (10 minutes) and walk the 1.5km down to the bay.

Marsalforn

Former fishing village Marsalforn (the name is possibly derived from the Arabic for 'bay of ships') is Gozo's main holiday resort. It's small-scale and has a pleasant feel; the promenade, lined by restaurants, is backed by developments of low-rise hotels and apartments.

At the head of Marsalforn's bay is a tiny scrap of sand, but better swimming and sunbathing can be found on the rocks out to the west. You could also hike eastward over the hill a couple of kilometres to Calypso's Cave (p130) and Ramla Bay (p132).

LOCAL KNOWLEDGE

SALT PANS

The salt pans set just outside Marsalforn are the island's most spectacular system. The northern coast of Gozo was particularly suited to salt production, as its area of flat limestone could be cut into by hand. Seawater ran into the shallow basins and the wind and sun did the rest; the salt pans on Gozo apparently date from Roman times. Small caverns were cut into the rock to store the salt. The Knights were in charge of salt harvesting and fined anyone who produced salt without permission. Nowdays the salt is still harvested between May and September, but only for local use. The sea and wind can be wild here, as they hammer the surrounding cliffs into sculptural shapes.

Marsalforn

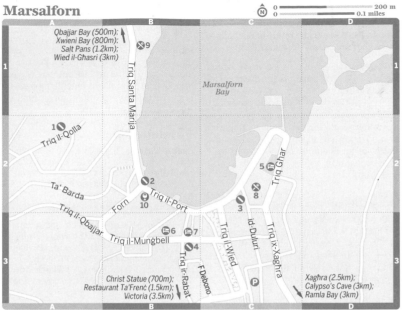

◉ Sights & Activities

★ Wied il-Għasri   BEACH

A 5km hike west along the coast from Marsalforn is the narrow, cliff-bound inlet of Wied il-Għasri. Here a staircase cut into the rock leads down to a tiny shingle beach at the head of the inlet. It's a gorgeously picturesque place and there is good swimming and snorkelling when the sea is calm, but it's best avoided in rough weather when the waves come crashing up the narrow defile.

You can also drive or walk to Wied il-Għasri from the village of Għasri, about 2km south. If you're coming from Marsalforn, there is a signposted turn-off about 300m after the coast road heads inland, where a rough track drops down to the right and leads to a rocky parking area; it's accessible in a regular car.

★ Beaches & Salt Pans   AREA

Walk or drive west from town along the promenade and you'll reach the tiny sand beaches at Qbajjar Bay, backed by buildings, and the more scenic Xwieni Bay, separated by a headland with a small fort. Beyond Xwieni, the road runs along a rocky shore that has been carved into a patchwork of salt pans, a wild and extraordinary landscape.

Marsalforn

◉ Activities, Courses & Tours

There's usually a small stall selling salt from the pans, which are owned by three families and still worked in summer.

Christ Statue   STATUE

As you enter Marsalforn from Victoria, you'll see the figure of Christ on a hill. The statue was erected in the 1970s, replacing earlier statues and a wooden cross from around the 1900s; the 96m-high hill is known as Tas-Salvatur (the Redeemer).

✖ Eating & Drinking

The majority of restaurants in Marsalforn have reduced hours in winter – call ahead to check they are open before setting off.

Otters Bistro   GOZITAN, ITALIAN €€
(☑2156 2473; Triq Santa Marija; mains €9-20; ☺11.30am-10.30pm Fri-Wed, to 5.30pm Thu) Waterfront Otters has a glorious, shady, outdoor terrace overlooking the bay. The menu has some great Gozitan choices, including braised lamb shank with fig and orange sauce, or spaghetti Gozitana (tossed with Maltese sausage, olives, capers, tomatoes and chilli).

Arzella   MEDITERRANEAN €€
(Triq Għar Qawqla; mains €9-22; ☺noon-3pm & 6.30-10.30pm Wed-Mon Apr-Oct, Fri-Sun Nov-Mar) Set high up to the east of the bay, family-run Arzella has a covered terrace with great views out to sea, and buzzes with locals who come for its fresh fish and convivial atmosphere.

La Trattoria   MEDITERRANEAN €€
(☑2155 9173; Triq il-Port; mains €8-24; ☺11am-10.30pm Wed-Mon) This welcoming family-run place has a small, arched interior and a cute little wooden terrace overlooking the town's tiny beach, The house speciality is *lampuka en paupiette* (rolled fillets of *lampuka* – dolphin fish – stuffed with prawns in a cream sauce), but the menu extends to pasta, risotto and pork and beef dishes.

Restaurant Ta'Frenċ   MEDITERRANEAN €€
(☑2155 3888; www.tafrencrestaurant.com; Triq ir-Rabat; mains €8.50-16.50, Maltese menu €35; ☺12.30-3pm & 7pm-late Wed-Mon; ☑) About 1.5km south of Marsalforn on the road to Victoria, this restaurant is in a beautiful setting (a 200-year-old converted farmhouse surrounded by garden) and has an impressive menu of French, Italian and Maltese

---

MARSALFORN DIVING

A number of Marsalforn dive operators can help you explore Gozo's great dive sites, including:

➡ **Atlantis** (p23)

➡ **Calypso** (p23)

➡ **Nautic Team** (p175)

➡ **Dolphins** (☑2702 8299; www.diving gozo.com; 17 Triq il Forn)

---

dishes, created from fresh local ingredients. There's also an extensive, award-winning wine list.

Piutrentanove   WINE BAR
(65 Triq il-Port; ☺4pm-3am; ☜) This small lounge bar on the waterfront has a sleek interior and a couple of outside tables, and is a lively place to be in the summer months. It also serves decent pizzas.

ℹ Information

Bank of Valletta (Triq il-Port; ☺8.30am-2pm Mon-Thu, to 3.30pm Fri, to 12.30pm Sat) You can change money at the Bank of Valletta on the promenade, which has an ATM.

ℹ Getting There & Away

Bus 310 runs between Marsalforn and Victoria (17 minutes, hourly). Bus 322 travels to/from Mġarr (38 minutes, every 1½ hours) via Ramla Bay (20 minutes) and Xagħra (14 minutes). Hire scooters or bikes from **On 2 Wheels Gozo** (☑2156 1503; www.on2wheelsgozo.com; Triq Rabat).

Xagħra

POP 4885

The pretty village of Xagħra (*shaa*-ra), one of Gozo's largest, spreads across the flat summit of the hill east of Victoria. The 19th-century Church of Our Lady of Victory looks down benignly on the tree-lined Pjazza Vittorja, where old men sit and chat in the shade of the oleanders – there's always something gossip-worthy going on in the village square.

◎ Sights & Activities

★ **Ġgantija Temples**   ARCHAEOLOGICAL SITE
(☑2155 3194; access from Triq I-Imqades; adult/child €9/5 incl admission to Ta'Kola Windmill; ☺9am-5pm) Perched on the crest of the hill to the south of Xagħra, the awe-inspiring megalithic Ġgantija Temples command soaring views over most of southern Gozo. As the name implies (*ġgantija* – dje-gant-ee-ya – means 'giantess'), these are the largest of the megalithic temples found on the Maltese Islands – the walls stand over 6m high, and the two temples together span over 40m.

The site has a wonderful new visitors centre, with displays putting the temples into context and showcasing many of the

Xagħra

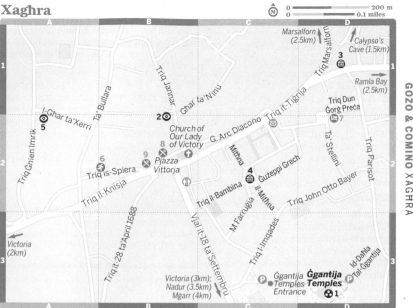

extraordinary carvings discovered here, including the famous 'fat ladies'.

Along with Ta'Ħaġrat and Skorba in Malta (p79), the Ġgantija Temples are thought to be Malta's oldest, dating from the period 3600 BC to 3000 BC. Both temples face towards the southeast, and both have five semicircular niches within. The south temple (on the left) is the older, and is entered across a huge threshold slab with four holes at each side, thought to be for libations. The first niche on the right contains an altar with some spiral decoration – there was once a pillar here with a snake carved on it, but the pillar now lives in Victoria's Archaeology Museum (p116). The left-hand niche in the inner chamber has a well-preserved trilithon altar; on the right is a circular hearth stone and a bench altar.

The outer wall of the later north temple complex is particularly impressive in scale. The largest of the megaliths measures 6m by 4m and weighs around 57 tonnes, and the wall may originally have stood up to 16m tall – it's incredible to contemplate how these huge stones were put in place. The exterior walls were built of harder-wearing coralline limestone, while the interiors were built of the lighter globigerina limestone – brought here from around a kilometre away.

Xagħra

◉ Top Sights
1 Ġgantija Temples D3

◉ Sights
2 Ninu's Cave B2
3 Pomskizillious Museum of Toys D1
4 Ta'Kola Windmill C2
5 Xerri's Grotto A2

◐ Activities, Courses & Tours
6 Lino's Stables B2

◒ Sleeping
7 Xagħra Lodge D2

◈ Eating
8 D-Venue B2
9 Oleander B2

Xerri's Grotto & Ninu's Cave   CAVE

In the backstreets to the north of the village square lie **Xerri's Grotto** (☎2156 0572; l'Għar ta'Xerri; adult/child €2.50/1; ⊙9.30am-4pm Sep-May, to 6pm Jun-Aug) and **Ninu's Cave** (Triq Jannar; donations appreciated; ⊙9.30am-6pm). These fun underground caverns, complete with stalactites and stalagmites, are unusual in that they are both entered through private houses. Having discovered the caves beneath their homes, the owners decided to cash in on the tourist potential. Xerri's Grotto was discovered in 1923, and Ninu's in 1888. They're both fascinating and incongruous.

Pomskizillious Museum of Toys MUSEUM
(☑2156 2489; www.themuseumoftoys.com; Triq Ġnien Xibla; adult/child €2.80/1.50; ⊙10.30am-1pm Thu-Sat Apr & Nov, 10.30am-1pm Mon-Sat May-Oct, 10.30am-1pm Sat Dec, Feb & Mar) This small labour of love has an impressive array of 19th-century and 1930s doll's houses, toy soldiers and spooky china dolls, mostly in glass cases. There's a display case devoted to nonsense poet Edward Lear, who coined the word 'pomskizillious' to describe Gozitan scenery.

Ta'Kola Windmill HISTORIC BUILDING
(☑2156 1071; Triq il-Bambina; adult/child €9/5 incl admission to Ġgantija Temples; ⊙9am-5pm) Built in 1725 at the instigation of the Knights, who built many such windmills to encourage the production of flour (this is one of the few left standing), Ta'Kola now houses a cute museum of country life, with displays of tools and living quarters. Best, though, is the climb up the narrow stairs to see the original milling gear, complete with huge millstones.

Calypso's Cave CAVE
Calypso's Cave overlooks the sandy beach of Ramla Bay (p132) – it's a 30-minute walk from the village square. The cave itself is hardly worth the hike – it's just a hollow under an overhang at the top of the cliff – but the views are worthwhile.

On a calm day you can see the remains of an artificial reef extending into the sea. This was part of the defences built by the Knights of St John to prevent attackers landing on the beach. In theory, the enemy ships would run aground on the reef, where they would be attacked using primitive mortar-like weapons.

Lino's Stables HORSE RIDING
(☑2156 2477; www.linostables.com; 16 Triq is-Spiera) These stables offer one-/two-hour horse rides to Marsalforn for €15/30 for both beginners and more experienced riders. Children over 10 may ride their own horses, but younger children ride with their accompanying adult or in a gig. Book in advance.

✖ Eating

Oleander GOZITAN €€
(☑2155 7230; Pjazza Vittorja; mains €7.50-20; ⊙9am-3pm & 6-10pm Tue-Sun) The much-loved Oleander, located on the pretty village square with tables outside, has a menu specialising in Maltese cuisine, with dishes including rabbit cooked in various ways, homemade ravioli with Gozitan cheese, and fresh fish of the day.

D-Venue MEDITERRANEAN €€
(☑7955 7230; www.dvenuerestaurant.com; Pjazza Vittorja; mains €8-20; ⊙noon-3pm & 7-11pm Tue-Sun) D-Venue has blonde-stone arches downstairs, and a great glass-covered terrace on the 1st floor. Food is equally stylish, with choices like spaghetti with prawns and rocket, calamari and rabbit.

ⓘ Getting There & Away

Bus 307 runs between Victoria and Xagħra (35 minutes, hourly). Bus 322 connects the town with Marsalforn (13 minutes, every 1½ hours), Ramla Bay (10 minutes) and Mġarr (25 minutes).

Nadur

POP 3970

Nadur is Gozo's 'second city', spreading along a high ridge to the east of Victoria. In Malti, Nadur means 'lookout', and a 17th-century watchtower overlooks the Comino sea lanes from the western end of the ridge. There's a large market every Wednesday from around 7am to 11am near the church.

◎ Sights

Church of Sts Peter & Paul CHURCH
(Pjazza San Pietru u San Pawl) Nadur's ornate Church of Sts Peter and Paul was built in the late 18th century – the entrance is framed by white statues of the two saints, giving the church its local nickname of iż-Żewġ (the pair). The interior is richly decorated with marble sculptures, and the vault is covered with 150 paintings.

Kelinu Grima Maritime Museum MUSEUM
(☑2156 5226; Triq il-Kappillan; adult/child €2.50/1.25; ⊙9am-4.45pm Mon-Sat) This charming museum contains fascinating ship models, relics and maritime memorabilia, collected over 65 years.

✖ Eating

Nadur is famous for its delicious *ftira* and pizza, sold at the two fantastic bakeries in town. Meals are sold as takeaways, so it's best to call around 30 minutes ahead to order.

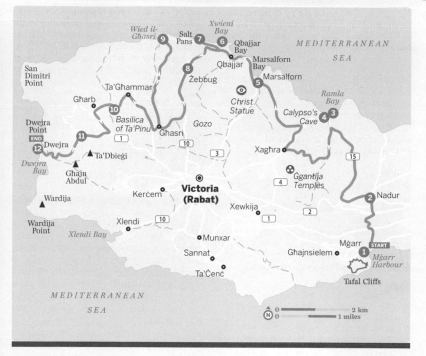

Driving Tour
Northern Gozo

START MĠARR
END DWEJRA
LENGTH 20KM; 1½ HOURS

This drive takes in some of Gozo's loveliest scenery. Begin at the port of **①Mġarr**, then take Triq Sant Antnin uphill towards **②Nadur**, perched on a hilltop and with great views from its modified watchtower. From Nadur, take the road through lovely countryside towards **③Ramla Bay**. When you reach the bay, stop for a look and perhaps a paddle, then on leaving take the first right-hand turn. You'll drive through a landscape of terraced fields and copper-coloured walls. On reaching the next junction, if you take the right-hand fork, you can drive round to **④Calypso's Cave** for a great view over the bay. Next, double back the way you came, taking the second right turn into Triq Tal-Masri, which will lead you down to Gozo's largest (yet still low-key) resort, **⑤Marsalforn**. Drive along the seafront and then take the coastal road. This will lead you to **⑥Xwieni Bay**, which is overlooked by the fabulously wild coast, where **⑦salt pans** are scooped out from the cliffs, and still in use. From here, take the road inland to the village of **⑧Żebbuġ** (the name means 'olives'), which is famous for the onyx found locally (check out the decoration of the Parish church) and for lace-making. Next drive around to visit the breathtaking gorge and bay of **⑨Wied Il-Għasri**. Head back to Għasri village and take Triq il Fanal towards the dramatically isolated pilgrimage **⑩Basilica of Ta'Pinu**. From here, take the road towards the pretty village of **⑪San Lawrenz** before finishing your drive at **⑫Dwejra**, an area featuring some of Gozo's most stunning coastal formations.

Mekrens Bakery PIZZA, BAKERY €

(☑2155 2342; Triq Hanaq; pizza from €4; ⊙4.30am-8pm) This is a great traditional bakery, serving up *ftira* and delicious pizza with all sorts of toppings.

Maxokk Bakery PIZZA, BAKERY €

(☑2155 0014; maxokkbakery.com; Triq San Ġakbu; pizza from €4, ftira €5.50; ⊙10.30am-7pm Mon-Sat, 1-7pm Sun) An excellent bakery, open since the 1930s, selling traditional *ftira* and pizza, freshly baked in a bread oven and with a wide range of toppings.

Anthony's Bar
& Restaurant MEDITERRANEAN €€

(☑2704 2210; 20 Triq Madre Ġ Camilleri; mains €4.50-14.75; ⊙5.30pm-late Wed-Mon) On the pretty square directly behind the church, this is a small, friendly place serving pizza, pasta and Maltese dishes.

❶ Getting There & Away

To get to Nadur, take bus 322, which runs from Mġarr (seven minutes), and goes on to Ramla Bay (eight minutes), Xagħra (18 minutes) and Marsalforn (21 minutes).

Ramla Bay, San Blas Bay & Daħlet Qorrot

◉ Sights

Ramla Bay BEACH

(Ir-Ramla) Ramla Bay is one of the prettiest sandy beaches on Gozo, with red-gold sand. The minimal remains of a Roman villa are hidden among the bamboo behind the beach, and Calypso's Cave (p130) looks down from the hilltop to the west. There's a cafe-restaurant and sunbed/sunshade hire.

Bus 322 travels to Ramla Bay from Mġarr (15 minutes, half-hourly) and on to Xagħra (10 minutes) and Marsalforn (25 minutes). The 302 runs between here and Nadur (five minutes, hourly) and Victoria (30 minutes).

The walk here from Nadur takes between 15 and 20 minutes. The beach is usually heaving with people in summer; it's more tranquil in spring and autumn, and in winter you can have the place almost to your (goose-pimpled) self.

★ San Blas Bay BEACH

San Blas, a tiny, rock-strewn bay with some patches of sand is backed by steep, terraced fields with prickly-pear hedges. There's parking space for only a handful of cars at the beginning of the very narrow track above the bay. It's a steep walk down to it, but you can take a jeep down or up (€2.50 per person).

It's a lovely place to take a picnic lunch and a good book, and perhaps a mask and fins for snorkelling – the water is quite shallow and very clear. You can walk to San Blas from Nadur in about 30 minutes; it's just over 2.5km from town (take Triq San Blas off Triq it-Tiġrija, two blocks north of Nadur's church). Bus 304 heads here every two hours from Victoria (18 minutes), via Nadur (five minutes).

Daħlet Qorrot BEACH

Attractive Daħlet Qorrot is popular with local weekenders. There's a tiny gravel beach, but most of the swimming is off the rocks beside the rows of little boathouses (carved out of the rock, and with brightly painted doors); there's usually plenty of space to park. It's within walking distance of Nadur: from Triq it-Tiġrija, head north for about 300m on Triq San Blas, then take the Triq Daħlet Qorrot turn-off; the bay is just over 2km away.

Qala

The village of Qala (a-la) has little to see except for a couple of 19th-century windmills. The road east of the village square (Triq il-Kunċizzjoni) leads down to the coast at Ħondoq ir-Rummien, a popular swimming cove with a scrap of sand, bathing ladders on the rocks and benches with a view across the water to Comino. There are toilets here and a kiosk catering to sunbathers.

COMINO

Comino (Kemmuna in Malti) is a small, barren chunk of limestone wedged smack-bang between Malta and Gozo. It was once reportedly the hideout of pirates and smugglers, and its remoteness saw it used as a place of isolation for cholera and plague victims in the early 19th century. The almost empty island – there's just one hotel here – is a breathtakingly beautiful place, ringed by caves and sea cliffs. It's home to the Blue Lagoon, one of Malta's loveliest but also most-visited natural attractions. In summer hordes of day trippers descend from Malta and Gozo, but in spring, autumn and winter you'll have a better chance of enjoying the turquoise waters.

Comino is only 2.5km by 1.5km. It's a nature reserve and bird sanctuary, and free of cars. A walk along the rough tracks affords some great views of northern Malta and of Gozo. It's impossible to get lost here.

The main part of the Comino Hotel is on San Niklaw Bay, and the Comino Hotel Bungalows are on Santa Marija Bay, 500m to the east. Triq Congreve, a rough track lined with oleander trees, runs from Santa Marija Bay south to St Mary's Tower. Side tracks lead to the Blue Lagoon and San Niklaw Bay.

The only buildings of note are the stark little **Chapel of Our Lady's Return from Egypt**, built in 1618, at Santa Marija Bay and the fortified **St Mary's Tower** (☑ 2122 5222; www.wirtghawdex.org; admisson €2.50; ☺ 10.30am-3pm Wed, Fri, Sat & Sun Apr-Oct, if flag is flying), built by the Knights in the same year. It was once part of the chain of signal towers between Gozo and Mdina. It may have served as an isolation hospital at some point, and was definitely used to house livestock, but was restored in 2004 and is now open to the public. Climb the steps and enjoy the views.

◉ Sights

Blue Lagoon LAGOON

Comino's biggest draw is the Blue Lagoon, a sheltered cove between the western end of the island and the uninhabited islet of Cominotto (Kemmunett in Malti). It's incredibly beautiful and inviting, with a white-sand seabed and clear waters. The blue is so intense it's as if you've stepped into an oversaturated postcard. The southern end of the lagoon is roped off to keep boats out; there is top-notch swimming and snorkelling here, plus you can swim over to Cominotto.

However, in summer the bay gets incredibly busy, particularly between 10am and 4pm. It's ideal to time your visit for later in the day if possible.

Take care in the unrelenting summer heat – there is no shade, and most sunbathing is done on the exposed rocky ledges surrounding the cove; also be careful of currents here on windy days. There are public toilets and a few kiosks selling cool drinks, ice creams and snacks (burgers, hot dogs and sandwiches). Deckchairs and umbrellas can be hired for extended luxurious lazing about.

❶ Getting There & Away

Numerous companies operate trips to Comino from Mġarr on Gozo. Return tickets for adults/children are around €10/5. Usually the trip includes a quick whiz around the island's caves.

Sightseeing trips operate to the Blue Lagoon from tourist areas like Sliema, Buġibba and Golden Bay in Malta, and Xlendi and Marsalforn in Gozo.

If you'd like to visit the Blue Lagoon from Malta without the crowds, take advantage of the trip leaving at 4pm from Golden Bay with Charlie's Discovery Speedboat Trips (p78).

Accommodation

Best Places to Stay

➡ Casa Ellul (p137)

➡ Valletta Vintage (p136)

➡ Hotel Ta'Ċenċ (p144)

➡ Thirtyseven (p144)

Best Atmospheric Apartments

➡ Palazzo San Pawl (p136)

➡ Valletta Suites (p137)

➡ Indulgence Divine (p138)

➡ Valletta G-House (p136)

Best B&Bs

➡ Mia Casa (p143)

➡ Julesys's B&B (p138)

➡ Nellu'n (p138)

➡ Knights in Malta (p142)

Where to Stay

In the last few years, something unprecedented has happened to Malta's accommodation choices. They've become exciting. As well as the islands' five-star grande dames and quaint family-run guesthouses, these days you can take your pick from bijou designer hotels, apartments and boutique hostels that offer inexpensive yet stylish sleeps.

Valletta, the Three Cities and Gozo have gained some small hotels, B&Bs and apartments so lovely it's tempting not to go out, and more are in the pipeline.

If you're after a beach holiday, your best best is to aim for the main resort towns on the northern coast, such as St Julian's, Buġibba and Mellieħa. Their resort hotels and apartments are often well appointed, sometimes with great sea views, and there are some budget gems.

Another option is to stay inland, where you'll feel more in touch with Maltese culture, in the atmospheric towns of Mdina, Rabat or Naxxar. The accommodation here tends to be small-scale hotels or top-notch B&Bs.

The islands are so small that wherever you base yourself you'll be in easy reach of all the island's destinations.

There are plenty of self-catering options all over Malta and Gozo, including some places in wonderful historic buildings in Valletta and the Three Cities; in Gozo, you can rent converted rustic farmhouses, which usually come with swimming pools and make for a relaxing base.

Pricing

The following price indicators refer to the cost of a double room in high season, including private bathroom and breakfast unless otherwise noted.

CATEGORY	COST
€ budget	less than €60
€€ midrange	€60–€140
€€€ top end	more than €140

Guesthouses

Guesthouses in Malta are usually small, simple, family-run places and are good value at around €30 to €50 per person. Most rooms will have a washbasin, but showers and toilets are often shared. A simple breakfast is normally included in the price. Facilities usually don't include air-con or a swimming pool, but there are a few exceptions. Bear in mind that some guesthouses in resort areas close in the low season.

B&Bs

The B&B is, surprisingly, a new concept in Malta, and there are some lovely examples springing up around the islands, usually with just two or three rooms, excellent attention to detail and delicious breakfasts. There are several great options in the Three Cities, central Malta and on Gozo.

Hostels

A fantastic development in Malta in recent years is the burgeoning number of lovely hostel options clustered in Sliema and St Julian's, usually small scale and with smart, attractive rooms and facilities at very reasonable prices. These are ideally located for students coming here to learn English, but attract a wide mix of tourists and students of all ages, and are sociable, friendly places to stay.

Hotels

Hotels in Malta range from simple seaside options to modern gilt-and-chrome five-star palaces overlooking private marinas. But there is also an increasing number of places to stay in Malta that ooze character and style, including in Valletta and on Gozo.

If you're after a more traditional glitzy large hotel, the main centres for these are the St Julian's and Sliema districts. Most of the large four- and five-star places offer the kind of holiday where you may not need to leave the hotel's grounds – they're fully equipped with cafes, bars and restaurants (most hotels include breakfast in their rates, and some offer half-board and full-board arrangements). At these places you'll usually find indoor and outdoor pools; a gym and/or sporting facilities; a program of children's activities; and quite possibly a health spa, a dive company and perhaps a beachside lido offering a pool and watersports, including water-skiing, boat trips, canoe or boat hire

and ringo rides (large rubber rings towed by speedboats). Three-star hotels vary from swish and contemporary to dated rooms, with bathroom and air-conditioning. Most hotels, big or small, offer free wi-fi.

Malta-specific hotel sites include **Holiday Malta** (www.holiday-malta.com) and **Malta Hotels** (www.malta-hotels.com). **Visit Malta** (www.visitmalta.com) also has lists.

Rental Accommodation

You'll get much more space for your money if you rent self-catering accommodation, and if you're travelling with a family, it's usually much easier (and cheaper) if you have facilities to cook some of your own meals. There are now plentiful gorgeous self-catering apartments on offer in Valletta and the Three Cities.

For the most outdoor space and laid-back holidays, you can rent a farmhouse on Gozo. These are usually several hundred years old and are often beautiful rental properties with swimming pools and garden courtyards. However, although they are usually called 'farmhouses', they are actually townhouses, where livestock were once kept in the basement or outhouse – so don't expect them to be in the open countryside. They're a particularly good option in the height of summer, when a swimming pool to cool off in is a boon. You can also occasionally find characterful self-catering townhouses or apartments on Malta as well, but these don't usually have pools attached.

In the major tourist centres, such as Buġibba or Qawra, there are hundreds of good-value self-catering apartments. Most have a private bathroom, a balcony and a kitchen area with fridge, sink and two-ring electric cooker. They are often excellent value at €30 to €40 per person, even in high season.

High & Low Seasons

The cost of accommodation in Malta can vary considerably according to the time of year, and low-season rates are often a bargain – frequently around half the high-season price. Low season is almost always November to March. High season generally refers to the period April to October, but some accommodation providers have a 'shoulder' or 'mid' season covering April, May and October, with high-season prices restricted to July and August (plus Easter

ACCOMMODATION

and Christmas). Some cheaper places don't vary their prices much across the year

Bear in mind that some establishments (small guesthouses and cheaper hotels) in some resort areas close in the low season. It's also not possible to stay on Comino from November to March.

Often there's a minimum-stay requirement at hotels or guesthouses, of three to seven nights. Some only require this in high season, while for others it's year-round. A few hotels offer discounts for longer stays.

VALLETTA & AROUND

Valletta and the Three Cities across the water have some wonderful places to stay, with a growing selection of bijou boutique hotels that are perfect for romantic sojourns, as well as upmarket antique-decorated apartments.

This is the best place in Malta to be based if you're interested in history and culture, and want easy access to a wide choice of restaurants and a growing selection of bars. However, you're also only around 30 to 40 minutes from a beach if you want to spend a day by the seaside. The main museums and attractions are within easy walking distance, and buses depart from Valletta bus station to all parts of the island. Many places have a minimum stay of three to seven nights, and accept over 5s only.

Valletta

Asti Guesthouse GUESTHOUSE €
(Map p48; ☑ 2123 9506; http://mol.net.mt/asti; 18 Triq Sant'Orsla; r per person with shared bathroom low/high season €25/35; �) This guesthouse is very much old school, in a 350-year-old townhouse, and run by the welcoming, determined and house-proud Mrs Galea. Breakfast is served in a cheery, plant-filled room with a vaulted ceiling and chandelier. Up the stairs on various levels

---

BOOK YOUR STAY ONLINE

For more accommodation reviews by Lonely Planet authors, check out hotels. lonelyplanet.com. You'll find independent reviews, as well as recommendations on the best places to stay. Best of all, you can book online.

---

are eight plain rooms, each with pine wooden furniture and a washbasin. Plants, wall hangings and ornaments give a warm and homely feel. Book ahead.

★**Valletta Vintage** APARTMENT €€
(Map p48; Triq ir-Repubblika; d €130; ✳奈) Three lovely rooms for rent, designed by renowned local architect Chris Briffa, with beautiful use of colour, poured concrete walls, design-classic furniture and restored original features. Each has its own rooftop terrace. Price doesn't include breakfast.

★**Palazzo Prince d'Orange** APARTMENT €€
(Map p48; www.palazzoprincemalta.com; Triq San Pawl; d from €120, 3-night min) Stay in style in this beautiful 17th-century baroque palazzo, which has been converted into suites that merge contemporary with the antique. The most spacious is the Wilhelmina Duplex Penthouse, which has a balcony with sea view, but there's also plenty of room in the Alexander Suite, with harbour views from the bedroom. No under 16s.

★**Valletta G-House** APARTMENT €€
(Map p48; www.vallettahouse.com; Triq it-Tramuntana; apt for 2 low/high season €89/105, 3-night min; 奈) Book ahead to snare time at this splendid apartment (over 20s only; no children). The artistic owner has restored a 16th-century, character-filled townhouse to offer romantic self-catering accommodation. The entrance area doubles as a small sitting room, downstairs is a rustic cellar kitchen and a small bathroom, and upstairs a sumptuous bedroom with a traditional Maltese balcony and striking floor tiles.

Palazzo San Pawl APARTMENT €€
(Map p48; ☑ 9942 3110; www.livinginvalletta.com; 318 Triq San Pawl; d low/high season €95/130, 3-night min; 奈) Housed in a beautiful 17th-century mansion are three graceful suites – 'Hompesch', 'Pinto' (with a Maltese balcony) and ground-floor 'del Monte'. Each has a sitting room and kitchenette. Decor is elegant, ceilings are high, and there's a lift to take you up to the roof terrace for stunning views. The 'Vilhena' suite is next door, with three 12-sq-metre rooms atop each other.

Grand Hotel Excelsior HOTEL €€
(☑ 2125 0520; www.excelsior.com.mt; Triq l-Assedju il-Kbir; r from €95; ✳@奈☲) The Grand lies outside the city walls, tucked beneath the northwestern bastions. It's a curvaceous concrete block; sea-front rooms have bal-

conies with fabulous views over Marsamxett Harbour; the less expensive rooms overlook the gardens or hotel plaza. Rooms are decorated in serene beiges, and the hotel's five-star rating is evident through its staff, service and food.

Grand Harbour Hotel HOTEL €€
(Map p48; ✆2124 6003; www.grandharbour hotel.com; 47 Triq il-Batterija; d €85, with sea view €120; @ ☎) The Grand Harbour Hotel has a great location, with astounding sea views. There are 30 rooms, which have been refurbished, but are nothing flash, though some have more flair than others. However, the view across to the Three Cities cannot be beaten. There's a roof terrace with even more astounding views.

Osborne Hotel HOTEL €€
(Map p48; ✆2124 3656; www.osbornehotel. com; 50 Triq Nofs in-Nhar; s/d low season €50/75, high season €125/135; ✳ @ ☒) The Osborne has a smart, red-shuttered exterior. Standard rooms are decorated with pearly greys and patterns. Superior sea-view rooms are grander, if a bit more old-fashioned, and have great views; deluxe sea-view rooms have recently been refurbished with shiny drapes and arty padded headboards. On the 6th floor there's a roof terrace with city views, and a small plunge pool.

Castille Hotel HOTEL €€
(Map p48; ✆2124 3678; www.hotelcastillemalta.com; Pjazza Kastilja; r €125; ✳ ☎) Castille has cheerful front-desk staff and a grand position in an old palazzo next to the ornate 16th-century Auberge de Castile. The hotel's small lobby and lounge make a good first impression, while guest rooms are dated, with faded charm, imperial blue walls and heavy Italianate furnishings. Ask for a view of the square.

British Hotel HOTEL €€
(Map p48; ✆2122 4730; www.britishhotel.com; 40 Triq il-Batterija; d €80-100; ✳ @ ☎) At the time of research, the public areas here were undergoing refurbishment. The hotel has its pros and cons – on the plus side it's affordable, welcoming and well located; it enjoys great views over the harbour and the Three Cities. The minuses: the rooms are simple and basic, it's a real rabbit warren; and aircon costs €7 per day. It's worth paying extra for a view.

★**Casa Ellul** BOUTIQUE HOTEL €€€
(Map p48; ✆2122 4821; www.casaellul.com; Triq it-Teatru l-Antik; d from €140; ✳ ☎) Converted from a townhouse that was a family home for five generations, Casa Ellul is Valletta's loveliest boutique hotel, with eight rooms beautifully designed by architect Chris Briffa. There are features such as free-standing bathtubs on the traditional Maltese balconies, and jacuzzis on terraces in two of the uppermost newly built rooms on the top floor. Older children only.

Trabuxu Boutique Living BOUTIQUE HOTEL €€€
(Map p48; ✆2122 6196; www.trabuxuboutique living.com; Triq i-Ispar l-Qadim; d low/high season €100/185; ✳ ☎) Nine eclectically decorated rooms, with themes such as an Italian-chic 'Dolce Vita', the Arabian-styled 'Araba', and even the arched cellar room 'Neoltica', surround a sunny courtyard in a 400-year-old house in this fabulous hotel. It's owned by a Maltese couple who have been pioneers in Valletta, running the excellent Trabuxu wine bar and restaurant. Older children only.

There's also a larger penthouse suite with its own entrance.

Valletta Suites – Maison La Vallette APARTMENT €€€
(Map p48; ✆7948 8047; www.vallettasuites. com; Triq San Patrizju; apt per night €132-158, 3-night min; ☎) Beautifully designed Valletta Suites have a few options around the city in boutique one-bedroom apartments, with plenty of style, antiques and all mod cons. Maison La Vallette is in a lovely 400-year-old townhouse, and handily located for both central Valletta and the Sliema ferry.

Valletta Suites – Valletta Nobile APARTMENT €€€
(Map p48; ✆7948 8047; www.vallettasuites. com; Triq San Nikola; apt per night €132-158, 3-night min; ☎) One of Valletta Suites' beautiful, boutique one-bedroom apartments, Valletta Nobile is in the northeast of Valletta, and is in a historic, wood-beamed house filled with antiques. It's furnished with style, and has a balcony with a view along Triq il-Merkanti.

Valletta Suites – Lucia Nova APARTMENT €€€
(Map p48; ✆7948 8047; www.lucianova.com; 88 Triq Santa Luċija; 2-4 people €158, 3-night min; ✳ ☎) Lucia Nova offers a large apartment with two double bedrooms, sitting room and roof terrace. Each room is atop the other, and all are connected by a traditional Maltese spiral stone staircase. The decor

is a thrilling mix of distressed original wall coverings, Philippe Starck chairs and silk Venetian headboards.

Floriana

Phoenicia Hotel HOTEL €€€
(Map p48; ☑ 2122 5241; www.phoeniciamalta. com; Il-Mall; r from €190; ❋ @ ☎) Just outside Valletta's main gate, this 1940s old grande dame feels like the kind of place Miss Marple might stay if she were in town, with its potted palms and art deco piano bar. The hotel is due to close for a €15-million refurbishment from November 2015 to April 2016. A higher rate gets you views of Marsamxett Harbour or Valletta's city walls.

In 1949, Princess Elizabeth (soon to be queen) and Prince Philip danced in the ballroom here.

Facilities include 24-hour room service, free parking, a business centre, lush 3-hectare gardens, a heated outdoor pool, a bar, and excellent brasserie and restaurant.

Vittoriosa, Senglea & Cospicua (the Three Cities)

Knight's Quarter RENTAL HOUSE €
(Map p60; ☑ 2137 0830; 8 Triq Gilormu; house (up to 4 people) €120; ☎) This lovely little house in Birgu's most photographed street has two bedrooms, a living room, a dining room with kitchenette and a roof terrace with sunbeds, barbecue and a sea view. There's underfloor heating, a washing machine and a tumble dryer, and the walls are decked with original artworks from local artists or international artists with a Maltese theme. Book ahead.

★Nelli's B&B €€
(☑ 7958 8897; s/d €65/90; ❋ ☎) This charming Belgian-run B&B has blue-shuttered windows right on the waterfront, with four harmonious, beautifully pared-down guest rooms featuring pale limestone walls and paintings, and walk-in showers in their en suites. A glorious breakfast is served on the roof terrace on the 4th floor overlooking the harbour.

Indulgence Divine APARTMENT €€
(Map p60; ☑ in UK +44 781 3988827; www.indulgencedivine.com; Triq Allesandru VII; apt low/high season €84/119, 5-7-night min; ☎) This sump-tuous and historic self-catering apartment (no children) is a romantic base, and you get lots of space for your money. It's a 16th-century townhouse for two that's been decorated with flamboyant shots of colour. It comprises a funky white-and-orange kitchen, a dining area with a pale blue Murano glass chandelier, a coolly minimalist living room and a sunny roof terrace.

★Julesys's B&B B&B €€€
(Map p60; ☑ 9995 3465; Julesysbnb.com; 105 Triq San Gorg; r low/high season €129/149; ❋ ☎) A topnotch B&B in an 18th-century townhouse in the local-feeling backstreets of Cospicua, this place is run by an Australian couple with Maltese heritage. There are two stone-walled rooms upstairs, one with lift access. There's a wine cellar housed in the 500-year-old cistern. Julie is a chef; she cooks gourmet breakfasts (the pancakes are renowned) and offers cooking lessons.

There's a roof terrace, and Roxy the labrador gives a warm welcome.

SLIEMA, ST JULIAN'S & PACEVILLE

Sliema is the quieter and more residential of these areas, and it has a bevy of gorgeous new hostel options that are very much at the boutique end of the spectrum, not party palaces for those in their teens and twenties, but catering to all ages. Both Sliema and St Julian's also have some grand five-star and midrange options. There's access to the rocky beach along Sliema's seafront from here. If you stay in St Julian's or Paceville you're nearer to the small sandy beach, and these districts form Malta's gastronomic and nightlife centre.

Sliema

★Hostel 94 HOSTEL €
(Map p68; ☑ 9949 7519; hostel94.com; 94 Triq Isouard; dm €16-18, d €35-80; ☎) In a converted townhouse on a quiet, residential Sliema backstreet, this is a fabulous, bright, fresh hostel, with a choice of male- or female-only dorms with sparkling bathrooms or two wellpriced double rooms, one of which has a balcony. There's a white-walled, fresh communal space downstairs and a kitchen where you can cook.

★**Hostel Jones** HOSTEL €

(Map p68; ☑9932 0003; maltahostel.com; Triq Adrian Dingli; dm €20-24, d €50-60) This is Sliema's most imaginative place to stay, a hostel decorated by local artists, with rooms called things like 'Tree', 'the Speech', 'Explosion' (covered in splattered paint) and the trippy 'Mush Room' where the murals glow in the dark; the bargain double is the romantic 'Lovers' Room'. There are original tiled floors and cool communal areas, including a kitchen and roof terrace.

Regular barbecues and yoga are a plus.

★**Corner Hostel** HOSTEL €

(Map p68; ☑2780 2780; www.cornerhostelmalta.com; 6 Triq Santa Margerita; dm low/high season €13/21, d €32/48; ❄🖥) Bright, breezy and sociable, Corner Hostel receives excellent reports. It has clean, small-scale mixed, male and female dorms, with funky 1970s duvet covers and peach or pale green walls, and double rooms in a converted townhouse, with colourfully tiled traditional floors. There's a rooftop where you can hang your washing, and a lift.

Two Pillows Hostel HOSTEL €

(Map p68; ☑2131 7070; www.twopillowsmalta.com; 49 Triq San Piju V; dm low/high season €16.50/25, studios €62/110; ❄🖥) A boutique hostel in a beautifully converted 300-year-old Maltese townhouse, bright and sparkling clean, with multiple small dorms (sleeping three to six) with flagstone walls and beamed ceilings. There is also a selection of open-plan studio apartments, which are themed by colour but mainly decorated in white with only flashes of the appropriate hue; several have sea views or terraces.

NSTS Hibernia Residence & Hostel HOSTEL €

(Map p68; ☑2558 8340; www.nsts.org; Triq Mons G Depiro; dm €10-15, s/d studio €30/40; @) Amid all of Sliema's new boutique hostels, Hibernia is looking left behind: it's institutionalised and old-fashioned. However, it proffers budget accommodation and a ready-made crowd (it's popular with English-language students). Shoestringers can camp out in the single-sex dorm sections, where three to four bedrooms (each with six to eight beds) share bathrooms and a generous kitchen-dining area.

The National Student Travel Service (p170), an associate member of Hostelling International (HI), operates this place.

Imperial Hotel HOTEL €€

(Map p68; ☑2134 4093; www.imperialhotelmalta.com; Triq Rudolfu; d low/high season €72/100; ❄🖥🖥) Things move slowly at the Imperial, in keeping with the old-world interior (dating from 1865) and vintage patrons. The lobby's chandelier and grand sweeping staircase impress. The rooms don't quite live up to the expectations raised by downstairs, but they're furnished by wrought-iron beds and are comfortable (you'll pay more for a garden/pool view and a balcony).

Pebbles ApartHotel APARTMENT €€

(Map p68; ☑2131 1889; www.pebblesaparthotel.com; 89 Triq ix-Xatt; d low/high season €48/120; ❄@🖥) This complex of 93 great-value studio apartments, decorated in cool greys and whites, is handy for the bus terminus and the ferry to Valletta. The apartments are not for the claustrophobic – don't expect a lot of living space: all studios have a private bathroom, kitchenette, phone and flatscreen cable TV. Pay a bit more for a sea view.

Preluna Hotel & Spa HOTEL €€

(Map p68; ☑2133 4001; www.preluna-hotel.com; 124 Triq it-Torri; d low/high season from €45/90; ❄@🖥🖥) This tall building offers sweeping views along the coast, and rooms are small but bright and fresh with touches of colour. Facilities are exhaustive (health spa, private beachfront lido, dive school and a choice of bars and restaurants). The extra cost for a sea view and balcony is worth it.

Palace Hotel HOTEL €€€

(Map p68; ☑2133 3444; www.thepalacemalta.com; Triq il-Kbira; r from low/high season €105/230; ❄@🖥🖥) Palace Hotel has a swish designer lobby and rooms that are pleasant, comfortable and decorated in neutral colours. For something a bit more out-there, try the concept suites, including the Music Suite with a drum kit. Facilities include a luxurious spa with indoor pool, and a roof terrace with outdoor pool and a superb view across the Sliema rooftops to Valletta's bastions.

Waterfront Hotel HOTEL €€€

(Map p68; ☑2133 3434; www.waterfronthotelmalta.com; Triq ix-Xatt; r low/high season from €70/150; ❄🖥🖥) The bright and breezy Waterfront has a nautically themed lobby, blue-and-white rooms and a rooftop pool and terrace with excellent panoramas across the harbour. Plus it's in a nice location on the Sliema waterfront. It's worth paying the €10 or so extra for a sea-view room.

ACCOMMODATION SLIEMA

Victoria Hotel
HOTEL €€€

(Map p68; ☎2133 4711; www.victoriahotel.
com; Triq Ġorġ Borg Olivier; r low/high season from
€76/200; ❄@🛜⊠) This hotel's lobby and
bar are full of dark wood and leather club
sofas – it's not exactly Victorian, but the
thought is there. Some rooms are equipped
with mahogany furniture, some with pale-
blue painted wood. The hotel is in a quiet location away from the seafront, and features
a rooftop pool, plus a small indoor pool on
the 7th floor.

St Julian's

Hostel Malti
HOSTEL €

(☎2730 2758; www.hostelmalti.com; 31 Birkirkara;
6-8-bed dm €12, 12-bed dm €10) Aimed squarely
at fun-loving backpackers, this is a sociable,
cheery hostel; a great place to meet people
and have a laid-back time. Lots of events,
barbecues and parties keep this feeling
like a happening place, and there are even
jacuzzis.

Boho Hostel
HOSTEL €

(☎2765 6008; www.bohohostel.com; Villa Cycas,
Triq Dun G Xerri; dm low/high season €10/22) In
a converted villa south of St Julian's, this
feels like the kind of enlightened place
you might find on the backpacker trail in
Southeast Asia – a fun place to stay, with
lots of laid-back attitude, a bamboo-framed
garden terrace with hanging chair, and
brightly painted dorms (and one double)
looking onto the garden.

★Hotel Juliani
BOUTIQUE HOTEL €€

(Map p72; ☎2138 8000; www.hoteljuliani.com;
12 Triq San Ġorġ; d low/high season from €70/120;
❄🛜⊠) This 44-room boutique hotel is in
a lovely restored seafront townhouse with a
great setting overlooking Spinola Bay. It has
chic guest rooms decorated in fresh sea-blue
hues and equipped with large flatscreen
TVs. It's worth paying extra for a more spacious room with a sea view (these come with
a jacuzzi), but there's no beating the views
from the rooftop pool and terrace.

There's an excellent restaurant, Zest
(p71), and a cafe.

Corinthia Hotel St George's Bay
HOTEL €€€

(☎2137 4114; www.corinthia.com; St George's Bay;
s/d €160/280; ❄🛜⊠) The Corinthia is an
iconic Maltese brand, and this is one of the
islands' classic hotels, with sea views from

most of the bedrooms, three pools and an
excellent spa, plus a private rocky beach.

Paceville

★Hotel Valentina
HOTEL €€

(Map p72; ☎2138 2232; www.hotelvalentina.
com; Triq Schreiber; d low/high season €56/120;
❄🛜) This is a small and appealing choice
tucked away in a relatively quiet Paceville
backstreet. Rooms have a jazzy contemporary look, with lots of pale grey and white,
and geometric patterns. The bright, contemporary lobby has a small, buzzing cafe.

Ir-Rokna Hotel
HOTEL €€

(Map p72; ☎2138 4060; www.roknahotel.com;
Triq il-Knisja; d low/high season €32/77; ❄🛜)
Stay within spitting distance of the glitzy
Portomaso marina, but a long way from
the Hilton price tag. You're also close to
the nightlife, but far enough away from the
noise. Ir-Rokna is decent value, with plain,
unfussy rooms with balconies overlooking
the busy square. Service is friendly and
the hotel is home to Malta's oldest pizzeria
(mains €7 to €10).

George Hotel
DESIGN HOTEL €€€

(Map p72; ☎2011 1000; www.thegeorgehotel
malta.com; Triq Paceville; r low/high season
€90/180; ❄🛜) A swish, well-designed place
that feels more like a designer urban hotel
than a seaside holiday locale, the George
Hotel attracts holidaymakers and business travellers for its serene, contemporary
rooms with iPod docks and access to the
spiffing spa. It's a great location in the heart
of Paceville, and excellent double glazing
blocks out the party noise from outside.

NORTHWEST MALTA

The resorts of Malta's northwest coast offer
a massive array of holiday accommodation,
and this is where you'll find Malta's most
competitivly priced budget hotels. Hotels
range from massive edifices with multiple
pools and facilities, to small family-run places
with a more intimate feel.

Golden Bay

Radisson Blu Resort & Spa
HOTEL €€€

(☎2000 1000; www.radissonblu.com; r €300/370;
❄@🛜⊠) The Radisson is a huge edifice

dominating one of Malta's loveliest beaches. It's a three-tower, 10-storey hotel with 329 rooms and chock-full of facilities. The 35-sq-metre 'Serene' deluxe rooms are welcoming; they're decorated in soothing sea colours, and fluffy robes, fancy toiletries and buffet breakfast are provided.

If you can afford it, fork out for a sea view, but it'll cost you around €70 more. The 'Zenith collection' comprises one-bedroom suites with a separate lounge, which are a wonderfully roomy 70 sq metres. All are great for families.

Mellieħa

Splendid Guesthouse GUESTHOUSE €
(Map p80; ☎2152 3602; www.splendidmalta.com; Triq il-Kappillan Magri; per person from €20, apt from €35; ❄@) This pleasant, pink-hued 14-room guesthouse is at the southern end of town in a residential area, a few minutes' walk from the main street. The spick-and-span guest rooms have plain, no-frills furnishings, private shower and washbasin (some have full en suite); there are a few apartments.

The friendly owners also have self-catering apartments available, and a large villa sleeping up to 10 people (€1300 to €2000 per week).

Maritim Antonine Hotel & Spa HOTEL €€
(Map p80; ☎2152 0923; www.maritim.com.mt; Triq Ġorġ Borg Olivier; d €70-170; ❄@🛜≋) The glossy Antonine dominates the main street in the middle of Mellieħa, with some sweeping views from its higher balconies, either over the pool or down towards the coast. Rooms and suites are decorated in soothing neutrals, each with balcony and satellite TV. There are restaurants, a health spa, a rooftop pool and sun terrace, and lovely lush gardens with a large pool.

Pergola Club Hotel HOTEL €€
(Map p80; ☎2152 3912; www.pergolahotel.com.mt; Triq Adenau; r from €16/106 low/high season, 2-person studio low/high season €32/120, 4-person apt low/high season €44/131; ❄@🛜≋) Pergola, across the bridge from Mellieħa's main road, offers comfortable, neutrally decorated hotel rooms and self-catering apartments (entry is at the top of the steps). The views from the sun terraces towards the church are lovely. There is also a health spa, an indoor pool, two outdoor pools and a children's splash pool, as well as a kids' play area.

Buġibba, Qawra & St Paul's Bay

Buccaneers Guesthouse GUESTHOUSE €
(Map p86; ☎2157 1671; www.buccaneers.com.mt; Triq Ġulju; r per person €20; ❄🛜≋) This friendly, family-run guesthouse is central and nicely small-scale, with just 30 rooms, and is surprisingly decent at a bargain price. Rooms are clean and well equipped – all with phone, private shower and washbasin (toilets are shared). There's a sun terrace on the roof with a pool that resembles an oversized paddling pool, and a lively bar and restaurant downstairs.

Sea View Hotel HOTEL €
(Map p86; ☎2157 3105; www.seaviewmaltahotel.com; cnr Dawret il-Gżejjer & Triq il-Imsell; r per person low/high season €18.50/30; ≋) Small-fry in comparison to the big boys in town, this cheap and cheerful hotel is on the promenade northeast of Misraħ il-Bajja and is open year-round. It's home to tiny, rather basic rooms (with fans, no air-con), but all have balconies, and there's a small pool, too, with terrace and bar, and pleasantly leafy surroundings.

Gillieru Harbour Hotel HOTEL €
(Map p86; ☎2157 2720; www.gillieru.com; Triq il-Knisja; r per person low/high season €25/35; ❄🛜≋) This small hotel on St Paul's Bay offers value for money, with decent rooms and a good pool and terrace above the restaurant. It's well located between Buġibba and St Paul's Bay. Upgrading to a sea view is worth it.

Sunseeker Holiday Complex APARTMENT €
(Map p86; ☎2157 5619; www.sunseekerholidaycomplex.com; Trejqet il-Kulpara; low/high season studio flat per person €26/50, 2-bed apt per person €39/77; ❄🛜≋) Tucked one block back from the waterfront in a quietish location, this central complex has indoor and outdoor pools, a gym, a sauna, a jacuzzi and a handy minimarket. On offer are one-, two- and three-bedroom self-catering apartments; all have ceiling fans, kitchenette and lounge area. Breakfast, a safety deposit box, and TV cost extra, and air-con is available in summer.

Apartments sleep up to seven, with families in mind.

db San Antonio Hotel & Spa
HOTEL €€€

(Map p86; ☑2158 3434; www.dbhotelsresorts.com/dbsanantonio; Triq it-Turisti; r low/high season from €100/180; ✱@☀) With a Med-themed whitewashed exterior and a colourful, light-filled lobby, this is one of Buġibba's best hotels, and has recently undergone a thorough refurb. The high standards carry through to the restaurants, the pool, the Moroccan-style spa and the garden areas. Standard rooms are kitted out in breezy blue, white and turquoise; deluxe ones have a low-key beige-and-white look but some great views.

Dolmen Resort Hotel
HOTEL €€€

(Map p86; ☑2355 2355; www.dolmen.com.mt; Triq il-Merluzz; r low/high season from €50/190; ✱@☀) This huge, plush waterfront hotel has the unusual combination of a casino *and* its own prehistoric temple on the grounds. Rooms are lush yet pleasingly plain, and some have great ocean views (worth the extra cost). Creature comforts include four outdoor swimming pools (one solely for kids), sports facilities, a spa and beach club.

Seashells Resort at Suncrest
HOTEL €€€

(Map p86; ☑2157 7101; www.suncresthotel.com; Dawret il-Qawra; d low/high season €92/150; ✱@☀☀) This 453-room hotel takes up a stretch of the Qawra waterfront facing Salina Bay. Rooms have been recently refurbished, the facilities are excellent and the clientele is diverse. There are plenty of restaurants, bars and a nightclub, and guests have free use of swimming pools, beachside lidos and a summer watersports centre.

CENTRAL MALTA

If you want to feel like you're staying in the real, local Malta, look inland. There are some fine choices here, with a particularly good selection of upmarket B&Bs, and the settings are usually glorious buildings that are several hundred years old. The advantages of staying in central Malta are also its local, untouristed feel and the sense of being off the beaten track, while you're actually in easy reach of everywhere (as you're never far from anywhere in Malta).

Mdina

Point de Vue Guesthouse & Restaurants
GUESTHOUSE €€

(Map p96; ☑2145 4117; www.pointdevuemalta.com; 5 Is-Saqqajja; low/high season d €70/85, large d €85/100; @) This guesthouse scores goals with a combination of affordable rates and a privileged position, just metres from the walled city. Rooms range from medium to huge, and are simply furnished, with tiled floors, whitewashed walls and white bed linen. Go for the larger rooms, which have covered balconies and are much better.

★ Xara Palace
HOTEL €€€

(Map p96; ☑2145 0560; www.xarapalace.com.mt; Misraħ il-Kunsill; r €120-200; ✱☀) This 17th-century palazzo contains 17 soft-hued duplex suites filled with antiques and original artworks; some have fabulous views. The rooftop fine-dining restaurant De Mondion (p95), with sweeping views, is considered by many to be Malta's best restaurant.

Rabat

★ Maple Farm Bed & Breakfast
B&B €€

(www.maplefarmbedandbreakfast.com; Triq il-Buskett; s/d €65/85; ☀) Just on the outskirts of Rabat, within walking distance of Mdina and the lovely wooded area of Buskett Gardens, this B&B is a fabulous choice, with a pool, gardens and sparkling-clean, simple double and twin rooms with garden views.

Casa Melita
RENTAL HOUSE €€

(Map p96; ☑7958 0800; 39 Triq Melita; per week low/high season €450/550; ☀) This restored townhouse sleeps six, and is on a lovely little pedestrianised lane. Facilities (including a kitchen and two bathrooms) are basic, and the house can feel damp outside summer months, but it's reasonably comfortable. The best thing about staying here is the location in the heart of Rabat, with its local feel. Wi-fi is available on request (at an extra charge).

Naxxar

★ Knights in Malta
B&B €€

(☑2143 2636; www.knightsinmalta.com; 138 Triq Santa Luċija; s/d from €60/70; ☀) This lovely guesthouse in a 17th century house, centred on a traditional courtyard, has airy rooms that have plenty of character. It's set in the historic centre of Naxxar, which has a few good restaurants. Best of all is the Grand Master suite, with a grand canopy over the bed. There's a sun terrace and jacuzzi.

Chapel 5 Suites B&B €€
(✍2757 7555; www.bedandbreakfast-Malta.com; Souq 5, Triq Santa Luċija; r €80-100; ❄🌐✉) Run by a welcoming couple who work in aviation, this place has five rooms in a converted townhouse set in central Naxxar, with Indonesian and Moroccan furniture and flagstone floors and walls. There's a great buffet breakfast served in the central dining room. They're due to add another five rooms next door.

The Three Villages

University Residence STUDENT ACCOMMODATION €
(✍2143 6168; www.universityresidence.com; Triq RM Bonnici; per person shared 2-bed dm €14-18, s €28-36; @🌐✉) The University of Malta's official student residence, 200m north of the San Anton Gardens, is 4km away from the centre of town and connected by a free bus service. It's a well-equipped, well-run facility offering two-bed rooms in eightroom townhouses, and is a good place to meet local and international students.

Beware, though, that securing shortterm accommodation here can be tough (especially from June to September).

Corinthia Palace Hotel HOTEL €€€
(✍2144 0301; www.corinthia.com; Vjal de Paule; r low/high season from €105/170; ❄@🌐✉) The grand old five-star Corinthia Palace, close to the San Anton Gardens, is a lovely grand mansion, and has plenty of grande dame atmosphere. It appeals to an older crowd who enjoy the discreet location, lush gardens, health spa and upmarket on-site restaurants. All rooms have a decent-sized balcony – request a pool view.

SOUTHEAST MALTA

Fewer foreign tourists stay in southeast Malta, and there's a sense of being off the beaten track. Marsaxlokk may be rammed on Sundays, but the rest of the week it's much less busy, and makes for a lovely harbourside base.

Marsaxlokk

★**Port View Guesthouse** B&B €
(✍9907 6004; portview.com; Triq il-Luzzu; d from €50) Carmel Azzopardi and his son Andrew run this smart, modern B&B that's set back from the harbour, with large rooms decorated with touches of blue, some with sea views. The rooftop breakfast terrace has a view over the harbour.

★**Quayside Apartments** APARTMENT €€
(✍9947 8225; www.quaysidemalta.com; Xatt is-Sajjieda; s/d/tr/q from €50/65/75/85; ❄🌐) With a set of different brightly coloured doors in the old harbourside building that looks ready to star in a paint commercial, Quayside Apartments are a row of studio apartments, with stone walls and beams, and doors that open directly onto the seafront. There's a patio garden at the back.

Duncan Guesthouse GUESTHOUSE €€
(✍2165 7212; www.duncanmalta.com; 33 Xatt is-Sajjieda; d €60-70; ❄🌐) Friendly Duncan's is above bustling Duncan Bar & Restaurant on the waterfront, and the spacious, aqua-hued guest rooms come in family-friendly configurations. They're well kitted out for lengthy stays, each with a sitting area, TV, small balcony and kitchenette. There's a rooftop sun terrace – the perfect vantage point for sundowner drinks and harbour-watching.

GOZO & COMINO

If you fancy slowing the pace down, take the 25-minute ferry trip to Gozo and over to another world. Malta's little sister moves at a slower pace, and it's a good plan to spend at least a few days here, or base yourself here for most of your holiday. When the sun is shining (which it reputedly does for over 300 days per year), there's plenty to do here, and it's an excellent choice for self-catering accommodation, as well as some lovely hidden-away B&Bs, and small and five-star hotels.

Victoria (Rabat)

★**Mia Casa** B&B €
(Map p119; ✍2730 0169; 23 Triq Santa Marija; d or tw €50-80) A fabulous deal, with three gorgeous rooms in a beautifully converted historic Gozo townhouse, which include

Maltese antiques and beautifully tiled floors and flagstone walls. One room has a balcony over the street. Children are not permitted.

Downtown Hotel HOTEL €€
(Map p119; ☑2210 8000; www.downtown.com.mt; Triq I-Ewropa; d low/high season €65/80; 🌣@🌊) Victoria's sole hotel offers bright, fuss-free, if uninspiring, rooms with respectable three-star amenities (cable TV, hairdryer, minibar). There's a family-friendly feel, with a rooftop pool (with magic views), soft-play kids club and bowling alley. From May to October there's a free bus service to Gozo beaches.

Mġarr

Grand Hotel HOTEL €€
(☑2156 3840; www.grandhotelmalta.com; Triq Sant'Antnin; s/d from €80/120; 🌣@🛜🌊) There's only one hotel in Mġarr – the butterscotch-bright, four-star Grand Hotel, which has a fine position overlooking the harbour. It has bright, airy, elegant rooms, and extensive facilities including a sauna, gym, games room, restaurant and cocktail bar. Its least expensive rooms have no view; from these it's a small step up to a 'country view' room.

Sea-view rooms with balcony or terrace are a worthwhile investment.

Ta'Ċenċ

★ **Hotel Ta'Ċenċ** HOTEL €€€
(☑2155 6819; www.tacenchotel.com; Triq Ta-Ċenċ; d €170-190; 🌣@🌊) Lovely, upmarket Ta'Ċenċ hides in 160 hectares on a remote clifftop plateau just east of Sannat; Brad Pitt and Angelina Jolie took it over for five months when filming *By the Sea* on Gozo. Built out of local stone, the simple, stylish rooms are housed in *trulli* (cone-shaped buildings). There are landscaped gardens, two outdoor pools and a rocky private beach, with a beautifully set restaurant.

Munxar

★ **Thirtyseven** GUESTHOUSE €€€
(☑2720 0069; www.thirtysevengozo.com; r €140-250, 3-night min; 🛜🌊) This stylish, rustic place has 10 rooms set around sunny courtyards in two adjoining farmhouses in one of Gozo's quietest villages. It's owned and run by a couple who used to work in the Milanese fashion scene – the decor combines exposed flagstone walls and floors with original artworks, one-off wallpapers and statement furniture.

GOZITAN FARMHOUSES

One of the best accommodation options for a stay on Gozo, especially if you're looking for a little local colour and rustic charm, is to rent a farmhouse. Gozo's farmhouses are in the villages, rather than set in open countryside – houses where farmers kept livestock on the ground floor. Dozens of these old, square-set buildings have been converted into accommodation, and many retain the beautiful stone arches, wooden beams and flagstone floors of their original construction (some are up to 400 years old). Most rental properties are very well equipped with everything you'll need for an easy holiday, including lush kitchens, a swimming pool, outdoor terrace and barbecue, laundry facilities and cable TV. They can sleep from two to 16 people, so are perfect for families or groups of friends, and the costs are very reasonable – from around €750 per week for two people in the high season (most high-season rentals are weekly), or from €60 per night for two people in the low season.

The farmhouses are usually inland in pretty, slow-paced villages. Almost anyone with a guesthouse or hotel on the island can arrange a farmhouse for visitors. The following websites specialise in these kind of properties:

➨ www.farmhousegozo.com

➨ www.gozo.com/gozodirectory/farmhouses.php

➨ www.gozofarmhouses.com

➨ www.facebook.com/il.Pellikan.Holiday.House

Each farmhouse has its own outdoor pool. Patti and Giuseppe offer lots of local information, and meals, cooking courses and trips in their vintage speedboat (around €200) are available.

Xlendi

St Patrick's Hotel   HOTEL €
(2156 2951; www.stpatrickshotel.com; Xatt ix-Xlendi; s €28-60, d €44-72; ※@☲) On the Xlendi waterfront is the friendly St Patrick's, with attractive, well-equipped rooms. The cheaper rooms face a pleasant-enough internal courtyard; the next step up sees larger rooms with a balcony and views over the town car park and valley beyond (it's worth paying more for the ones with sea views). The rooftop terrace has a spa and pool.

San Antonio Guesthouse   GUESTHOUSE €€
(2156 3555; www.clubgozo.com.mt; Triq it-Torri; s/d from €45/55; ※☎☲) This lovely, leafy guesthouse is a fair climb up the hill on the south side of Xlendi Bay. The 13 rooms are good value, large, bright and spotless, with chunky pine furniture and balconies/terraces. There's a garden, a nice swimming pool (with views) and a kiddies' pool. For optimum views, request a pool-facing room on the 1st floor.

San Andrea Hotel   HOTEL €€
(2156 5555; www.hotelsanandrea.com; Xatt ix-Xlendi; d low/high season from €26/38; ※) This little hotel with a great location on the Xlendi waterfront has plenty of sunny rooms with balconies looking out to sea (€14 extra). Rooms are unexciting, but made by the views, and are small but comfortable.

San Lawrenz

★Kempinski Hotel San
Lawrenz   HOTEL €€€
(2211 0000; www.kempinski.com; Triq ir-Rokon; d around €200; ※@☲) The Kempinski, close to the wondrous coastline around Dwejra, is a swish hideaway set in lush, palm-shaded landscaped grounds. Rooms are warmly decorated in polished wood and make use of smooth, pale, local limestone. Staff are obliging and there is a wealth of facilities, including a spa with *hammam*, and restaurants where ingredients come from the organic garden.

Marsalforn

Lantern Guesthouse   GUESTHOUSE €
(Map p127; 2155 6285; www.gozo.com/lantern; Triq il-Mungbell; r per person €25-30; ※) The Lantern is a cosy guesthouse with clean, homely rooms, all with en suite, cable TV and fridge (air-con available at extra charge). The friendly owners can also hook you up with reasonably priced apartments around town.

★Maria-Giovanna
Guesthouse   GUESTHOUSE €€
(Map p127; 2155 3630; www.gozohostels.com; cnr Triq il-Mungbell & Triq ir-Rabat; s/d from €50/80; @) This place has 15 rooms, each decorated in rustic style, with funky cast-iron or wooden beds, polished wooden furniture and colourful linen and rugs. Guests have use of the hostel's kitchen, dining area, courtyard and TV lounge.

It's run by helpful twin sisters who live across the road; they can arrange all sorts of extras (for a small fee): laundry, home-cooked local meals, taxi service and a water taxi to Comino.

Calypso Hotel   HOTEL €€€
(Map p127; 2156 2000; www.hotelcalypsogozo.com; Triq il-Port; low/high season s from €60/90, d from €85/145; ※@☎☲) The Calypso is a custard-coloured Maltese building on Marsalforn's waterfront with 100 smart, bright rooms hued in warm blues. There's a handful of on-site restaurants, cafes and a sweet shop, plus a diving school, and a lovely pool, bar and sun terrace on the roof.

Xagħra

Xagħra Lodge   GUESTHOUSE €
(Map p129; 2156 2362; gozo.com/xaghralodge; Triq Dun Gorg Preca; d €50-60; ※☲) This old-school homely guesthouse is in a quiet neighbourhood, and run by a friendly English couple. The rooms feel as though you could be in a nice British B&B. It's good value, with cable TV and balconies, a flowering garden with pool and aviary, and an adjacent bar and Chinese restaurant. Located a five-minute walk east of the town square.

Cornucopia Hotel   HOTEL €€
(2155 6486; www.galahotels.com; Triq Gnien Imrik; d €70-120, bungalow or farmhouse €130-150; ※@☎☲) Cornucopia and its copious

accommodation options are set in and around a converted farmhouse about 1km north of the village square. Four-star accommodation is available in its 48 hotel rooms and suites arranged around a courtyard, pool and pretty garden, or in self-catering villas, bungalows, apartments and farmhouses. Request a valley view for sweeping countryside vistas.

Nadur

★Quaint Boutique Hotel   BOUTIQUE HOTEL €

(☑2210 8500; www.quainthotelsgozo.com; Triq 13 Dec St; r from €55) The first of what promises to be a four-hotel chain across Gozo, this place is in a historic 19th-century building sympathetically converted in contemporary style, with bargain 'comfort' rooms, duplex and penthouse suites with terraces. Downstairs is the Fat Rabbit restaurant, for breakfast.

Qala

Ferrieha Farmhouse   GUESTHOUSE €€

(☑2155 3819; www.ferriehafarmhouse.com; d €70-80; ☎☒) This large house, perched on a hilltop, is built in traditional style, with lots of space and fantastic views over the sea and over to Comino. There are four spacious guest rooms, all with sandstone walls, views and a great pool and splash pool. The Swedish owners have also installed a wood-heated sauna in an outhouse.

Comino

Comino Hotels   HOTEL €€€

(☑2152 9821; www.cominohotel.com; half-board d low/high season from €50/180, 3-night min, full-board/sea-view supplement €14/8; ✳@☒) This old-fashioned four-star hotel is the only place to stay and eat (guests only) on the island. It has 95 rooms at San Niklaw Bay and 46 bungalows at Santa Marija Bay, but no self-catering options. Bungalows are a larger option than the hotel rooms, with a sitting area. It's open Easter to October only.

By day there are hotel-organised activities (at additional cost) to occupy your time – the most popular is scuba diving, taking advantage of Comino's excellent dive sites. Instruction and courses for beginners, experienced divers and kids are available through the hotel's dive school.

Other diversions include a private beach (in San Niklaw Bay), swimming pools, tennis courts, bikes and watersports (including rental of windsurfing equipment, canoes, and sailing and motor boats). There are also boat excursions. Or you can simply recharge your batteries in your bright, bland but perfectly adequate room (featuring air-con, phone, cable TV, fridge and balcony).

Day trippers can use the hotel's facilities for €47 a day, but this must be booked in advance through the hotel. The price includes a buffet lunch, return boat ticket and use of the pool and private beach. Casual visitors might like to escape the Blue Lagoon and dine at the cafe or buy a drink at the bar.

Understand Malta & Gozo

Malta & Gozo Today

Malta is a microcosm of the Mediterranean, with a powerful enough character to measure up to any larger nation. The country emerged relatively unscathed from the global financial crisis and has enjoyed steady growth. Compared to many of its neighbours, Malta appears to be positively basking in a sense of well-being, enhanced by Valletta being named European Capital of Culture for 2018.

Best on Film

Malta Story (1953) WWII epic about the embattled island starring Sir Alec Guinness.

Simshar (2014) Critically acclaimed Maltese movie about migrants and a Maltese family shipwreck.

By the Sea (2015) Angelina Jolie writes and directs, and stars alongside Brad Pitt. Shot on Gozo.

Best in Print

The Great Siege: Malta 1565 (Ernle Bradford) Rip-roaring read about the epic battle between the Ottoman Turks and the Knights of Malta.

Fortress Malta: An Island Under Siege 1940–1943 (James Holland) Evocative account of Malta's fascinating and essential role in WWII.

Earthly Powers (Anthony Burgess) Set in a fictionalised Malta and written while the author lived here in the 1960s.

Politics & the Economy

The smallest state in the EU has largely ridden out the European storm: EU membership led to a flood of foreign investment, and strict banking regulations prevented the kind of financial meltdown seen elsewhere. Locals enjoy a good standard of living, with low inflation and relatively low unemployment. Government debt is also low.

Dependent on foreign trade, manufacturing and tourism, the Maltese economy could not entirely escape being hurt by the global economic situation, but its recession was short and shallow. A weakened euro and the arrival of budget carriers on Malta's deregulated airline scene helped to keep the tourist industry afloat, as has Valletta's status as European Capital of Culture in 2018, which has led to many hotel and restaurant openings and museum renovations. Construction and speculative property development remain strong areas, digital gaming is one of Malta's most dynamic sectors, and tax incentives have led numerous companies to base their operations here.

Since Maltese independence in 1964, the political scene has been dominated by two main parties: the Christian democratic Nationalist Party (Partit Nazzjonalista) and the social democratic Labour Party (Partit Laburista). After 15 years in opposition, the Labour Party, headed by former journalist Joseph Muscat, won a decisive victory in 2013. Labour promised to address high energy prices and tackle corruption, though opinions are divided on how successful they have been so far.

Migration

There are around 24,000 overseas-born residents in Malta; the largest group is British, followed by Libyans, Italians, Somalis and Russians. Before Malta joined the EU, in 2004, immigration was very low, but since then the country has become a gateway for migrants fleeing war and unrest in North Africa, who make the dangerous journey across the Mediterranean to apply for asylum in Europe.

Racial tensions have been evident since the increase in migrant numbers, and the islands' size makes migration a controversial issue. Malta has been criticised for its mandatory detention policy, of up to 18 months, which Amnesty International and others believe is at odds with international human rights obligations. A tragedy in April 2015, in which more than 800 asylum seekers died off the coast of Italy, prompted EU leaders to work harder to address the migration crisis, funding the search-and-rescue Operation Triton and agreeing on measures to try to disrupt the trafficking networks.

In 2013 Malta introduced the 'individual investor program', which allows outsiders to achieve Maltese citizenship if they invest in the country. Those who can pay €650,000, buy government bonds of €150,000, purchase/rent a house at €350,000/€16,000 per annum and prove a genuine attachment to the country can receive a Maltese passport within 12 months.

Environment

Key environmental concerns in Malta are land use, increased development and the pressures of population. The country only grows around 20% of its food and has no domestic energy sources (almost all of its electricity is generated using oil-fired power stations), so it is heavily reliant on imports. There is also a severe shortage of fresh water – the only natural supply comes from ground water.

Malta has the highest rate of asthma of all Mediterranean countries, with air (and noise) pollution caused by construction, traffic and discharges from power stations and factories. With such a small land area, disposal of rubbish in landfill sites is increasingly problematic, though recycling is on the rise.

Plans to site a new American University of Malta campus on 90,000 sq metres of pristine land in the southeast at Zondoq inspired protests about building on Malta's increasingly scarce countryside. The government is keen to promote the university, which is backed by a Jordanian company, because of the opportunities and students it will bring, so the search continues for an alternative site.

Hunting is a popular sport in Malta, with around 31 hunters per sq km. In 2015 a referendum was held on stopping the spring hunting of quail and turtle doves. The extremely close vote split the country, but the hunters won by a narrow margin.

For more information on environmental issues, see Flimkien ghal Ambjent Ahjar (FAA; www.faa.org.mt), an NGO that campaigns to preserve the islands' heritage and environment.

POPULATION: **412,650**

AREA: **316 SQ KM**

MOBILE PHONE SUBSCRIBERS: **581,000**

INFLATION: **0.3%**

UNEMPLOYMENT: **5.7%**

if Malta were 100 people

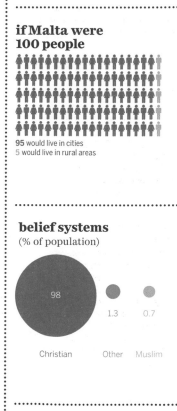

95 would live in cities
5 would live in rural areas

belief systems
(% of population)

98 Christian   1.3 Other   0.7 Muslim

population per sq km

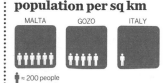

MALTA   GOZO   ITALY

 ≈ 200 people

History

Inhabited for millennia, the tiny Maltese Islands have a rollicking history and some of the world's most sophisticated prehistoric architecture. The islands' destiny has been shaped by geography, with their natural harbours and prime location attracting a series of masters – the Phoenicians, Romans, Arabs and Normans among them. However, the most influential settlers were the Knights of St John, who held sway until the arrival of Napoleon. Under British rule, Malta showed incredible bravery during WWII, and finally achieved independence in 1964.

Renowned British archaeologist and scholar David H Trump wrote *Malta Prehistory & Temples*, the definitive guide to Malta's prehistory. This comprehensive book includes detailed visual treatment of 30 key sites.

The Mystery of the Temple Builders

About 1000 years before the construction of the Great Pyramid of Cheops in Egypt, the people of Malta were manipulating megaliths that weighed up to 50 tonnes and creating elaborate buildings that appear to be oriented in relation to the winter solstice sunrise. The Maltese megalithic temples, built between 3600 and 2500 BC, are the oldest surviving free-standing structures in the world. It's thought that their builders were descended from the islands' neolithic inhabitants, rather than being new settlers, yet it appears they started building these structures quite suddenly.

It was a seemingly peaceful era, perhaps due to the islands' then geographical isolation, as no evidence of defensive structures remain. The society that built the temples must have been sophisticated, as indicated by the scale and complexity of the buildings and the evidence of delicate sculpture and decoration (mostly now displayed in Valletta's National Museum of Archaeology). The builders were also significantly wealthy enough to pay for the materials and extra labour beyond the needs of everyday life. Although the materials were mainly local, they often were transported from a distance of around 1km. It's thought that the massive slabs of stone were moved by rolling them on ball-shaped rocks – such stones have been discovered at the sites. The buildings have been termed 'temples' but, while there is evidence of ritual activity, it's not known definitively what they were used for.

TIMELINE	c 5200 BC	c 3600–2500 BC	c 2000 BC
	Arrival of first known inhabitants, by primitive boats or rafts from Sicily. The Maltese Islands are more wooded, fertile and richer in animal life at this time.	Megalithic temples are built.	Bronze Age culture develops.

It's a mystery why this population died out: some theories are drought and famine, an epidemic or an attack from overseas – or perhaps a combination of these afflictions. Whatever the reason, temple building appears to have come to a sudden stop around 2500 BC. The temples fell into disrepair, and the Bronze Age culture that followed was completely different in its practices (for example, cremation rather than burial) and its artworks, which were heavier and rougher than the fine work of the mysterious temple builders.

A Trading Post

Phoenicians & Romans

As sea travel developed, so did Malta's significance. It was impossible for ancient vessels to sail overnight or attempt long, continuous trips, so Malta was the ideal place to stop on a journey between mainland Europe and Africa.

From around 800 to 218 BC, Malta was ruled by the Phoenicians and, for around the last 250 years of this period, by Phoenicia's principal North African colony, Carthage. There is a direct legacy of this period visible in contemporary Malta: with watchful eyes painted on their prow, the colourful Maltese fishing boats – the *luzzu* and the *kajjik* – seem little changed from the Phoenician trading vessels that once plied the Mediterranean.

During the Second Punic War (218–201 BC) Rome took control of Malta before finally crushing Carthage in the Third Punic War (149–146 BC). The island was then given the status of a *municipium* (free town), with the power to control its own affairs and to send an ambassador to Rome. However, there is evidence that Malta retained a Punic influence. The 1st-century-BC historian Diodorus Siculus described the island as a Phoenician colony, and the biblical account of St Paul's shipwreck on Malta in AD 60 describes the islanders as 'barbarous' (that is, they did not speak the 'civilised' languages of Latin or Greek). St Paul's shipwreck was also particularly significant because he brought Christianity to the islands.

Malta seems to have prospered under Roman rule. The main town, called Melita, occupied the hilltop of Mdina but also spread over an area around three times the size of the later medieval citadel. The excavated remains of townhouses, villas, farms and baths suggest that the inhabitants enjoyed a comfortable lifestyle and occupied themselves with the production of olives, wheat, honey and grapes.

It wasn't till 1934 that Malti became the co-official language of Malta (alongside English), and the use of Italian was officially dropped. The first-ever grammar of the Maltese language was published at this time.

800–480 BC	480–218 BC	218 BC– AD 395	41 BC
Malta is occupied by the Phoenicians, a seafaring people based in present-day Lebanon.	Malta is controlled by the Carthaginian Empire, based in present-day Tunisia.	The Romans take over Malta, having destroyed Carthage in the Punic Wars.	The Romans make Malta a *municipium* (free town). The islands prosper through trade, as an outpost of Roman Sicily.

Arabs

The rapid expansion of Islam in the 7th to 9th centuries saw an Arab empire extend from Spain to India. Arab armies invaded Sicily in 827 and finally conquered it in 878; Malta fell into Arab hands in 870. Both Malta and Sicily remained Muslim possessions until the end of the 11th century, though the Arab rulers tolerated the Christian population. They had a strong influence on the Malti language – apart from the names Malta and Gozo, which are thought to have Latin roots, most Maltese place names date from after the Arab occupation.

Normans

For 400 years after the Norman conquest of Malta and Sicily (1090–91), the histories of these two Mediterranean islands were linked – their rulers were a succession of Normans, Angevins (French), Aragonese and Castilians (Spanish). Malta remained a minor pawn on the edge of the European chessboard, and its relatively small population of downtrodden islanders paid their taxes by trading, slaving and piracy, and were repaid in kind by marauding Turks and Barbary corsairs. This was th\e scene when the Knights of St John arrived, having been given the islands (much to the islanders' dismay) by the Holy Roman Emperor Charles V. The Knights were to rule the islands until the arrival of the French in the 18th century.

East Versus West

Swapped for a Falcon

In 1479 the marriage of Catholic monarchs Fernando II of Aragon and Isabella of Castile led to the unification of Spain. Under their grandson, the Holy Roman Emperor Charles V, Malta became part of the vast Spanish Empire. One of the greatest threats to Charles' realm was the expanding Ottoman Empire of Süleyman the Magnificent in the East. Sultan Süleyman had driven the Knights of St John from their island stronghold of Rhodes between 1522 and 1523. When the Knights begged Charles V to find them a new home, he offered them Malta along with the governorship of Tripoli, hoping that they might help to contain the Turkish naval forces in the eastern Mediterranean. The nominal rent was to be two falcons a year – one for the emperor and one for the viceroy of Sicily. Malta consequently found itself at the heart of a struggle between two religious philosophies, Islam and Christianity, and became the location for one of the mightiest clashes between East and West, which was to shape the nation's future and the landscape of the island as we see it today.

Didier Destremau, former French ambassador to Malta, wrote *Malte Tricolore – The Story of a French Malta 1798–1964*, a lighthearted, satirical history of Malta 'as it might have happened', had Napoleon not got the boot.

AD 60	395–870	870–1090	1090–1530
St Paul is shipwrecked on Malta and introduces Christianity to the population.	After the Roman Empire split in AD 395, Malta is believed to have fallen under Byzantine rule.	North African Arabs occupy Malta, introducing irrigation and the cultivation of cotton and citrus fruits.	Normans take over. During their rule, a Maltese aristocracy is established, and the architectural style referred to as Siculo-Norman developed.

WIIO WERE THE KNIGHTS OF ST JOHN?

The Sovereign and Military Order of the Knights Hospitaller of St John of Jerusalem had its origins in the Christian Crusades of the 11th and 12th centuries.

A hospital for poor pilgrims in Jerusalem was founded by some Italian merchants from Amalfi in 1070. The hospital, operated by monks, won the protection of the papacy in 1113 and was raised to the status of an independent religious order known as the Hospitallers. The Order set up more hospitals along the pilgrimage route from Italy to the Holy Land, and the knights who had been healed of their wounds showed their gratitude by granting funds and property to the growing Order.

When the armies of Islam recaptured the Holy Land in 1291, the Order sought refuge in the Kingdom of Cyprus. In 1309 they acquired the island of Rhodes, planning to stay close to the Middle East in the hope of reconquering Jerusalem. And there they remained for over 200 years, building fortresses, auberges and a hospital, and evolving from a land-based army into the medieval world's most formidable naval fighting force.

The Order consisted of European noblemen who lived the lives of monks and soldiers. Their traditional attire was a hooded monk's habit emblazoned with a white Maltese cross. This eight-pointed cross is said to represent the eight virtues the Knights strove to uphold: to live in truth; to have faith; to repent of sins; to give proof of humility; to love justice; to be merciful; to be sincere and whole-hearted; and to endure persecution. The Order comprised eight nationalities or langues (literally 'tongues' or languages) – Italian, French, Provencal, Auvergnat, Castilian, Aragonese, German and English.

The hospitals created by the Order – first in the Holy Land, then in Rhodes and finally in Malta – were often at the forefront of medical development. Ironically, although the Knights had sworn to bring death and destruction to the 'infidel' Muslims, much of the Order's medical knowledge was gleaned from the study of Arabic medicine.

The Great Siege of 1565

Grand Master Philippe Villiers de L'Isle Adam (1530–34) of the Knights of St John was not particularly impressed by the gift of the Maltese Islands, which seemed to him barren, waterless and poorly defended. Equally unimpressed were the 12,000 or so local inhabitants, who were given no say in the matter, including the aristocracy, who remained aloof in their palazzi in Mdina. However, determined to make the best of a bad job and hoping one day to return to Rhodes, in 1530 the Knights settled in the fishing village of Birgu (now Vittoriosa), on the south side of Grand Harbour, and set about fortifying their defences.

While in Rhodes, the Knights had been a constant thorn in the side of the Ottoman Turks. In Malta their greatest adversary was the Turkish admiral Dragut Reis, who invaded Gozo in 1551 and carried

1530	1565	1566	1798
The Knights of St John arrive in Malta, having been gifted the islands by Emperor Charles V.	The Knights defeat Turkish invaders in the Great Siege of Malta.	Valletta is founded, and is the first planned city in Europe.	Napoleon's fleet calls at Malta and captures the island with hardly a fight.

off almost the entire population of 5000 into slavery. Not much later, in 1559, the Knights lost half their galleys in a disastrous attack on Dragut's lair on the island of Djerba (Tunisia). With the power of the Knights at a low ebb, Süleyman the Magnificent saw an opportunity to polish off this troublesome crew, while at the same time capturing Malta as a base for the invasion of Europe.

Jean Parisot de la Valette, Grand Master between 1557 and 1568, was a stern disciplinarian and an experienced soldier. He foresaw the threat of a Turkish siege and prepared for it well, renewing Fort St Angelo and building Fort St Michael and Fort St Elmo. The Knights' galley fleet was taken into the creek below Birgu, and a great chain was stretched across the harbour entrance between Fort St Angelo and Fort St Michael to keep out enemy vessels. Food, water and arms were stockpiled, and la Valette sent urgent requests for aid to the emperor, the pope and the viceroy of Sicily. No help came. In May 1565, when an Ottoman fleet carrying more than 30,000 men arrived to lay siege to the island, la Valette was 70 years old and commanded a force of only 700 Knights and around 8000 Maltese irregulars and mercenary troops.

The Turkish force, led jointly by Admiral Piali and Mustafa Pasha, dropped anchor in the bay of Marsaxlokk, and its soldiers set up camp on the plain of Marsa. The entire population of Malta took refuge within the walls of Birgu, Isla and Mdina, taking their livestock with them and poisoning the wells and cisterns they left behind. The Turks began their campaign with an attack on Fort St Elmo, which guarded the entrance to both Grand and Marsamxett Harbours. The fort was small, holding a garrison of only 60 Knights and a few hundred men – Mustafa Pasha was confident that it would fall in less than a week.

Despite continuous bombardment and repeated mass assaults on its walls, Fort St Elmo held out for over four weeks, and cost the lives of 8000 Turkish soldiers before it was taken. When the fort finally fell, not one of the Christian defenders survived.

Looking across at the looming bulk of Fort St Angelo from the smoke and rubble of St Elmo, Mustafa Pasha is said to have muttered, 'Allah! If so small a son has cost us so dear, what price shall we have to pay for so large a father?'

Hoping to intimidate the already demoralised defenders of Fort St Angelo, Mustafa Pasha ordered that several of the leading Knights be beheaded and their heads fixed on stakes looking across towards Birgu. The Turks nailed the decapitated bodies to makeshift wooden crucifixes and sent them floating across the harbour. La Valette's response was immediate and equally cruel: all Turkish prisoners

The Order of Malta website (www.orderof-malta.org) covers the long, illustrious history of the Knights, as well as information about present-day knightly activities.

The Great Siege, by Ernle Bradford, is a page-turning account of the epic 1565 battle between the Ottoman Turks and the Knights of St John.

1800	1814	1814–1964	1853–56
The Maltese rebel against the French garrison and ask the British for assistance. Following a naval blockade, the French surrender in September.	Malta becomes a prosperous trading port and entrepôt; after the 1814 Treaty of Paris it is formally recognised as a Crown Colony of the British Empire.	The British rule Malta, allowing varying levels of Maltese self-government.	Malta is the headquarters of the British Mediterranean Fleet, and is used as a base and supply station for the Royal Navy during the Crimean War.

were decapitated and their heads used as cannonballs, fired across the harbour to St Elmo.

Then began the final assault on the strongholds of Birgu and Isla: the Turks launched at least 10 massed assaults, but each time they were beaten back. Turkish morale was drained by the long, hot summer, increasing casualties and the impending possibility of having to spend the entire winter on Malta (the Mediterranean sailing season traditionally ended with the storms of late September). The ferocity of their attacks decreased. On 7 September, the Knights' long-promised relief force from Sicily finally arrived – 28 ships carrying some 8000 men landed at Mellieħa Bay and took command of the high ground around Naxxar as the Turks scrambled at Marsamxett.

Seeing the unexpectedly small size of the relief force, Mustafa Pasha ordered some of his troops to land again at St Paul's Bay, while the rest marched towards Naxxar from Marsamxett. But the tired and demoralised Turkish soldiers were in no mood to fight these fresh and ferocious soldiers, and turned and ran for the galleys now anchored in St Paul's Bay. Thousands were hacked to pieces in the shallow waters of the bay as they tried to escape. That night the banner of the Order of St John flew once again over the battered ruins of St Elmo.

The part played in the Great Siege by the ordinary people of Malta is often overlooked, but their courage and resilience was a deciding factor in the Turkish defeat. Besides the defence force made up of 5000 or so Maltese soldiers, the local women and children contributed by repairing walls, supplying food and ammunition and tending the wounded. The date of the end of the siege, 8 September, is still commemorated in Malta as the Victory Day public holiday.

It's no small feat to cover a country's past in fewer than 300 pages, but *A Concise History of Malta*, by Carmel Cassar, is an entertaining introduction to Maltese history.

From Heroism to Hedonism

The Knights of St John, previously neglected, were now hailed as the saviours of Europe. Money and honours were heaped on them by grateful monarchs, and the construction of the new city of Valletta – named after the hero of the siege – and its enormous fortifications began. Although sporadic raids continued, Malta was never again seriously threatened by the Turks.

The period following the Great Siege was one of building – not only massive new fortifications and watchtowers, but also churches, palaces and auberges (residences). The military engineer Francesco Laparelli was sent to Malta by the pope to design the new defences of Valletta, and Italian artists arrived to decorate its churches, chapels and palazzi. An influx of new Knights, eager to join the now prestigious Order, swelled the coffers of the treasury. The pious Grand

1887	1914–18	1919	1921
For the first time in its history, Malta acquires representative government through a legislative council, composed of a majority of Maltese elected members. This is later revoked in 1903.	Malta serves as a military hospital during WWI.	There is a growing desire for Maltese self-government. Tension comes to a head on 7 June when riots break out.	The British respond to Maltese unrest by granting a new constitution that provides for a limited form of self-government. Joseph Howard becomes the first prime minister of Malta.

Master Jean de la Cassière (1572–81) oversaw the construction of the Order's new hospital, the Sacra Infermeria, and the magnificent St John's Co-Cathedral.

In later years, with the Turkish threat removed, the Knights occupied themselves less with militarism and monasticism, and more with piracy, commerce, drinking and duelling.

Following their 1798 expulsion from Malta by Napoleon and the loss of their French estates, the Knights sought refuge first in Russia and later in Italy. After several years of uncertainty, they finally made their headquarters in the Palazzo di Malta (the former Embassy of the Hospitallers) in Rome. The Order continues to this day; since 2008 the Grand Master has been Englishman Fra' Matthew Festing. See www.orderof malta.org/english for more details.

A Military Linchpin

Napoleon in Malta

In the aftermath of the French Revolution, Grand Master Emmanuel de Rohan (1775–97) provided money for Louis XVI's doomed attempt to escape from Paris. By the late 18th century around three-quarters of the Order's income came from the Knights of the French langue (division), and when the revolutionary authorities confiscated all of the Order's properties and estates in France, the Order was left in dire financial straits.

In 1798 Napoleon Bonaparte arrived in Malta aboard his flagship *L'Orient,* at the head of the French Navy, on his way to Egypt to counter the British influence in the Mediterranean. He demanded that he be allowed to water his ships, but the Knights refused. The French landed and captured the island with hardly a fight – many of the Knights were in league with the French, and the Maltese were in no mood for a battle. On 11 June 1798 the Order surrendered to Napoleon.

Napoleon stayed in Malta for only six days (in the Palazzo de Parisio in Valletta), but when he left, *L'Orient* was weighed down with silver, gold, paintings and tapestries looted from the Order's churches, auberges and infirmary. (Most of this treasure went to the bottom of the sea a few months later when the Royal Navy under Admiral Nelson destroyed the French fleet at the Battle of the Nile.) The French also abolished the Maltese aristocracy, defaced coats of arms, desecrated churches and closed down monasteries.

Napoleon left behind a garrison of 4000 men, but they were taken unawares by a spontaneous uprising of the Maltese and had to

The Malta Story (1953), starring Alec Guinness and Jack Hawkins, involves men in spiffy uniforms fighting dangerous battles, performing heroic acts and winning hearts (of course). Surprisingly, it's the only movie made about the dramatic WWII events in Malta.

1930s–50s	1940	1940–43	1942
Economic depression and political turmoil result in large numbers of Maltese emigrating to the US, Australia, Canada and the UK.	Mussolini's Italy enters WWII on 10 June. On 11 June Italian bombers strike at Malta's Grand Harbour. Three ageing biplanes take to the air to defend the islands.	Malta assumes huge strategic importance as a WWII naval and air force base; the country experiences heavy bombing and great hardship.	King George VI awards the George Cross, Britain's highest award for civilian bravery, to the entire population of Malta.

retreat within the walls of Valletta. A Maltese deputation sought help from the sympathetic British, who enforced a naval blockade. The French garrison finally capitulated in September 1800 – but the British government, having taken Malta, was somewhat unsure what to do with it.

British Rule

The Treaty of Amiens (March 1802) provided for the return of Malta to the Order of St John, but the Maltese, not wanting the Order back, petitioned the British to stay. Their pleas fell on deaf ears, and arrangements were made for the return of the Order. But when war between Britain and France broke out again in May 1803, leaving the British government faced with the blockade of European ports against British trade, they soon changed their mind regarding the potential usefulness of Malta.

While the latter stages of the Napoleonic Wars wore on, Malta rapidly became a prosperous entrepôt, and with the Treaty of Paris in 1814 it was formally recognised as a Crown Colony of the British Empire.

The end of the Napoleonic Wars brought an economic slump to Malta as trade fell off and little was done in the way of investment in the island. But its fortunes revived during the Crimean War (1853–56), when it was developed by the Royal Navy as a major naval base and supply station. With the opening of the Suez Canal in 1869, Malta became one of the chief coaling ports on the imperial steamship route between Britain and India.

The early 19th century also saw the beginnings of Maltese political development. In 1835 a Council of Government made up of prominent local citizens was appointed to advise the governor and a free press was established.

In the second half of the 19th century vast sums were spent on improving Malta's defences and dockyard facilities as the island became a linchpin in the imperial chain of command. The Victoria Lines and several large dry docks were built during this period. Commercial facilities were also improved to cater for the busy trade route to India and the Far East. In 1883 a railway was built between Valletta and Mdina (it closed in 1931).

During WWI Malta served as a military hospital, providing 25,000 beds for casualties from the disastrous Gallipoli campaign in Turkey. But prices and taxes rose during the war and the economy fell. During protest riots in 1919, four Maltese citizens were shot dead by panicking British soldiers and several more were injured.

WWII

The day after Mussolini's Italy entered WWII, one of that country's first acts of war was to bomb Malta.

1943	1947	1958	1964
In July Malta serves as the operational headquarters and air support base for the Allied invasion of Sicily. Captured Italian warships are anchored in Marsaxlokk Bay.	A measure of self-government is restored with a general election, but a post-war economic slump creates more political tension.	Pivotal and pugnacious Dom Mintoff resigns as prime minister following a clash with the British and the Maltese church.	On 21 September, Malta gains its independence from Britain, but Queen Elizabeth II remains the head of state.

The British government responded to the unrest by giving the Maltese a greater say in the running of Malta. The 1921 constitution created a diarchic system of government, with a Maltese assembly presiding over local affairs and a British imperial government controlling foreign policy and defence.

WWII

The outbreak of WWII found Britain undecided about the strategic importance of Malta. The islands' need for defence did not seem crucial at a time when Britain was itself poorly armed, and the Italian threat was remote until the Fall of France in June 1940. Thus Malta was unprepared and undefended when on 11 June, the day after Mussolini entered the war, Italian bombers attacked Grand Harbour.

Malta suffered 154 days and nights of nonstop bombing in 1942. By comparison, at the height of London's Blitz there were 57 days of continuous bombing.

The only aircraft available on the islands at this time were three Gloster Gladiator biplanes – quickly nicknamed Faith, Hope and Charity – whose pilots fought with such tenacity that Italian pilots estimated the strength of the Maltese squadron to be in the region of 25 aircraft. The Gladiators battled on alone for three weeks before squadrons of modern Hurricane fighters arrived to bolster the islands' air defences. The remains of the sole surviving aircraft, Faith, can be seen at Valletta's National War Museum.

Malta effectively became a fortified aircraft carrier, a base for bombing attacks on enemy ships and harbours in Sicily and North Africa. It also harboured submarines that preyed on Italian and German supply ships. Malta's importance was clear to Hitler too, and crack squadrons of Stuka dive bombers were stationed in Sicily with the objective of pounding the Maltese Islands into submission.

Malta's greatest ordeal came in 1942, when the country came close to starvation and surrender. In April alone some 6700 tonnes of bombs were dropped on Grand Harbour and the surrounding area. On 15 April, King George VI awarded the George Cross – Britain's highest award for civilian bravery – to the entire population of Malta.

Just as Malta's importance to the Allies lay in disrupting enemy supply lines, so its major weakness was the difficulty of getting supplies to the island. At the height of the siege in the summer of 1942 the governor made an inventory of remaining food and fuel, and informed London that Malta would only last until August without further supplies. A massive relief convoy known as Operation Pedestal, consisting of 14 supply ships escorted by three aircraft carriers, two battleships, seven cruisers and 24 destroyers, was dispatched to run the gauntlet of enemy bombers and submarines. It suffered massive attacks, and only five supply ships made it into Grand Harbour – the crippled oil tanker

1974	1980	1984	1989
Under returned Prime Minister Dom Mintoff, Malta becomes a republic, with a parliament-appointed president now the head of state.	The USSR opens an embassy on Malta as Mintoff forges strong links with North Korea, the USSR and Libya.	Dom Mintoff again resigns as prime minister, but continues to play an important backbench role until 1998.	Neutral Malta hosts a summit between Mikhail Gorbachev and George Bush Sr, marking the end of the Cold War.

Ohio, with its precious cargo of fuel, limped in on 15 August, lashed between two warships.

Malta was thus able to continue its vital task of disrupting enemy supply lines. The aircraft and submarines based in Malta succeeded in destroying or damaging German convoys to North Africa to the extent that Rommel's Afrika Korps was low on fuel and ammunition during the crucial Battle of El Alamein in October 1942, a situation that contributed to a famous Allied victory and the beginning of the end of the German presence in North Africa.

In July 1943 Malta served as the operational headquarters and air support base for Operation Husky, the Allied invasion of Sicily. The Italian Navy finally surrendered to the Allies on 8 September, after which Malta's role in the war rapidly diminished.

Independence to the Present Day

WWII left the islands with 35,000 homes destroyed and the population on the brink of starvation. In 1947 the war-torn island was given a measure of self-government and a £30-million war-damage fund to help rebuilding and restoration. But Britain's reductions in defence spending and the loss of jobs in the naval dockyard led to calls either for closer integration with Britain or for Malta to go it alone. Malta's prime minister from 1955 was the Labour Party's Dominic (Dom) Mintoff, a politician who never shied away from controversy. He took on the Roman Catholic Church, which he saw as hampering progress, and proposed not independence but that the Maltese government should integrate with that of the UK, with Maltese MPs at Westminster and the islanders given British citizenship. The British Government refused and Mintoff resigned in 1958. His clash with the church was instrumental in his subsequent electoral defeats in 1962 and 1966.

On 21 September 1964, with Nationalist Prime Minister Dr George Borg Olivier at the helm, Malta finally gained its independence. It remained within the British Commonwealth, with Queen Elizabeth II as the head of state represented in Malta by a governor-general.

Dom Mintoff took over once again in 1971, and Malta became a republic in 1974. In 1979 links with Britain were reduced further when Mintoff expelled the British armed services, declared Malta's neutrality and signed agreements with Libya, the USSR and North Korea. His government brought in measures on housing, nationalised many industries, and made all schools comprehensive. He forged a strong, if erratic, relationship with Colonel Muammar Gaddafi, and in 1980 the USSR opened an embassy on the island. In 1984 Mintoff stood down as prime minister but continued as an

When Malta gained independence in 1964 it was the first time since prehistory that the country had been ruled by the native Maltese and not by an outside power.

2003–04	2008	2012	2015
In a 2003 referendum with a voter turnout of 92%, just over half the electorate votes to join the EU. On 1 May 2004 Malta joins the EU, along with nine other states.	On 1 January Malta kisses goodbye to the Maltese lira, its currency since 1972, and adopts the euro. Maltese euro coins proudly display the Maltese cross.	Former prime minister Dom Mintoff dies, aged 96.	Malta votes to retain the tradition of spring bird hunting in a nationwide referendum.

influential backbencher. When he died in 2012, thousands of Maltese united in mourning and assessed the legacy of their most prominent contemporary politician.

In the 1987 election, the conservative Nationalists achieved a majority and retained power for most of the next 26 years. In 1989 Malta was the scene for the historic summit between USSR and US leaders Mikhail Gorbachev and George Bush Sr that signalled the end of the Cold War. The meetings took place on board the Soviet cruise ship SS *Maxim Gorkiy,* anchored off the coast of Marsaxlokk, in choppy seas.

In 2004 Malta joined the EU, and in 2008 became part of the Eurozone, which brought much inward investment and helped diversify the local economy. More recently the islands have been buffeted by, but largely rode out, the European financial crisis, experiencing reasonably steady growth.

The Maltese Way of Life

The Maltese have many passions: Roman Catholicism, band clubs, sport, cars, fireworks, swimming, sailing, food and family. And almost as many cultural influences from the nation's string of occupiers: the Phoenicians, Carthaginians, Romans, Byzantines, Arabs, Normans, Sicilians, Knights of St John, French and British. This is a society with a unique, powerful identity that harbours numerous contradictions – it's old-fashioned yet forward-thinking, bureaucratic yet rule-bending, a defensive small island that extends a warm welcome.

Psyche

The Maltese are friendly and warm, yet it can take a long time for outsiders to feel integrated into society, despite the many different nationalities who've made their home here over millennia. Malta has one of the highest per capita refugee acceptance rates in the world but the issue of migrants from North Africa is fiercely debated, and Malta was rated 33rd out of 38 countries in the 2015 Migrant Integration Policy Index.

Church buildings and parish activities remain at the core of village life, and the Catholic Church still exerts a strong influence. If you're here during an important religious festival such as Holy Week or any of the festas (celebrating villages' patron saints, from June to September) you'll experience firsthand how people of all ages take part, from young children in costume to the frailest elderly locals lined up in wheelchairs to watch the procession pass.

Family values are held in high regard, as is the love of socialising common to southern European countries – Sunday in particular is the day to gather with family and friends, and enjoy good food and company. In some ways Malta feels wedded to tradition, but it also embraces the new – it's an important iGaming centre, for example. There are strong class divisions, perhaps a hangover from British rule, and the elite tend to speak English and attend English schools. The south is more Maltese and slightly looked down upon by the more cosmopolitan north but, on such a small island, everyone mingles in any case.

The Maltese are justifiably proud of their small country's historical importance and the local grit and determination (well demonstrated during WWII). The vast majority of the population take great interest in political matters and love discussing politics – the accessibility of politicians in this small population probably plays a large part. The locals also put their money where their mouth is: voter turnout is among the highest in the world (over 90%) but, interestingly, margins are usually close – the country seems fairly evenly split on major issues. In the 2015 hunting referendum the pro-hunting side won 50.44% to 49.56%. The Maltese relish taking sides in other areas too: there is fierce competition between the local band clubs, the local football teams, and about who has the best local festa.

Aspiring anthropologists should seek out Tarcisio Zarb's book *Folklore of an Island – Maltese Threshold Customs*, which covers Maltese traditions related to all of life's big occasions, including birth, puberty, marriage and death.

The Church

Malta's Roman Catholic Church exerts a powerful influence, and the important events of people's lives are all celebrated in church: christenings, first communions, weddings and funerals. One indicator of the Church's strength is the fact that divorce only became legal here in 2011 (it's been legal in Italy since 1974). Under the Maltese constitution, Roman Catholic Christianity is the official state religion and must be taught in state schools, though the constitution guarantees freedom of worship.

Though the Roman Catholic Church plays a major role in everyday life, there is evidence that its influence is waning. Around 95% of Maltese are Catholic, but the Church estimates that only around 40% now attend Sunday Mass – a drop of around 20% in 20 years (but still larger than in Italy, where the figure is more like 20% to 30%).

Religious occasions are celebrated with food and drink, socialising, music, processions and fireworks, and the most important event in the calendar is the annual parish festa, which is held on the day of the village's patron saint.

Malta is among the most densely populated countries in the world, with 1336 people per sq km, slightly more than Bangladesh, which has 1218.

Women in Malta

Women have been traditionally expected to stay at home to look after their children or elderly parents, or to be supported by their husbands – it's still thought of as unusual for women to be completely financially independent. Malta's gender employment gap is the largest in the EU, with around 60% of women not employed. The government has been trying to address this issue, introducing lots of incentives for women to work; for example, tax incentives for married women over 40 who return to work, and free childcare centres. The costs of childcare appear low compared with the UK or other European countries, but so are many of the rates of pay. After-school clubs, which most schools have, cost 80c per hour, while a childminder costs around €3 per hour (the minimum wage is €4.16 per hour). There are lots of free or inexpensive sports-centred courses for children over the long summer months (school holidays run from June to September) as the government tries to address the child obesity problem: one in four Maltese children are judged to be obese (rates elsewhere in Europe are around one in five).

Locals talk of low official wages spurring the creation of a parallel economy of cash work on the side. Taking on two to three jobs is common, and many qualified women work from home, in positions such as hairdressing and dressmaking, which is another contributor to the low official percentage of women in employment.

Interestingly, the birth rate is fairly low at around 1.4 children per woman of child-bearing age, a little higher than its famously non-procreative and Roman Catholic neighbour Italy, but not much.

Etiquette

Do dress respectfully when visiting a church.

Don't go topless on the beach.

Do avoid eating meat on a Friday, traditionally the day Roman Catholics eat fish.

A LINGUISTIC MELTING POT

The native language of Malta is Malti (also called Maltese). Some linguists attribute its origins to the Phoenician occupation of Malta in the 1st millennium BC, but most link it to North African Arabic dialects. The language has an Arabic grammar and construction but is formed from a morass of influences, laced with Sicilian, Italian, Spanish, French and English loan-words. Until the 1930s, Italian was the official language of the country, used in the Church and for all administrative matters, even though only the aristocracy could speak it. Malti only became an official language in 1934 (alongside English).

English is taught to schoolchildren from an early age, and almost everyone in Malta speaks it well. Many also speak Italian, helped by the fact that Malta receives Italian TV. French and German are also spoken, though less widely.

Malta at Play

Music

The Maltese are great music lovers and the *għana* (*ah*-na; folk song) is Maltese folk music at its most individual and traditional. A tribute to Malta's geographic location, *għana* verses are a mixture of the Sicilian ballad and the rhythmic wail of an Arabic tune, and were traditionally viewed as the music of the farmers, labourers and working classes. In the genre's truest form, lyrics are created fresh each time and tell stories of village life and events in local history. The verses are always sung by men with guitar accompaniment.

The St James' Cavalier Centre for Creativity in Valletta organises *għana* nights, as do other venues across Malta, especially in the centre and south. You might see performances at various heritage events, or even chance upon an impromptu *għana* performance in a rural bar. Għanafest takes place in mid-June in Floriana, with three days of live concerts.

Etnika is one traditional folk group that has revived ethnic Maltese musical forms and instruments. Their style of music, using traditional bagpipes, horns and drums, was once part of Malta's daily life, and was used in a variety of social contexts, including weddings and funerals. Etnika reinterpret this musical heritage for a contemporary audience and sometimes fuse it with *għana,* jazz and flamenco, for a unique sound.

Traditional band music is one of the most popular traditions on the islands, with bands playing a vital role in the village festa and other open-air events. Every town and village has at least one band club and they are often engaged in strong rivalry.

There's a great deal of live music in Malta over the spring and summer months, with gigs at pubs and bars and the Jazz Festival, Arts Festival, Music Week and the Isle of MTV.

For Rozina...a Husband, by playwright and novelist Francis Ebejer (1925–93), is a collection of short stories (in English) that seeks to capture the essence of Maltese village life.

Crafts

Malta is noted for its fine crafts, especially its handmade lace, hand woven fabrics and silver filigree.

Lace-making probably arrived with the Knights in the 16th century. It was traditionally the role of village women. Although the craft has developed into a healthy industry, you still occasionally see women making lace in villages around Gozo.

The art of producing silver filigree was probably introduced to the islands in the 17th century via Sicily, which was then strongly influenced by Spain. Malta's silversmiths still produce beautiful filigree by traditional methods, yet it's mostly created in large quantities to meet tourist demand.

Other handicrafts include weaving, knitting and glass-blowing; the latter is an especially healthy small industry that produces glassware exported throughout the world. Head to Ta'Qali Crafts Village near Rabat or its smaller Gozitan equivalent, Ta'Dbieġi, for the opportunity to see locals practising their craft and to buy souvenirs. Malta Artisan Markets (www.maltaartisanmarkets.com) are regular events held in locations such as Palazzo Parisio, where you can find contemporary crafts made by artisans around the islands.

The Cultural Events section of www.maltaculture.com (from the Malta Council for Culture & the Arts) is a great starting point for information about forthcoming cultural events, including literary recitals, traditional folk music performances and lunchtime concerts.

Sport

Football (Soccer)

The Maltese are staunch, passionate football fans and follow the fortunes of local sides and international teams (especially British and Italian) with equal fervour – countless bars televise matches. The local and Maltese Premier League season runs from October till May; league and international matches are held at the 20,000-seat **Ta'Qali National**

BIRD HUNTING

One of Malta's favourite traditional sports is bird hunting; there are around 14,000 registered hunters and trappers in the country. Most birds are shot or trapped while migrating between Africa and Europe; Malta is one of the major flyways for migrating birds and more than 384 species have been recorded here.

The spring hunting season is open between 12 and 30 April; the autumn season runs from 1 September to 31 January. Two species of bird – turtle dove and quail – may be legally hunted; shooting at any other bird is illegal. There has been a decline in illegal shootings but they do happen, and in 2015 the spring hunting season was closed three days early by the prime minister after a kestrel – a protected bird of prey – was shot by a hunter and landed in a school playground.

Since 2007 BirdLife Malta has kept a centralised database on illegal hunting and trapping incidents witnessed by ornithologists, members of the public and the organisation's staff and volunteers.

Malta is the only EU member state that still allows hunting during the spring season. In 2015 there was a national referendum to decide whether spring hunting should be banned completely. Polls prior to the vote showed the conservationists with a strong lead, but the pro-hunting camp won by a slim majority of 2220, to maintain the tradition.

It is estimated that there are as many Maltese living abroad as there are in Malta.

Stadium (☑2143 6137; www.mfa.com.mt), which is situated between Mosta and Rabat, and results are reported in the local newspapers. The Malta Football Association (www.mfa.com.mt/en/home.htm) and Malta Football (www.maltafootball.com) are good resources.

Water Polo

As the heat of summer increases, football gives way to water polo. Between July and September, the fans who were once shouting on the terraces now yell from the pool side. Games are fierce and physical – it's worth trying to take in a match during your stay. The important clashes are held at the Tal-Qroqq National Swimming Pool Complex on Triq Maria Teresa Spinelli in Gżira. Further information is available from the Aquatic Sports Association (www.asaofmalta.com).

Racing

Another of Malta's much-loved spectator sports is horse racing. Race meetings are held at the Marsa Racecourse (part of the Marsa Sports Club outside Valletta) every Sunday, and sometimes on Friday and Saturday, from January to July. Races are mostly harness racing – and the betting is frantic. In season, some tour operators offer a day trip to the races. For more information see www.maltaracingclub.com.

In car-loving Malta, motor racing is also hugely popular; the Mdina Grand Prix Classic Car Event (www.vallettagrandprix.com) takes place annually in October, with a challenging 2.2km circuit outside the city walls.

5000 Years of Architecture

Malta's architectural history kicked off in spectacular fashion. Here is some of the world's most extraordinary prehistoric architecture, great temple-like buildings both above and below ground. The next inhabitants to leave such a powerful mark on the islands were the Knights of St John, with their stately 16th- and 17th-century fortified towns and gilded baroque cathedrals. You won't just be astounded by the buildings of the past but also by those of today, most notably Renzo Piano's dramatic additions to new-look Valletta.

The architecture on Malta and Gozo is partly shaped by geology: the islands are predominantly made up of layers of limestone. This type of stone, with its natural faults, allows rocks to be levered out with simple tools. Prehistoric builders exploited the weaknesses in the rock to carve out their mammoth slabs. The stone, while soft when first quarried, becomes harder when it dries out, making it ideal for carving and moulding.

Historical context is also of huge importance. Grand defensive structures are abundant, signalling how often the islands were fought over throughout their history. There are the great forts and walled cities constructed by the Knights of St John; the Victoria Lines, built by the British, running across the Maltese hills; and castellated watchtowers, which stalk the coastline like sentinels.

Malta's prehistoric temples predate the Egyptian pyramids by around 1000 years.

Prehistoric Innovation

The islands are home to a series of extraordinary megalithic monuments constructed between the 4th and 3rd millennia BC. A model made by the temple builders has been discovered, which shows the corbelled roof of a temple made of stone, indicating the extraordinary sophistication of the ancient builders.

The Hal Saflieni Hypogeum, a multi-level underground burial complex hewn out of Globigerina limestone, dates from 5000 years ago. The builders carved out the stone in such a way as to imitate structures above ground, with rock-cut decoration, smoothed walls and curved ceilings. The well-preserved forms of this underground complex have also cast light on the less enduring monuments above ground, such as the Tarxien Temples and Ħaġar Qim on Malta and Ġgantija on Gozo. Where the roofs of the above-ground temples have collapsed, the Hypogeum's parallel subterranean architecture provides an invaluable reference point.

Best Prehistoric

Hal Saflieni Hypogeum, Malta

Tarxien Temples, Malta

Ħaġar Qim & Mnajdra, Malta

Ġgantija, Gozo

Early Prosperity

Malta's urban architecture developed during prosperous times. The Carthaginians built Malta's first towns, although little remains from this period. Some significant Roman relics have been preserved, including the grand villa complex at Rabat in central Malta, a typically Roman structure centred on a peristyle courtyard. Although the cultural impact

MALTA'S CHURCHES

The Maltese claim to be one of the earliest Christian peoples in the world, having been converted by St Paul after his shipwreck on Malta in AD 60, and ecclesiastical architecture certainly dominates the landscape.

There are 64 Catholic parishes and 313 Catholic churches on Malta, and 15 Catholic parishes and 46 Catholic churches on Gozo. The main period of church-building in Malta took place after the arrival of the Knights of St John, in the 16th, 17th and 18th centuries; the oldest surviving church is the tiny medieval Chapel of the Annunciation at Ħal Millieri near Żurrieq, which dates from the mid-15th century.

In the 16th century the Knights imported the Renaissance style from Italy. This was supplanted by the more elaborate forms of Maltese baroque, which evolved throughout the 17th century and culminated in the design of St Paul's Cathedral in Mdina. The 19th and 20th centuries saw the addition of several large churches in the neo-Gothic style, including St Paul's Anglican Cathedral in Valletta and the Church of Our Lady of Lourdes in Mġarr, Gozo. Two huge rotundas were also built by public subscription: the vast Church of St Mary at Mosta (1833–60) and the Church of St John the Baptist (1951–71) at Xewkija, Gozo, which has space to seat 4000 people.

of the later Islamic period was extremely significant, it left little architectural trace.

For over 2000 years Mdina was the island's major town. Originally a Phoenician settlement, it was enlarged and built upon by the Romans, and developed further by the Byzantines, Arabs, Normans and Aragonese. Mdina reached its current form in the 15th and 16th centuries, though the 1720s saw major redevelopment as the fortifications were bolstered.

At Ġgantija, the finer interior work was created from Globigerina limestone, dragged from over a kilometre away.

Military Might

When the Knights of St John arrived in Malta in the 16th century they set about building defences, particularly around Birgu (Vittoriosa); they also rebuilt the fortifications around Mdina. They based themselves at Birgu, and here constructed splendid hostels, or auberges, where the members of the Order lived.

After the Knights fought off the Ottoman threat in the Great Siege of 1565, grateful European allies poured money into Malta. With this largesse the Knights built Valletta, surrounding it with huge bastions. Because the island is so rocky, the fortifications were often carved into the rock, rather than built upon it, which helped increase their strength. The well-connected Knights had access to all the leading courts of Europe, so were able to call on the great military engineers of the era to create cutting-edge defences, which remain vastly impressive today. These constructions are not merely intimidating, but also beautiful, with delicate decorative elements that exalt their builders – intricacies that helped reinforce the power of the Order.

Read *Malta: Phoenician, Punic & Roman*, by Anthony Bonanno, to learn about the island's early history.

However, the extent of the building was vastly expensive, and by the late 1600s the order was bankrupted by its cost. Built by conflict but untested, these fortifications were the nuclear weaponry of their day, acting as a deterrent to potential invaders.

Baroque Splendours

Together, the Knights of St John and the Church created a distinctive variation of baroque, the ornate style that dominated Europe from the 16th to the 18th centuries. This frenzy of decoration was a visual form of propaganda, exalting God, Christianity and the nobility of its builders.

The greatest Maltese architect of the 16th century was Gerolamo Cassar (1520–86). He was born in the fishing village of Birgu 10 years before the Knights of St John arrived from Rhodes, and worked as an assistant to Francesco Laparelli, the military engineer who designed the fortifications of Valletta. Cassar studied architecture in Rome and was responsible for the design of many of Malta's finest buildings, including the Grand Master's Palace, the facade of St John's Co-Cathedral and many of the Knights' auberges.

Prolific architect Tommaso Dingli (1591–1666) created many of Malta's parish churches. His masterpiece is the Church of St Mary in Attard, which he designed when he was only 22 years of age. Lorenzo Gafa (1630–1704) designed many of the finest examples of Maltese baroque, among them the cathedrals of Mdina and Gozo.

Valletta's Manoel Theatre is an architectural treasure, with a magnificent auditorium. Founded by the Portuguese Grand Master Antonio Manoel de Vilhena in 1731, it was used regularly by the Knights for their productions, and is one of the oldest working theatres in Europe.

Great Mansions

Malta is not only rich in ecclesiastical and military architecture, but has some splendid noble houses, several of which are open to the public. These include Casa Rocca Piccola in Valletta, Palazzo Faison in Mdina, and Villa Bologna in Attard, which provide a glimpse into the gilded world of the Maltese aristocracy. The grandest of them all is the largely 19th-century Palazzo Parisio in Naxxar, once a summer house belonging to Maltese-Sicilian gentry, and later transformed by a wealthy Maltese marquis, who added extravagant murals and a mirror-lined ballroom to create a mini-Versailles.

Contemporary Style

Malta has been blighted in the modern period by overdevelopment in many places, though building in its historical centres has remained strictly controlled. While the contemporary scene is not all bad news, every new major development has been dogged by controversy.

One of Malta's foremost architects is Richard England (www.richard england.com), whose work has included transforming Valletta's St James' Cavalier (originally designed by military engineer Laparelli de Cortona) into its contemporary guise as the Centre for Creativity. England is also responsible for the striking design of St Joseph's Church in Manikata on the outskirts of Mellieħa, for which he used the *girna* (a small circular building farmers construct in the middle of fields) as inspiration.

Another well-known contemporary local architect is the prolific Chris Briffa, who has been responsible for many architectural projects around Malta in recent years, and has won plaudits for his sympathetic approach to converting historic buildings. One of his architectural innovations has been to open up the traditional *gallarija* (Maltese balcony) in such a way that none of the view is obscured. He's also converted Casa Ellul,

Best Baroque

St John's Co-Cathedral, Valletta

St Paul's Shipwreck Church, Valletta

St Paul's Cathedral, Mdina

Gozo Cathedral, Victoria

THE MALTESE BALCONY

The first recorded *gallarija* in Valletta was the long gallery that lines the Grand Master's Palace, built in the late 17th century. When the city of Valletta was first built in the 16th century, open balconies were very popular, but this palatial enclosed gallery sparked a trend that everyone began to copy. At first people merely enclosed the top part of their existing balconies, but then they started to add lower panels to match, resulting in the unique Maltese style of balcony seen today.

the Harbour Club, designed the stylish Ġgantija Temples visitor centre, and is working on projects to develop a row of bars in Valletta's Strait St.

There have been a remarkable number of architectural developments in Malta in recent years, including the sleekly remodelled Valletta, Cottonera (Vittoriosa), Senglea and Qawra waterfronts; Tigne Point; the Mdina Ditch Gardens; the starfish-shaped Malta National Aquarium; and the huge SmartCity development, an entire town to house Malta's emerging tech industry. All of these projects have provoked debate.

Without doubt the most high-profile and controversial project is that of Italian architect Renzo Piano in Valletta. Piano's City Gate consists of a breach in the city walls, replacing the 1960s development that previously framed the entrance. Just inside the gate and forming part of a harmonious ensemble, his modernist Parliament Building supports huge golden-stone blocks on a steel structure, and uses the latest ecological architectural innovations to heat and cool the building. Alongside the Parliament Building is Piano's Opera House, an open-air auditorium above the ruins of the former building, which had been destroyed in WWII and left as a ruin as a reminder of the past. Like the islands' prehistoric builders, Piano has been inspired by the local stone, and the complex includes piazzas, staircases and walkways that have turned the area into a dynamic public space. The project has sparked masses of debate, about its expense and contemporary style, the position of the buildings, the open-air design of the auditorium, and the use of a foreign-born architect. Others consider it a masterpiece.

5000 Years of Architecture in Malta, by Leonard Mahoney, provides comprehensive coverage of Malta's archaeological history, from Neolithic temples to the auberges of the Knights and beyond.

Survival Guide

Directory A–Z

Climate

Valletta

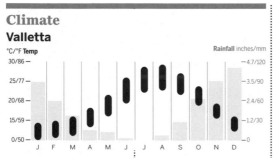

°C/°F **Temp**

Rainfall inches/mm

Customs Regulations

There are no restrictions if you're travelling from another EU country, though you're likely to be questioned if amounts seem excessive. If you're entering Malta from outside the EU, the duty-free allowance per person is 1L of spirits, 4L of wine, and 200 cigarettes or 100 cigarillos or 50 cigars or 250g of tobacco. Duty will be charged on any gifts over €430 that are intended for local residents.

Discount Cards

If you're planning to visit more than a few of Malta and Gozo's cultural treasures, it's a good idea to purchase a multisite pass from Heritage Malta, which covers 21 Heritage Malta sites and the Malta National Aquarium. Admission fees are so high that a single adult ticket to the Armoury and State Rooms in Valletta costs €10, the Ħaġar Qim & Mnajdra Temples cost €10, and most other sites cost €5 or €6.

The pass offers 30 days of free admission to most Heritage Malta sights (the Hypogeum is an exception; see www.heritagemalta.org for a full list). An adult/child pass costs €50/25, while a family ticket (two adults and two children) is an even better bargain at €110.

Other discounts:

➡ **Malta Pass** (maltapass. com.mt; 1/2/3 days €24.95/39.95/49.95) allows admission to over 40 attractions, plus a harbour cruise and open-bus tour. Buy online.

➡ People over 60 years are entitled to discounted admission to all government-owned museums.

➡ A valid ISIC card (www.isic. org) or European Youth Card (www.euro26.org) will gain you discounts.

➡ The **National Student Travel Service** (NSTS; ☎2558 8000; www.nsts.org; 220 Triq San Pawl, Valletta) can provide information about where you can get student reductions. Admission to state-run museums is discounted for card-carrying students.

Electricity

240V/50Hz

Embassies & Consulates

Full lists of Maltese embassies and consulates and foreign embassies in Malta can be found at www.foreign.gov.mt.

Australian High Commission (☎2133 8201; www.malta.embassy.gov. au; Villa Fiorentina, Rampa Ta'Xbiex, Ta'Xbiex)

Canadian Consulate (☎2552 3233; www.canada international.gc.ca; 103 Triq L-Arċisqof; ⊙8.30am-1.30pm Mon-Fri)

French Embassy (☎2248 0600; www.ambafrance-mt.org; 130 Triq Melita, Valletta)

German Embassy (☎2260 4000; www.valletta.diplo.de; Entrance B, 1st fl, Il-Piazzetta, Triq it-Torri, Sliema)

Irish Embassy (☎2133 4744; www.embassyofireland.org. mt; Whitehall Mansions, Ix-Xatt Ta'Xbiex, Ta'Xbiex)

Italian Embassy (☎2123 3157; www.amblavalletta.esteri. it; 5 Triq Vilhena, Floriana)

Netherlands Embassy (☎2131 3980; netherlands. visahq.com/embassy/Malta; Whitehall Mansions, Ix-Xatt Ta'Xbiex, Ta'Xbiex)

UK High Commission (☎2323 0000; www.gov.uk; Whitehall Mansions, Ix-Xatt Ta'Xbiex, Ta'Xbiex)

US Embassy (☎2561 4000; http://valletta.usembassy.gov; Ta'Qali, Attard)

Gay & Lesbian Travellers

Homosexual sex was legalised in Malta in 1973. In 2014 the government passed a bill approving same-sex civil unions and gay adoption. Gay marriages contracted abroad are also recognised by the state. However, Malta is a conservative, very Catholic country and public affection (straight or gay) is generally frowned upon. Still, while Malta is not a very 'out' destination, it is gay-friendly. For more information see www.gozoandmalta.com/gay and www.gaytravel.com/gay-guides/malta.

Malta Gay Rights Movement (www.maltagayrights. org) staged its first Gay Pride march in Valletta in July 2004, and the marches have been held annually ever since. Although the march and surrounding festivities are tiny in comparison to the large gatherings elsewhere in Europe, they're a chance for Malta's LGBT community to gather, celebrate diversity and push for an end to discrimination.

Health
Availability of Health Care in Malta

High-standard health and dental care is readily available in Malta, and for minor illnesses pharmacists can give valuable advice and sell over-the-counter medication. They can also advise when more specialised help is required and point you in the right direction.

There are pharmacies in most towns; these are generally open from 9am to 1pm and 4pm to 7pm Monday to Saturday. On Sundays and public holidays they open by roster in the morning – the local Sunday newspapers print details of the roster, and it can be found online at www. ehealth.gov.mt.

Malta's public general hospital is **Mater Dei Hospital** (☎2545 0000, emergency 112; www.ehealth.gov.mt; Tal-Qroqq), 2km southwest of Sliema and accessible by bus 75 from Valletta. Gozo's smaller **General Hospital** (☎2156 1600; Triq I-Arċisqof Pietru Pace) may also be of use. General practitioner service is available at a network of health centres (at Floriana, Gżira, Qormi, Paola, Ċospicua, Mosta, Rabat and on Gozo) as well as some pharmacies. English is spoken at all pharmacies, hospitals and health centres.

Medical Insurance

Citizens of the EU, Iceland, Liechtenstein, Norway and Switzerland receive free or reduced-cost state-provided health care with the European Health Insurance Card (EHIC) for medical treatment that becomes necessary while in Malta. The EHIC will not provide cover for non-emergencies or emergency repatriation home. Each family member will need a separate card. The EHIC is free; full details are online at www. ehic.org.uk.

Malta has reciprocal health agreements with Australia and the UK. Australians are eligible for subsidised health care for up to six months from their date of arrival in Malta; UK residents for up to 30 days. Details of these arrangements and various health services can be found on the website of the Maltese Ministry of Health (http:// health.gov.mt).

If you need health insurance, strongly consider a policy covering the worst possible scenario, such as an accident requiring an emergency flight home.

Insurance

A travel insurance policy to cover theft, loss and medical problems is always a good idea. Worldwide travel insurance is available at www. lonelyplanet.com/travel-insurance. You can buy, extend and claim online anytime – even if you're already on the road.

Some insurance policies specifically exclude 'dangerous activities', which can include scuba-diving. Note that policies don't usually cover dental work, only pain relief. Check the small print before signing up.

PRACTICALITIES

Newspapers & Magazines

➡ *The Times of Malta* (www.timesofmalta.com) Good mix of local, European and world news; English-language daily.

➡ *The Independent* (www.independent.com.mt) Coverage of domestic social issues; English-language daily.

➡ *Malta Today* (www.maltatoday.com.mt/en/home) Local and international news.

Radio & TV

➡ More than 20 local radio stations broadcast, mostly in Malti but occasionally in English.

➡ TVM is the state-run TV channel.

➡ Most of the main Italian TV stations, such as RAI-1, RAI-2 and RAI-3 can be received in Malta.

➡ Satellite and cable TV are widely available in hotels and bars.

Weights & Measures

➡ Metric system, like elsewhere in Europe. The British legacy persists in the use of pint glasses in some pubs.

Smoking

➡ Banned in any enclosed private or public premises open to the public except in designated smoking rooms.

➡ People can smoke freely outside.

You may prefer to have an insurance policy that pays doctors or hospitals directly rather than you having to pay on the spot and claim later. If you have to claim later, make sure you keep all documentation. Some policies ask you to call (reverse charges) a centre in your home country, where an immediate assessment of your problem is made.

Internet Access

Malta has extensive wi-fi coverage – most towns and even some of the sleepiest villages have a wi-fi hotspot in their main square. Many establishments, including hotels, cafes, bars and restaurants, also offer wi-fi. The wi-fi at most guesthouses, hostels and hotels is free; very occasionally there may be a charge of around €3 per hour. Signals are of varying quality.

If you're visiting from outside Europe, you may need a voltage converter to adjust the current in Europe (240V) to one your electronic device can handle. You do not usually need these for laptop computers and digital camera battery chargers.

Language Courses

The Maltese Islands are renowned as an enjoyable place to study English, and young people flock to the more than 40 language schools across the islands. Schools are mainly clustered in Valletta, St Julian's and Paceville. For a comprehensive list, see www.visitmalta.com.

Legal Matters

All towns and most villages have their own police station; the smaller ones are staffed by a single officer and often marked by a classic, British-style blue lamp.

If you are arrested or detained by the police you have the right to be informed, in a language that you understand, of the reasons for your arrest or detention, and if the police do not release you they must bring you before a court within 48 hours. You also have the right to inform your consulate and to speak to a lawyer.

For an emergency requiring help from the police (*pulizija* in Malti), call ☎112.

Gozo Police Headquarters (☎2156 2040; Triq ir-Repubblika, Victoria) Gozo's main police station is located near the corner of Triq ir-Repubblika and Triq Putirjal.

Malta Police Headquarters (☎2123 6719)

Money

Malta abandoned the Maltese lira and adopted the euro (€) on 1 January 2008. To prevent retailers from rounding up prices, the rate of exchange was fixed at Lm1 to €2.33, which is why you'll still sometimes see euro prices in fractions or multiples of 2.33.

The reverse sides of Maltese coins feature a uniquely Maltese design (a Maltese cross, for example), but are legal tender in all countries in the Eurozone.

ATMs

There are plentiful ATMs at Malta International Airport, Valletta's waterfront and in all the main towns in Malta, where you can withdraw euros using a credit or debit card and PIN.

ATM withdrawals may incur a transaction charge of around 2.75% and an ATM charge of around 1.5% to 2% of the amount withdrawn – check with your bank before departing. You may also need to inform your bank before you travel, to avoid your card being blocked.

Cash

Cash can be changed at hotels, banks, exchange bureaux and some tourist shops. There are also 24-hour exchange machines at banks in the main tourist towns, including Valletta, Sliema and Buġibba, where you can feed in foreign banknotes and get euros back.

You'll need to carry cash because many smaller restaurants and hotels don't accept cards.

Credit Cards

Visa, MasterCard and Amex credit cards and charge cards are widely accepted in larger hotels, restaurants and shops, though smaller places only deal in cash. Travel and car-hire agencies accept cards.

Taxes & Refunds

VAT (value-added tax) was reintroduced to Malta in 1999, with two rates: accommodation is charged at 5% (and is usually included in the rates quoted) and the rate for other items is 18%. Food, medicine, education, maritime services, air, sea and public transport are exempt from VAT.

Visitors to Malta can reclaim VAT on their purchases provided they are residents outside the EU, and will be taking the goods outside the EU when they depart from Malta. Repayment of VAT applies only on single items valued at not less than €55 and bought from a single registered outlet as shown on the receipt, and where the total value of all items is not under €315. If you wish to get a VAT refund, you fill out an application form, available at the custom exit points at the airport or sea port. Previously there was a lengthy wait to receive the refund, but the government took action to address this in 2015, so it may be that you receive your refund before leaving the country.

Tipping & Bargaining

➡ Tipping etiquette is like on mainland Europe (ie tipping is not expected, but appreciated). In restaurants where no service charge is included in the bill, leave 10% for good service. Baggage porters should get about €1 per piece of luggage, car-park attendants around €1. Taxi drivers don't expect a tip, but it's nice to round up a fare in order to leave a small tip (up to 10%) if warranted.

➡ You may bargain for handicrafts at stalls or markets, but shops have fixed prices.

➡ You can often angle for lower prices from hotels and car-hire agencies in the off season (October to mid-June) and stays/rentals of a week or more will often get a 10% discount.

Opening Hours

Banks

➡ 8.30am to 12.30pm Monday to Friday (some banks will stay open until 2pm, or even slightly longer on Friday)

➡ 8.30am to around noon on Saturday

➡ From 8am mid-June to September

Museums

➡ 9am to 5pm daily (last entry at 4.30pm)

➡ Closed 24, 25 and 31 December, 1 January and Good Friday

Pharmacies

➡ 9am to 1pm and 4pm to 7pm Monday to Saturday

➡ Duty pharmacies that open late and on Sunday or public holidays are listed in local newspapers

Restaurants

➡ Lunch: noon to 3pm, dinner: 7pm to 11pm

➡ Some restaurants close for three or four weeks in August

Shops

➡ 9am to 1pm and 4pm to 7pm Monday to Saturday

➡ In tourist areas in summer they are often open all day

➡ Most shops are closed on Sunday and public holidays

Photography

Memory cards and camera equipment are easily obtained at photographic shops in all the main towns.

For tips on taking the perfect holiday snaps, look out for Lonely Planet's *Travel Photography* book.

Post

Malta Post (www.maltapost. com) operates a reliable postal service. Post office branches are found in most towns and villages (in some towns the local newsagent/ souvenir shop acts as a branch agent).

Local postage costs €0.26 up to 50g; a 20g letter or postcard sent airmail to the UK or Europe costs €0.59, to the USA €0.51 and to Australia €0.63. Stamps are frequently available from hotels and souvenir shops as well as from post offices.

Safe Travel

Swimming

Malta and Gozo's waters are not really tidal, and when the weather is calm it's usually completely safe to swim. However, the Maltese often repeat the saying, 'The sea has a soft belly, but a hard head', a warning to be wary of the sea around the islands because of its powerful undercurrents in windy weather. Locals advise never to swim in rough sea.

Major beaches, such as Golden Bay on Malta and Ramla Bay on Gozo, have lifeguards patrolling and a flag system operating from June to September; take note of the flags. If there's no flag system operating and if you're in doubt, ask a local about whether it's safe and where to swim.

Hunting

If you go walking in the countryside, be aware of the common pastime of shooting and trapping birds – the little stone shacks that pepper the clifftops are shooters' hides. You will hear the popping of shotguns before you see the shooters. There are usually two short hunting seasons, in spring and autumn.

Road Conditions & Driving

Much of the road network in Malta is badly in need of repair, which means that driving is often an uncomfortably bumpy experience. Rules of the road are rarely observed, which adds to the stress of driving in unfamiliar territory, especially during rush-hour conditions around Sliema and St Julian's.

Take special care on roundabouts and always wait to see what other drivers are doing, even if it's your right of way (never assume they will stop for you!) A sat-nav will also enormously reduce the stress of driving, particularly as signposting can be erratic off the main routes.

Theft & Violence

Malta has a low rate of violent crime, and crimes against visitors are a rarity. Incidents involving pickpockets and purse-snatchers are uncommon, but in past years there have been increasing reports of thieves breaking into cars parked in quiet areas including Marfa and Delimara Point. Lock your car and don't leave anything of value in it.

There have been occasional incidents of drunken violence in Paceville late at night; exercise caution in this area.

Telephone

Mobile Phones

There are 130 mobile phones per 100 population in Malta, so not only are mobiles widespread, but many locals have more than one number. Mobile-phone numbers begin with either ☑79 or ☑99. Malta uses the GSM900 mobile phone network which is compatible with the rest of Europe, Australia and New Zealand, but not with the USA and Canada's GSM1900. If you have a GSM phone, check with your service provider about using it in Malta and beware of calls being routed internationally (expensive for a 'local' call).

You may consider buying a Maltese SIM card, which gives you a Maltese mobile number. (Your mobile may be locked to the local network in your home country, so ask your home network for advice before going abroad.) Prepaid vouchers for topping up credit are available at many places and kiosks throughout Malta.

Phone Codes

The international direct dialling code is ☑00, followed by the relevant country code and then the number. To call Malta from abroad, dial the international access code, ☑356 (the country code for Malta) and then the number.

There are no area codes in Malta; all Maltese phone numbers are eight-digit numbers.

Public Phones & Phonecards

Public telephones are widely available, and most are card-operated (there are also coin-operated phones, but these are not as common). You can buy phonecards at many kiosks, post offices and souvenir shops. Go Easyline cards (www.go.com.mt) can be used from any line (including payphones, mobiles and even from hotels) and can be used in a range of overseas destinations. They are available in denominations of €5, €10 and €20.

Local calls using a Go Easyline card cost €0.05 per minute to landlines, and €0.25 per minute to mobiles, and you can also make calls overseas.

Time

Malta is in the same time zone as most of Western Europe: one hour ahead of GMT/UTC on standard time, and two hours ahead from the last Sunday in March to the last Sunday in October (the daylight saving period).

Toilets

Malta is well equipped with public toilets, often at the entrance to a public garden or near the village square. They are usually clean and in good order. If there is an attendant, it is good manners to leave a tip of a few cents in a dish by the door.

Tourist Information

Local Tourist Offices

As well as the useful and comprehensive **Malta Tourism site** (www.visitmalta.com), there are tourist information offices in Valletta, Mdina, Buġibba, at Malta International Airport, and in Victoria and at the Ferry Terminal in Mġarr on Gozo.

Tourist Offices Abroad

The Malta Tourism Authority has overseas representation that can help with enquiries from potential holiday-makers.

Germany (☎069-247503135; www.visitmalta.com/de; Fremdenverkehrsamt Malta, Schillerstrasse 30-40, D-60313 Frankfurt-am-Main)

UK (☎020-8877 6990; office.uk@visitmalta.com; Malta Tourist Office, Unit C, Park House, 14 Northfields, London SW18 1DD)

Travellers with Disabilities

Maltese government policy is to improve access for people with disabilities, but many of Malta's historic places – notably the steep, stepped streets of Valletta – remain difficult, if not impossible, to negotiate for those with restricted mobility. Several sights are accessible, however, including Fort St Elmo and the National War Museum, the Grand Master's Palace, the Malta Experience and the National Museum of Archaeology in Valletta.

A good number of the more expensive hotels have wheelchair access and some have rooms specially designed for guests with disabilities. Sliema, with its long promenade, is a good place to be based. The Malta and Gozo bus services have wheelchair-accessible buses.

The **Nautic Team** (☎2155 8507; www.nauticteam.com; Triq il-Vulcan) on Gozo are equipped for divers with disabilities, offering courses and equipment hire.

The Malta Tourism Authority (www.visitmalta.com) can provide information on hotels and sights that are equipped for wheelchair users.

The **National Commission for Persons with Disabilities** (Centru Hidma Soċjali; ☎2278 8555; www.knpd.org; Triq Braille, Santa Venera) can provide information on facilities and access for travellers with a disability in Malta.

Lonely Planet has a Travel for All community on Google+, where you can find out and share information about accessible travel, as well as the Thorntree community at www.lonelyplanet.com/thorntree/forums/travellers-with-disabilities.

Visas

Everyone is required to have a valid passport (or ID card for EU citizens) to enter Malta. EU citizens are entitled to travel freely around the member states of the EU, and settle anywhere within its territory.

Malta is part of the Schengen area. Citizens from some non-EU countries are required to hold a visa when travelling to the Schengen area. Generally, a short-stay visa issued by one of the Schengen states entitles its holder to travel throughout the 25 Schengen states for up to three months within a six-month period. Visas for visits exceeding that period are at the discretion of the Malta authorities. Citizens of Australia, Canada, Israel, Japan, New Zealand and the US can stay for up to three months without a visa; other nationalities can check their visa requirements on www.foreign.gov.mt (click on the Services/Travelling to Malta link).

If you wish to stay for more than 90 days, you will have to apply for a Temporary Residence Permit via the Department for Citizenship and Expatriates Affairs (eresidence.mhas@gov.mt). You will need two photographs, a letter regarding your reasons for staying (an English-language course, employment etc), a completed application form, evidence of your means of support, and documents showing your health insurance. More information is available at www.mfa.gov.mt and http://identitymalta.com/citizenships-expatriates.

Visit Lonely Planet's website for up-to-date visa information: www.lonelyplanet.com/malta/practical-information/visas.

Transport

GETTING THERE & AWAY

Air

Malta is well connected to Europe and North Africa, but there are no direct flights into Malta from places further afield. If you're flying from elsewhere, it's best to travel to a major European hub, such as London, Amsterdam or Brussels, then join a direct connecting flight to Malta.

Airports & Airlines

All flights arrive and depart from **Malta International Airport** (MLA; ☑2124 9600; www.maltairport.com; Luga), 8km south of Valletta. The airport has good facilities, including ATMs and currency exchange, internet access, a tourist office (open daily), left luggage, and regular, inexpensive bus connections to Malta's major towns and to the Gozo ferry. The Maltese national airline is **Air Malta** (KM; ☑2166 2211; www.air malta.com), a small airline with a good safety record.

Land

You can travel by bus from most parts of Europe to a port in Italy and catch a ferry from there to Malta. Euro-lines (www.eurolines.com) is a consortium of coach companies that operates across Europe, with offices in all major European cities.

With your own vehicle, you can drive to northern Italy and take a car ferry from Genoa, or drive to southern Italy and take a car ferry from Salerno or from Pozzallo or Catania (Sicily) to Malta. From northern Europe the fastest road route is via the Simplon Pass to Milan, from which Italy's main highway, the Autostrada del Sole, stretches all the way to Reggio di Calabria. From London the distance is around 2200km.

Car drivers and motorbike riders will need the vehicle's registration papers, a Green Card, a nationality plate and their domestic licence. Contact your local automobile association for details about necessary documentation.

Sea

Ferry

Malta has regular sea links with Sicily (Pozzallo and Catania), central Italy (Civitavecchia) and northern Italy (Genoa). Ferries dock at the Sea Passenger Terminal beside the Valletta Waterfront in Floriana, underneath the southeast bastions of Valletta.

Virtu Ferries (☑2206 9022; www.virtuferries.com) offers the shortest, fastest Malta–Sicily crossing with its catamaran service (carrying cars and passengers)

CLIMATE CHANGE & TRAVEL

Every form of transport that relies on carbon-based fuel generates CO_2, the main cause of human-induced climate change. Modern travel is dependent on planes, which might use less fuel per kilometre per person than most cars but travel much greater distances. The altitude at which aircraft emit gases (including CO_2) and particles also contributes to their climate change impact. Many websites offer 'carbon calculators' that allow people to estimate the carbon emissions generated by their journey and, for those who wish to do so, to offset the impact of the greenhouse gases emitted with contributions to portfolios of climate-friendly initiatives throughout the world. Lonely Planet offsets the carbon footprint of all staff and author travel.

to/from Pozzallo, with bus transfers to Catania (two hours).

The Pozzallo–Malta crossing takes 1½ hours and operates year-round, with daily sailings from June to August, dropping to four or five days a week in September, weather permitting. The return passenger fare in high/low season is €150/113 (day return €136/85).

Tickets for children under four years are free but there is a charge of €10 for local transport where applicable; children aged four to 14 years pay around 50% of the adult fares.

Public transport links from the ferry terminal at Valletta's waterfront have vastly improved with the new Upper Barrakka Lift, which connects the waterfront with Upper Barrakka Gardens in Valletta. However, if you have luggage you'll probably prefer to catch a taxi to your destination. Set fees are established – head to the information booth at Valletta Waterfront (to Valletta is €10, to Sliema/St Julian's €18).

Yacht

Malta's excellent harbour and its strategic location at the hub of the Mediterranean has led to its development as a major yachting centre.

There are berths for 720 yachts (up to 22m length overall) in the Msida and Ta' Xbiex marinas (www.marinamalta.com) near Valletta; Mgarr Marina (www.gozomarina.net) on Gozo has space for more than 200 boats. There are also marinas at the Portomaso complex (www.portomasomarina.com) in St Julian's, and the Grand Harbour Marina (www.cnmarinas.com/en/marinas/grand-harbour-marina) in Vittoriosa.

For more information on these marinas and details of the logistics and formalities of sailing to Malta, contact **Transport Malta** (☑2122 2203; www.transport.gov.mt).

EXCURSIONS TO SICILY

Virtu Ferries (☑2206 9022; www.virtuferries.com) runs 90-minute passenger catamaran services to Pozzallo that enable travellers to make a day trip to the Italian island of Sicily. You take the boat at 6.30am and return on the 9.30pm boat; the itinerary takes in Mt Etna and the town of Taormina; Syracuse, the Marina di Ragusa and Modica; or Mt Etna and Modica (adult/child four to 14 years €124/92).

It also runs the 'Godfather Excursion' to Taormina and Savoca, where some scenes from the Coppola films were shot (€136; children are free with two adults). Other themed excursions include a culinary tour and quad bike adventure.

Prices include taxes but exclude lunch; transfers in Malta cost €10. You can book a trip online or through most hotels and travel agents in Malta.

Malta's popularity with the yachting fraternity means that it is possible to make your way there as unpaid crew. Yachts tend to leave Gibraltar, southern Spain and the Balearics in April and May to head towards the popular cruising grounds of the Greek Islands and the Turkish coast. It's possible to just turn up at a marina and ask if there are any yachts looking for crew, but there are also agencies that bring together yacht owners and prospective crew (for a fee). One such agency is UK-based **Crewseekers** (☑0238-115 9207; www.crewseekers.net), which charges £70/95 for a six-/12-month membership.

Tours

There are loads of companies offering tours around the islands, by boat/bus/4WD or a combination of the three. Prices vary (as does what's included), so shop around. If you're pushed for time these trips can be a good way to see the highlights, but itineraries can be rushed, with little free time.

Tours include half-day tours to the Blue Grotto or Valletta's Sunday market; full-day trips to the Three Cities, Mosta and Mdina; or evening trips to take in

festa celebrations. Day trips to Gozo and Comino are also common. Tours can be arranged through most hotels and travel agents.

Captain Morgan Cruises (☑2346 3333; www.captainmorgan.com.mt; adult/child harbour cruise €16/13, round Malta €35/free, Blue Lagoon €25/free, underwater safari €17/11; jeep safari Malta €55/45, Gozo €65/55) Offers a wide range of cruises, including the Grand Harbour, round Malta, and day trips to the Blue Lagoon. These trips depart from the ferry area in Sliema; some include transfers to/from your accommodation in the price. On some under 12s go free when with two adults. There are also 'underwater safari' cruises from Bugibba, on boats with underwater viewing areas.

It also offers popular chauffeur-driven jeep safaris to remote parts of Malta and Gozo.

CitySightseeing Malta (☑2346 7777; www.citysightseeing.com.mt; adult/child €17/9; ☉half-hourly 9am-3pm Mon-Sat, 9am-1pm Sun) Operates tours of Malta in open-top buses: hop on and off any of the buses at any of the 20 or so stops. You can board and buy a ticket at any stop.

Hera Cruises (☑2133 0583; www.heracruises.com) Various boat tours leaving from Sliema waterfront, including all-day cruises (adult/child €58/30), and trips to Comino and the Blue Lagoon (€30/20) or Comino and Gozo (€50/30, includes lunch) in a regular boat, or to the Blue Lagoon in a Turkish *gulet* (old-style sailing boat; €58/30, includes lunch).

Luzzu Cruises (www. luzzucruises.com; 2-harbour cruise adult/child €16/13, Gozo, Comino & Blue Lagoon €40/20, Comino, Blue Lagoon & caves €20/15, boat & jeep Gozo €55/40) A range of trips, including a two-harbour cruise and day-long trips taking in Gozo, Comino and the Blue Lagoon. Also arranges boat trips to Marsaxlokk (adult/child €17.50/12.50) for the Sunday market.

Malta Sightseeing (☑2169 4967; www.maltasightseeing. com; per day adult/child €20/13; ⊙north & south tours depart Sliema 9am-3pm Mon-Sat & 9am-2pm Sun & public holidays; Gozo tours depart Mġarr Harbour 9.30am-3pm) Hop-on, hop-off tours around north (blue tour) or south (red tour) Malta, or around Gozo.

GETTING AROUND

Bicycle

Cycling on Maltese roads can be nerve-wracking – the roads are often narrow and potholed, there's lots of traffic, and drivers show little consideration for cyclists. However, things are considerably better on the back roads and also on Gozo – the roads can still be rough, but there's far less traffic, and more and more visitors are opting to cycle around the island rather than rely on the buses.

You can rent bikes from **Magri Cycles & Spares** (☑2141 4399; www.magri cycles.com; 135 Triq il-Kungress Ewkaristiku, Mosta, Malta) and **Victoria Garage** (☑2155 6414; www.victoriagaragegozo. com; Triq Putirjal, Victoria, Gozo; bicycle per day from €5, car per day €21). You can rent electric bikes from **Eco Bikes** (www. bikerentalmalta.com; bike/e-bike per day €10/20).

Bus

The bone-shaking, charming, brightly painted vintage buses that were so characteristic of Malta were taken out of service in 2011, replaced by boring-looking but more efficient modern buses, which have disabled access. These are operated by **Malta Public Transport** (www.publictransport.com.mt), which is presently run by the Spanish company Autobuses Urbanos de León.

Many bus routes on Malta originate from the Valletta Bus Station and radiate to all parts of the island, but there are also many routes that bypass the capital; bus timings range from every 10 minutes to hourly for less-visited places. On Gozo the bus system is much more efficient than previously, though some places are only served by an hourly bus.

Tickets

You can buy single tickets as you board the bus or from ticket machines, which are found near numerous bus stops. Blocks of tickets and

---

BIG YELLOW BUSES

Malta's old buses were a tourist attraction in themselves, and it's a shame in terms of local colour and photo opportunities that they're no longer rattling around the islands' potholed roads at unsettling speeds. Run as independent businesses by their drivers, they were lovingly customised with handmade parts and decorations. They were known as *xarabank,* a derivation of *charabanc* (a carriage or an old-fashioned term for a motor coach).

On the other hand, they probably also contributed to Malta being the most car-dense country in Europe. Quaintness of buses is not necessarily an endearing quality when you have to use them day to day, and the bus system is much more efficient nowadays. You will spot the occasional old bus on the road: the classic Bedfords, Thames, Leylands and AECs dating from the 1950s, '60s and '70s, brightly painted in a livery of yellow, white and orange, have not completely disappeared. Numerous well-preserved vintage buses have been retained as tourist attractions, and now run sightseeing trips around the islands. Try **Malta Sightseeing** (☑2169 4967; www.maltasightseeing.com; per day adult/child €20/13; ⊙north & south tours depart Sliema 9am-3pm Mon-Sat & 9am-2pm Sun & public holidays; Gozo tours depart Mġarr Harbour 9.30am-3pm), which offers a tour from Sliema around the Three Cities for €15/9 adult/child. A vintage bus also runs from Valletta's waterfront up to Floriana.

The Malta Buses by Michael Cassar and Joseph Bonnici is an illustrated history of the islands' celebrated public transport.

seven-day passes must be bought in advance from ticket offices or Agenda bookshop outlets. If you're caught travelling without a ticket, there's a penalty charge of €10.

➡ €2/1.50 July to September/October to June single ticket (valid two hours): may be bought on the bus

➡ €3 night fare (on night buses): year-round

➡ Block of 12 tickets €15: this is a multi-user option, so if two people are travelling together, they can scan the ticket twice. A ticket is valid for two hours from when it's scanned. On night buses, you pay double (ie scan two tickets for one journey).

➡ Explorer seven-day ticket adult/child €21/15: valid on both Malta and Gozo, unlimited journeys, day or night

➡ Tallinja stored value card: for this you need to register at Valletta Bus Station or online two weeks in advance to allow for delivery. You have to provide an ID card number, but this can be Maltese, a foreign ID or your passport number. You have also to give your Malta address, which may be the address of your hotel in Malta – the card will be delivered there. With the Tallinja card, a single journey costs €0.75/0.25 adult/child. Night buses cost €2.50.

Routes & Timetables

At the time of research, some bus numbers and timetables were about to change. To see up-to-date, full bus timetables and route maps, check online at www.publictransport.com.mt.

There are six different express services running between the airport and various parts of the island, including St Julian's, Sliema and Ċirkewwa. The X4, X5 and X7 run between Valletta and the airport, and take just over 20 minutes.

Most buses run from around 5.30am to 11pm, and frequency varies depending on the popularity of the route. In towns and villages the bus terminus is usually found on or near the parish church square.

Car & Motorcycle

The Maltese love their cars. At weekends (Sunday in particular) they take to the road en masse, visiting friends and family or heading for the beach or a favourite picnic site. This means that there is often serious congestion on the roads around Valletta, Sliema and St Julian's. Friday and Saturday night in Paceville is one big traffic jam. However, renting a car gives you more flexibility, particularly to discover out-of-the-way beach coves.

Distance isn't a problem – the longest distance on Malta is 27km and the widest point is around 15km. On Gozo the longest distance is about 14km and the widest only 7km.

Automobile Associations

If you're renting a car, you'll be provided with a telephone number to contact in the event of mechanical difficulties or breakdown. If you're bringing your own vehicle, it's a good idea to take out European breakdown cover (offered in the UK by both the RAC and the AA). For roadside assistance in Malta, contact **RMF** (☑2124 2222; www.rmfmalta.com) or **MTC** (☑2143 3333; www.mtctowing-malta.com).

Bringing Your Own Vehicle

Tourists are permitted to use their vehicles for a maximum of six months in any given year without the need to apply for a permit. A motor vehicle entering a foreign country must display a sticker identifying its country of registration.

Driving Licences

All EU member states' driving licences are fully recognised throughout Europe. For those with a non-EU licence, an International Driving Permit (IDP) is a useful adjunct, especially if your home licence has no photo or is in a language other than English. Your local automobile association can issue an IDP, valid for one year, for a small fee. You must carry your home licence together with the IDP.

Fuel

The price of fuel is set by the government and at the time of research was €1.35/1.28 a litre for unleaded/diesel. Petrol is dispensed by attendants and garages are generally open from 7am to 7pm (6pm in winter) Monday to Saturday; most are closed on Sunday and public holidays – though a few are open from 8am to noon on a roster system. Larger stations have a self-service, cash-operated pump (€5, €10 and €20 notes accepted) for filling up outside opening hours.

Hire

Car rental rates in Malta are among the lowest in Europe. If you hire a car on Malta you can take it over to Gozo on the ferry without a problem. Rental rates on Gozo are lower (but with an extra charge for taking the car to Malta), but if you're visiting both islands the inconvenience of hiring a car in both places would outweigh any benefits. Supply is limited on Gozo so for July and August you'll need to book in advance to be assured of a vehicle.

Most of the car-hire companies have representatives at the airport, but rates vary so it's worth shopping around. Make sure you know what is included in the quoted rate – many of the local agencies quote very low rates that do not include full insurance against theft and collision damage.

Obviously rates will vary with season, length of rental period and the size and make of car (plus extras like air-con). Rates for the smallest vehicles start from around €25 a day (for rental of seven days or longer) in the high season. A child seat costs around €4 per day – but confirm whether it's a booster seat or full child seat.

The age limit for rental drivers is generally 21 to 70 years, but drivers between 21 and 25 years may be asked to pay a supplement of up to €10 a day. You will need a valid driving licence that you have held for at least one year. Rental rates often include free delivery and collection, especially in the Valletta-Sliema-St Julian's area.

Many accommodation providers offer car-rental arrangements – it pays to ask when you're making a booking. Most will drop off and collect cars (usually for a small fee). As well as all the major international compa-nies, such as Avis, Budget and Hertz, there are dozens of local car-hire agencies.

Billy's (☑2152 3676; www.billyscarhire.com; 113 Triq Ġorġ Borg Olivier, Mellieħa, Malta)

Mayjo Car Rentals (☑2155 6678; www.mayjocarhire.com; Triq Fortunato Mizzi, Victoria, Gozo; per day €28) A large range of cars at good rates.

Wembleys (☑2137 4141, 2137 4242; http://wembleys.com; 50 Triq San Ġorġ, St Julian's, Malta)

Insurance

Car-hire companies offer col-lision damage waiver (CDW) and/or theft damage protec-tion insurance at extra cost (usually charged per day). Be sure to read the fine print and understand what you're covered for, and what excess charges you'll be up for in the case of an accident.

If you are bringing your own car, check with your local insurance company before you leave to make sure you are covered.

Parking

Parking can be tricky in the Sliema-St Julian's and Bugib-ba-Qawra areas. While there are car parks available, it's far more difficult to find parking in the high season. There's a large car park next to the Malta National Aquarium (from €2). In Valletta you can park within the city walls in the blue parking bays, but those delineated in green are reserved for residents. If you can't find parking within the walls, you can use the large MCP underground car park near the bus terminus, close to the Hotel Phoenicia, which is only a short walk from Valletta's City Gate and sights. Parking in the MCP costs €2.50 for up to two hours and €5 for over four hours. Alternatively, you can use the Park & Ride facility, just south of Floriana, where parking costs €0.40 per day and shuttle buses run to the City Gate in Valletta. Parking elsewhere costs €1 to €2 per hour.

Local traffic police are swift and merciless in the imposition of on-the-spot fines. Most main towns, tourist sights and beaches have a car park, with an attendant dressed in a blue shirt and cap and usually wearing an official badge. These attendants will expect a tip of around €1 upon your departure.

Road Rules & Conditions

Unlike most of Europe, the Maltese drive on the left. Speed limits are 80km/h on highways and 50km/h in urban areas, but are rarely observed. Wearing a seat belt is compulsory for the driver and front-seat passenger. Any accidents must be re-ported to the nearest police station (and to the rental company if the car is hired); don't move your vehicle until the police arrive, otherwise your insurance may be nullified.

Road signs and regu-lations are pretty much the same as the rest of Europe, with one important difference – in Malta no-one seems to pay attention to any of the rules. Be prepared for drivers overtaking on the inside, ignoring traffic lights, refusing to give way at junctions and hanging on your rear bumper if they think you're going too slowly. All rental cars have registra-tion numbers ending in K, so tourists can be spotted easily. Vehicles coming from your right are supposed to have right of way at round-abouts, but don't count on vehicles on your left observ-ing this rule.

You should also be aware that many of the roads are in a pitiful condition, with cracks and potholes, and there are very few road mark-ings. In winter, minor roads are occasionally blocked by wash-outs or collapsed retaining walls after heavy rain. Signposting is variable – some minor sights are easy to find, while major towns remain elusive. Often places seem to be well signposted, and then the signposts peter out. A sat-nav or a detailed road map will help ease the way.

The maximum allowable blood-alcohol concentration in drivers in Malta is 0.08%.

Ferry

To/from Valletta
Valletta Ferry Services (☑2346 3862; www.valletta-ferryservices.com) operate regular ferries between Valletta's Marsamxett har-bour and **Sliema** (single/return adult €1.50/2.80, child €0.50/0.90; ⏱7.15am-7.15pm Oct-May, to 12.45am Jun-Sep), as well as from near Valletta Waterfront to Cospicua (Bormla) and on to Seng-lea (L'Isla) in the **Three Cities** (single/return adult €1.50/2.80, child €0.50/0.90;

⊘half-hourly 7am-7pm Oct-May, to midnight Jun-Sep).

Water taxis, run by **A&S Water Taxis** (⏿9812 9802; www.maltesewatertaxis.com; Valletta–Three Cities/Sliema/ St Julian's €3/10/12, harbour cruise €30) and **Malta Water Taxis** (⏿9993 9443; www.maltawatertaxis.com. mt; Valletta–Three Cities €3, harbour cruise €10), also take people back and forth between Valletta and the Three Cities, and Valletta and Sliema, but it's a question of luck whether you'll find one, unless you call ahead to book.

To/from Gozo & Comino

Gozo Channel (⏿2155 6114; www.gozochannel.com; foot passenger day/night €4.65/4.05, child €1.15, car & driver day/night €15.70/12.80) operates the car ferry that shuttles between Malta's Ċirkewwa and Gozo's Mġarr every 45 minutes from 6am to around 6pm (and roughly every 1½ hours throughout the night). If travelling by vehicle you pay on your return leg, when leaving Mġarr (Gozo), so there's no need to buy a ticket in Ċirkewwa on the way out.

Gozo Channel also operates a cargo ferry from Sa Maison near Valletta to/ from Gozo (90 minutes; usually twice weekly, on Tuesday and Thursday), which takes some foot passengers (€4.65), but you'll have to call on the day to see if there is space available.

KARROZZIN

The *karrozzin* – a traditional horse-drawn carriage with seats for four passengers – has been in use in Malta since 1856. Many of the carriages are treasured family possessions passed down through generations, and are cared for with obsessive pride.

You can catch a *karrozzin* at Valletta's City Gate, Marsamxetto Ferry, Fort St Elmo, Valletta Waterfront and Mdina's Main Gate. There is an unfortunate tendency in some drivers to overcharge unwitting tourists. Haggle with the driver and be sure to agree on a fare before getting in. The fixed fare is €35 for 35 minutes.

Taxi

Official Maltese taxis are white (usually Mercedes, with a taxi sign on top; www.maltataxi.net). To combat regular complaints of overcharging, taxi drivers must by law use the meter to determine the fare (except from the airport and sea port, where there are set fares).

Details of the fixed fares from the airport are available at the taxi desk in the arrivals hall, where you can pay in advance and hand a ticket to the driver. These were the fares at the time of research:

➡ Valletta/Floriana €15

➡ Three Cities area €18

➡ Mdina/Rabat €18

➡ Sliema/St Julian's area €20

➡ Buġibba/St Paul's Bay €25

➡ Golden Bay area €25

➡ Mellieħa €30

➡ Ċirkewwa €32

There are taxi ranks at City Gate and outside the Grand Master's Palace in Valletta, and at bus stations and major hotels in the main tourist resorts. Within Valletta, **Smart Cabs** (⏿7741 4177; 3 people within city perimeter/ to cruise-ship terminal €5/8) provide an electric-powered taxi service for a flat fare of €5/8 for three people inside/ outside the city walls.

As an alternative to the official Maltese white taxis, unsigned black taxis are owned by private companies and usually offer cheaper set fares (similar to the UK's minicabs). To order a taxi, it's best to ask your hotel reception for the name and number of their preferred service. There are several 24-hour companies.

Belmont Garage (⏿2155 6962; Nadur, Gozo)

Freephone Taxis (⏿8007 3770, 2138 9575; St Julian's, Malta)

Wembley's (⏿2137 4141, 2137 4242; St Julian's, Malta) Reliable 24-hour radio taxi service. Rates are generally cheaper than official taxi rates (from St Julian's to Valletta it's €13, to the airport €18, to the Gozo ferry €28).

Language

Malti – the native language of Malta – is a member of the Semitic language group, which also includes Arabic, Hebrew and Amharic. It's thought by some to be a direct descendant of the language spoken by the Phoenicians, but most linguists consider it to be related to the Arabic dialects of western North Africa. Malti is the only Semitic language that is written in a Latin script.
Both Malti and English are official languages in Malta, and almost everyone is bilingual. Travellers will have no trouble at all getting by in English at all times. This chapter provides a basic introduction to Malti.

PRONUNCIATION

Most letters of the Maltese alphabet are pronounced as they are in English, with the following exceptions:

ċ	as the 'ch' in 'child'
ġ	soft, as the 'j' in 'job'
għ	inaudible; lengthens the preceding or following vowel
h	inaudible, as in 'hour'
ħ	as the 'h' in 'hand'
ij	as the 'ai' in 'aisle'
j	as the 'y' in 'yellow'
q	a glottal stop, which is similar to the pause in the middle of 'uh-oh'
x	as the 'sh' in 'shop'
z	as the 'ts' in 'bits'
ż	soft, as in 'zero'

BASICS

Hello.	Merħba.
Good morning./day.	Bonġu.
Good evening.	Bonswa.
Goodbye.	Saħħa.
Yes.	Iva.
No.	Le.
Please.	Jekk jogħġbok.
Thank you.	Grazzi.
Excuse me.	Skużani.
How are you?	Kif inti?
I'm fine, thank you.	Tajjed, grazzi.
Do you speak English?	Titkellem bl-ingliż?
What's your name?	X'ismek?
My name is ...	Jisimni ...
I love you.	Inħobbok.

ACCOMMODATION

Do you have any rooms available?	Għad fadlilkom xi kmamar vojta?
Can you show me a room?	Tista' turini kamra?
How much is it?	Kemm hi?
I'd like a room ...	Nixtieq kamra ...
with en suite	bil-kamra tal-banju
with one bed	b'sodda waħda
with two beds	b'żewġ sodod

SIGNS

Dħul	Entrance
Ħrug	Exit
Magħluq	Closed
Miftuħ	Open
Nisa	Women
Rġiel	Men
Sqaq	Lane/Alley
Twaletta	Toilet
Vjalq	Avenue

NUMBERS

0	xejn
1	wieħed
2	tnejn
3	tlieta
4	erbgħa
5	ħamsa
6	sitta
7	sebgħa
8	tmienja
9	disgħa
10	għaxra
11	ħdax
12	tnax
13	tlettax
14	erbatax
15	ħmistax
16	sittax
17	sbatax
18	tmintax
19	dsatax
20	għoxrin
30	tletin
40	erbgħin
50	ħamsin
60	sittin
70	sebgħin
80	tmienin
90	disgħin
100	mija
1000	elf

EMERGENCIES

Help!	Ajjut!
Police!	Pulizija!
Call a doctor!	Qibgħad ghat-tabib!
I'm lost.	Ninsab mitluf.

ambulance	ambulans
hospital	sptar

SHOPPING & SERVICES

At what time does it open/close?	Fix'ħin jiftaħ/jagħlaq?
How much?	Kemm?

bank	ħank
... embassy	ambaxxata ...
hotel	hotel/il-lukanda
market	suq
pharmacy	ispiżerija
post office	posta
public telephone	telefon pubbliku
shop	ħanut

TIME, DATES & NUMBERS

What's the time?	X'ħin hu?

morning	fil-għodu
afternoon	wara nofs in-nhar
yesterday	il-bieraħ
today	illum
tomorrow	għada

Monday	it-tnejn
Tuesday	it-tlieta
Wednesday	l-erbgħa
Thursday	il-ħamis
Friday	il-gimgħa
Saturday	is-sibt
Sunday	il-ħadd

January	Jannar
February	Frar
March	Marzu
April	April
May	Mejju
June	Ġunju
July	Lulju
August	Awissu
September	Settembru
October	Ottubru
November	Novembru
December	Diċembru

TRANSPORT & DIRECTIONS

I'd like a ticket.	Nixtieq biljett.
When does the boat leave/arrive?	Meta jitlaq/jasal il-vapur?
When does the bus leave/arrive?	Meta titlaq/jasal il-karoz za?

I'd like to hire a car/bicycle.	*Nixtieq nikri karozza/rota.*
Where is a/the ...?	*Fejn hu ...?*
Go straight ahead.	*Mur dritt.*
Turn left.	*Dur fuq ix-xellug.*
Turn right.	*Dur fuq il-lemin.*
far	*il-boghod*
near	*il-viċin*
left luggage	*hallejt il-bagalji*

GLOSSSARY

AFM – Armed Forces of Malta

auberge – the residence of an individual langue of the Knights of St John

bajja – bay

bastion – a defensive work with two faces and two flanks, projecting from the line of the rampart

belt – city

bieb – gate

cavalier – a defensive work inside the main fortification, rising above the level of the main rampart to give covering fire

ċimiterju – cemetery

curtain – a stretch of rampart linking two bastions, with a parapet along the top

daħla – creek

dawret – bypass

demi-bastion – a half-bastion with only one face and one flank

dgħajsa – a traditional oar-powered boat

festa – feast day

fortiżża – fort

foss – ditch

għajn – spring (of water)

għar – cave

ġnien – garden

Grand Master – the title typically given to the head of an order of knights, including the Knights of Malta

kajjik – fishing boat

kappillan – parish priest

karrozzin – traditional horse-drawn carriage

kastell – castle

katidral – cathedral

kbira – big, main

knisja – church

kwartier – quarter, neighbourhood

langue – a division of the Knights of St John, based on nationality

luzzu – fishing boat

marsa – harbour

medina – fortified town, citadel

mina – arch, gate

misraħ – square

mitħna – windmill

mużew – museum

palazzo – Italian term for palace or mansion

parroċċa – parish

passeggiata – evening stroll (Italian term)

pjazza – square

plajja – beach, seashore

pont – bridge

pulizija – police

rabat – town outside the walls of a citadel

ramla – bay, beach

ras – point, headland

razzett – farm, farmhouse

sqaq – alley, lane

suq – market

sur – bastion

taraġ – stairs, steps

telgħa – hill

torri – tower, castle

triq – street, road

trulli – cone-shaped buildings that echo the traditional architecture of Puglia in Southern Italy

vedette – a lookout point, watchtower

vjal – avenue

wied – valley

xatt – wharf, marina

Behind the Scenes

SEND US YOUR FEEDBACK

We love to hear from travellers – your comments keep us on our toes and help make our books better. Our well-travelled team reads every word on what you loved or loathed about this book. Although we cannot reply individually to your submissions, we always guarantee that your feedback goes straight to the appropriate authors, in time for the next edition. Each person who sends us information is thanked in the next edition – the most useful submissions are rewarded with a selection of digital PDF chapters.

Visit **lonelyplanet.com/contact** to submit your updates and suggestions or to ask for help. Our award-winning website also features inspirational travel stories, news and discussions.

Note: We may edit, reproduce and incorporate your comments in Lonely Planet products such as guidebooks, websites and digital products, so let us know if you don't want your comments reproduced or your name acknowledged. For a copy of our privacy policy visit lonelyplanet.com/privacy.

OUR READERS

Many thanks to the travellers who wrote to us with helpful hints, useful advice and interesting anecdotes:

Ailyn Garley, Anne Kent, Carl Boyer, David Betts, Jesmond Muscat, Judi Ewings, June Cahill, Lucy Connell, Maggie Gjessing, Monica Costoya, Neil Pearce, Peter Connors, Ron Wilcox, Sain Alizada, Sascha Kreuziger, Stefan Krista, Trevor Coultas

AUTHOR THANKS
Abigail Blasi

Many thanks to Anna Tyler for commissioning me and her editorial knowhow, and to Helen Caruna Galizia, Julia Tomkins, Philip Manduca, Denise Briffa, Lisa Grech, Patti Piazzi, Chris Briffa, Giuseppe Bonanci Schembri, Sarah Williams, and Remco Slik for local recommendations and advice. Thanks to Simon Sciberras and Robert Magri for help with diving information, and to Steve Zammit Briffa for help with nightlife recommendations. Grateful thanks to Martin Morana and Jenciute Gabija at Malta Tourism, and to Marcia Grima at Heritage Malta.

ACKNOWLEDGEMENTS

Climate map data adapted from Peel MC, Finlayson BL & McMahon TA (2007) 'Updated World Map of the Köppen-Geiger Climate Classification', *Hydrology and Earth System Sciences*, 11, 163344.

Cover photograph: Valletta, Interpixels/ Shutterstock

THIS BOOK

This 6th edition of Lonely Planet's *Malta & Gozo* guidebook was researched and written by Abigail Blasi. The 5th edition was also written by Abigail Blasi and the 4th edition by Neil Wilson. This guidebook was produced by the following people:

Destination Editor
Anna Tyler
Product Editors
Penny Cordner, Vicky Smith, Tracy Whitmey
Senior Cartographer
Anthony Phelan
Book Designer
Mazzy Prinsep
Assisting Editors
Nigel Chin, Anne Mulvaney, Kirsten Rawlings

Cartographer
James Leversha
Cover Researcher
Campbell McKenzie
Thanks to Joel Cotterell, Grace Dobell, Ryan Evans, Larissa Frost, Andi Jones, Anne Mason, Claire Murphy, Karyn Noble, Samantha Russell-Tulip, Dianne Schallmeiner, Angela Tinson, Lauren Wellicome, Tony Wheeler, Amanda Williamson

Index